Jonathan Sewall
Odyssey of an American Loyalist

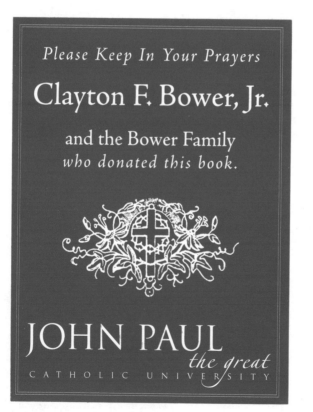

Jonathan Sewall

Odyssey of an American Loyalist

Carol Berkin

COLUMBIA UNIVERSITY PRESS
NEW YORK AND LONDON
1974

Library of Congress Cataloging in Publication Data

Berkin, Carol.
   Jonathan Sewall; odyssey of an American loyalist.

   Originally presented as the author's thesis,
Columbia University.
   Bibliography: p.
   1. Sewall, Jonathan, 1728–1796. 2. American
loyalists.
E278.S48B47 1974   973.3'14'0924 [B]   74–10795
ISBN 0–231–03851–8

For my father, Saul Berkin
To my mother, Marian Goldreich Berkin

Acknowledgments

No dissertation becomes a book without the help of professors, colleagues, and friends.

Debts accrue in the earliest stages of research. For her unselfish sharing of the secrets of the Public Record Office, I would like to thank Mary Beth Norton of Cornell University, whose own work on the Loyalists has done much to revive historical interest in these American exiles. I thank also Eileen McIlvaine, Reference Librarian at Columbia University, who often persevered in search of Sewall material when I was ready to concede defeat. I am grateful to those responsible for making the Public Archives of Canada in Ottawa the most pleasant and well-organized archive a historian could hope to work in. Finally, I appreciate Steven Shane and Shulamit many hours as research assistants and the editorial aid of Messrs. Bernard Gronert and Lesilie Bialler of Columbia University Press.

My work was supported by a grant from the Leopold Schepp Foundation and by the City University of New York Research Foundation, whose New Faculty Research Grant in 1973 made possible the necessary reexamination of Sewall's legal materials in Boston.

Several colleagues read and reread the manuscript as it progressed. For their patience as much as for their helpful criticism, I would like to acknowledge Roy Bartolomei, Jordy Bell, Eli Faber, Thomas Frazier, Aron Halberstam, Ene Servit, and Judith Walsh. I am also indebted to Alden Vaughan and Herman Ausubel of Columbia University for their critical reading of the original manuscript and for their generous recommendation, as members of my dissertation defense committee, that my work be considered for the Bancroft Award. I offer special thanks to Norman Cantor and Sidney Burrell, two men whom I have been pleased to call teachers, colleagues, and friends, whose support and encouragement began in my college days.

There is, of course, no satisfactory way to thank Richard B. Morris, who taught me, as he taught so many graduate students, the historian's craft. His support and advice, and above all his own contagious enthusiasm for the study of the American past, spurred me to complete my own work.

There are two final thank you's. To the New York Knicks, for that always necessary link with pure enjoyment. And to my husband, John Harper, who has long been my most respected colleague, my most valued critic, and my best friend.

Abbreviations

I *Manuscripts and Documents*

Ad Mss	Adams Papers, Massachusetts Historical Society
B–T Mss	Bowdoin-Temple Papers, Massachusetts Historical Society
CP–HU	Harvard College Papers, Harvard University Archives
CR–HU	Harvard College Records, Harvard University Archives
DAB	*Dictionary of American Biography*
EW Mss	Papers of Edward Winslow, Public Archives of Canada
FB Mss	Papers of Sir Francis Bernard, Letterbooks, Houghton Library, Harvard University
FR–HU	Faculty Records, Harvard University Archives
H–W Mss	Hutchinson-Watson Mss., Massachusetts Historical Society
JOURNALS	*Journals of the Hon. House of Representatives of his Majesty's Province of the Massachusetts-Bay, in New England*
JS Mss	Papers of Jonathan Sewall, Public Archives of Canada
JSC	George A. Ward, ed. *The Journal and Letters of the Late Samuel Curwen.* New York, 1845
Lf Mss	Lee Family Mss., Massachusetts Historical Society

LPJA	Hiller Zobel and L. Kinvin Wroth, eds. *Legal Papers of John Adams*. 3 Vols. Cambridge, 1965
MINUTES	Public Record Office. Great Britain. Commissioners of Customs in America. Records and Minutes, 1762–1770, Volume V. Minutes Extracted from the Board's Records. Book I, 1767–1769
PRO/AO–821	Public Record Office. Audit Office, Declared Accounts. Customs Bundle 821
PRO/AO/ 12–48	Public Record Office. Audit Office 12. Bundle 48
PRO/AO/ 13–137	Public Record Office. Audit Office 13. Bundle 137
PRO/T/1– 463, 465, 468, 771	Public Record Office. Treasury 1. Bundle 463, 465, 468, or 771
R–S Mss	Robie-Sewall Collection, Massachusetts Historical Society
RSCM	Records of the Superior Court of Massachusetts, Suffolk County Court House, Boston
RTP Mss	Robert Treat Paine Papers, Massachusetts Historical Society
SC Mss	Papers of Samuel Curwen, Essex Institute, Salem
SMC Mss	Smith-Carter Mss., Massachusetts Historical Society
TC Mss	Thomas Coffin Papers, Massachusetts Historical Society
TH Mss	Papers of Thomas Hutchinson, Massachusetts Archives
WC Mss	Papers of Ward Chipman, Lawrence Collection, Public Archives of Canada
WJA	Charles F. Adams, ed. *The Works of John Adams*. 10 Vols. Boston, 1851–1866

II *Books and Journals*

Dickerson, BUMR	Oliver M. Dickerson. *Boston Under Military Rule, 1768–1769, as Recorded in a Journal of the Times.* Boston, 1936
Freiberg, "Prelude"	Malcolm Freiberg. "Prelude to Purgatory: Thomas Hutchinson in Provincial Massachusetts Politics, 1748–1776." Ph.D. diss., Brown University, 1950
Hutchinson, *History*	Thomas Hutchinson. *The History of the Colony and Province of Massachusetts-Bay,* ed. by Laurence Shaw Mayo. 3 Vols. Cambridge, 1936
MHSC	*Massachusetts Historical Society Collections*
MHSP	*Massachusetts Historical Society Proceedings*
Murrin, "Anglicizing"	John Murrin. "Anglicizing an American Colony: The Transformation of Provincial Massachusetts." Ph.D. diss., Yale, 1966
NEQ	*New England Quarterly*
Norton, *British-Americans*	Mary Beth Norton. *The British-Americans: The Loyalist Exiles in England, 1774–1789.* Boston, 1972
Novanglus	John Adams. *Novanglus and Massachusettensis; Or Political Essays, published in the years 1774 and 1775, on the Principal Points of Controversy, Between Great Britain and her Colonies.* New York, 1968
Washburn, *Sketches*	Emory Washburn. *Sketches of the Judicial History of Massachusetts from 1630 to the Revolution in 1775.* Boston, 1840
WMQ	*William and Mary Quarterly*
Zobel, *Massacre*	Hiller Zobel. *The Boston Massacre.* New York, 1970

Contents

Jonathan Sewall
Odyssey of an American Loyalist

CHAPTER ONE

The Legacy of Six Generations: Jonathan Sewall
1728-1757

THE SEWALL FAMILY had been in Massachusetts for a century when Jonathan Sewall was born in 1728. Generations before him of judges, militia officers, and legislators bore witness to the accretion of wealth and power to that family within Massachusetts society. The Sewall roots lay in Northern England, where Henry Sewall was born in Coventry in the 1540s.[1] Henry lifted the family from a comfortable anonymity into local importance through the successful management of his draper's business. He acquired an extensive estate and, as befit a man of wealth, he entered political life. For many years he served as Mayor of Coventry. The Mayor's heir and namesake was baptized in 1576. But this Henry proved no joy to his father's old age. From childhood he was rebellious, unreliable and erratic in his personal behavior; he had an unruly temper and an affinity for unorthodox views on society and politics. His mother, Margaret, grew so weary of her son's behavior that she wrote Henry out of her will. When she died in 1629, the reading of that document left her 53-year-old son in no doubt as to the reasons for his exclusion.

Perhaps Henry's own dissatisfaction with life in England prompted him to send his son to New England. In 1634, this young Henry was packed on board the *Elizabeth and Dorcas;* with him went a generous supply of cattle and other provisions considered necessary for a plantation life in the colonies. His obviously ample means made the new immigrant welcome in Massachusetts, and John Cotton himself urged Henry to remain in Boston. Henry chose, however, to settle in the smaller town of Newbury.

Henry's father joined him shortly afterward. During the twelve prosperous years that followed, the elder Sewall's querulous and erratic temperament grew worse, and he became subject to fits of mental derangement. When the younger Henry married, his father dramatically fled the comforts of Newbury for the isolation of the frontier town of Rowley. Here, in a self-imposed solitude, he lived out his remaining years in a precarious state of melancholia.

The newly married Henry also left Newbury, returning with his wife and her parents to England. Here five of Henry's eight children were born: Hannah, Samuel, John, Stephen, and Jane. But thirteen years later the family journeyed back to America. The decision to return was prompted in part by economic considerations. The absentee arrangements for his Newbury estate and rental properties were costing Henry considerable profit, and with a growing family he now wished to manage these affairs himself. There were political considerations as well, for the Stuart restoration brought little comfort to Henry, who had personally served the Protector Richard Cromwell during the Puritan ascendancy.

In Newbury Henry enjoyed wealth, and the local prestige that accompanied it. He was frequently his community's representative in the General Court, serving terms in 1661, 1663, 1668, and 1670. His success enabled him to provide well for the future of his children. To his satisfaction his daughters made good, if not exceptional, marriages. Only Mehitabel Sewall might have caused Henry some concern, for her romantic inclinations led her to marry the local midwife's grandson, a Mr. William Moody. Henry's sons, enjoying the advantages of their father's prestige and connections, as well as varying portions of his wealth, all managed to replicate his position in provincial society. The eldest son, Samuel, was able to surpass his father in both wealth and status by means of an excellent marriage and a brilliant career as a jurist. It was through Samuel that the family name was raised to prominence on a provincial rather than a local level.

Henry's fourth son, Stephen, was Jonathan Sewall's grandfather. Stephen made his home in Salem, Massachusetts, where he carved out a comfortable position in his father's mold as local political leader and militia officer. When he died in 1725, Major Sewall left nine adult children, most of whom were also firmly established in the colony's squirearchy. In Stephen's family, as in his own generation of Sewalls, the elder son surpassed the father. Young Stephen entered the circles of the provincial elite, as his uncle Samuel had done before him, through the judicial system. He too rose to the office of Chief Justice of the Superior Court.

But not every Sewall of this Salem branch was able to maintain or improve upon his father's status. Unfortunately, Jonathan Sewall's own father, Stephen Sewall's fourth son, was one of those whose financial failures carried him to the peripheries of the family circle. As a young man he had moved from the family seat in Salem to Boston, where he established himself as a merchant. He married in 1718, but his wife soon died, leaving Sewall no heirs. He married again in 1724. Although his second wife, Mary Payne Sewall, bore six children, only a daughter, Jane, and the merchant's namesake, Jonathan, survived.

For a few years Sewall managed to care for his small family with the profits from his faltering enterprises. But whatever expectations the merchant might have had for his business were not to be realized. For his health too was faltering. On the morning of November 22, 1731, Samuel Sewall gave to Benjamin Sewall the "sorrowful Tidings of ye Death of our Dear Bro. Jonathan who died yesterday morning about 8 Clock ye Change being sudden having three or four Large Stools of Clear Blood ye Last of which Carried him off he remaining perfect in his reason to ye Last—We would be glad you would Come down Immediately—particularly It will be Necessary about ye Cloaths—God Grant we May be all ready for this great Change." [2] An inventory of Sewall's business showed him to be bankrupt.[3]

Thus the young Jonathan Sewall was left heir to only two of the advantages of the family name—its prestige and the social and political connections accrued throughout the generations. Wealth, which made a man master of the other advantages, was missing. For the three-year-old boy, such questions of mastery mattered little. It was enough, throughout his childhood and youth, that the family name saved him from the poverty and obscurity to which his own lack of inheritance doomed him. Neither his uncles nor the elite Boston society of which his father had been a marginal member would allow this fate for Mary Payne Sewall's only son.

Family and friends saw to it that Sewall was properly schooled. His early education was financed by Reverend Samuel Cooper, minister of the exclusive Brattle Street Church Sewall's family had attended. Cooper raised funds from among his wealthy parishioners to finance this college preparatory training for Sewall. When the proper time came, Jonathan's uncle, Chief Justice Stephen Sewall, enrolled him at Harvard.[4]

Sewall was fifteen and one-half when he began his college training in 1743. If he had not yet recognized the tenuous nature of his social position in Massachusetts society, Harvard itself was certain to force his awareness. The Harvard of the 1740s was not a school exclusively for the sons of the province's wealthy and politically powerful; its classes were open to prosperous middle class families as well. But despite this broadened base, Harvard remained an elite institution, and the social consciousness of the school's administration had not been relaxed. The members of each entering class were subjected to a public ranking, based not on scholastic achievement but on their family standing within the province. Three categories for ranking were recognized: first, sons of the province's political bureaucracy; next, sons of university graduates; finally, a category covering one-half the class—"all others."[5] Within this ranking system, Sewall's own place was far from clear. His immediate background implied a low ranking, but he was bolstered by the prestige of his uncle, Judge Sewall, and edged upward by the connection of a cousin among the Fellows of the College. In the end, Sewall was established in a comfortable, though not prominent rank, eleventh in his class of twenty-four.[6]

If Sewall's social status remained ambiguous, his personal status among the students was quickly established: he was an acknowledged ringleader in the student rebellions common to Harvard College life. These rebellions were a response to the constraining life at Harvard. The boys were permitted only six weeks' vacation during the year, and the remaining months were filled with daily schedules of prayers, classes, indigestible meals, and long afternoons of study.[7] The pattern hardly took into account the private inclinations of the student himself. Though in theory the educational fare was appetizing—promising mastery of Greek, Hebrew, logic, rhetoric, and exploration of the newer fields of science—the student's actual experience with these subjects was the tedious daily encounter with dry lectures and copybook exercises. This strict regimen provoked most boys to small rebellion, despite the formidable array of punishments and fines which could be brought down upon the heads of those who failed to comply. But if most students ran afoul of authority at some point during their years at Harvard, Sewall's name steadily found its way into the records of disciplinary actions. He seemed determined not to allow his dependence upon family, charity, or the university fellowships he received to curb his impulses.

As an underclassman Sewall received routine punishment for destroying school property and for disobeying instructions.[8] But as an upperclassman he was the organizer of a series of destructive pranks and practical jokes inflicted upon his tutor, the famous divine Jonathan Mayhew. These pranks climaxed in an acrimonious conflict between the old scholar and his chief tormentor.

Late one evening, Sewall, with his roommates and cronies, positioned themselves beneath Mayhew's window. The students began a noisy torrent of taunts, shouting for Mayhew to awaken. Then someone hurled a brick into the tutor's room. The group dispersed, but its members were soon caught. The boys named Sewall as the chief instigator of the disturbance, and conceded that it was he who threw the brick. But when Sewall was called upon to confess he stubbornly refused to admit his guilt. His defiance infuriated Mayhew, who resolved to waste little time in this battle of wills. Such a battle implied an equality that was wholly illusory. The older man brought down the full weight of his power and authority; he threatened Sewall with civil action if he did not confess at once. With that, Sewall capitulated. Having won his point, Mayhew had Sewall expelled.[9]

The affair did not end there. For two years Sewall kept school at Watertown, hoping for a pardon and readmittance to the College. Although he regularly petitioned for that pardon, it was denied him. Mayhew's lesson in the price of rebellion was to be learned through these repeated rejections. Finally, in June 1751, terms for Sewall's readmittance were set. These terms, too, carried Mayhew's lesson on rebellion, for Sewall was required to offer a series of humbling public apologies before classmates and faculty.[10]

Sewall spent two more years at Harvard, finishing undergraduate work and getting his Masters degree as well. When he left the college, he took up schoolkeeping again, this time in Salem.[11] Although many Harvard graduates started their careers as teachers, few remained long in the classroom. The lesson-giving and discipline-dispensing that passed for pedagogy in that day was far from a satisfying or profitable career. For most of these young men teaching was a temporary employment, which offered a pause before a career decision was made.[12] In Worcester, for example, a young Harvard graduate named John Adams was also keeping school, and while his students daydreamed over their lessons Adams argued with himself the relative advantages of the ministry, medicine, and the law.[13]

Sewall too may have seen his schoolkeeping as a temporary arrangement. But his hesitancy in choosing his profession did not, like Adams's, stem from the difficulties of selecting among many options. Sewall's choices were distinctly limited. He had no farmlands to return to and none of the capital essential for his establishment in the business world. The logical choice before him was the ministry, for it offered him status and a sufficient, if modest, income. But Sewall seems never to have considered this option seriously. What talents and energies he had appeared likely to be wasted for lack of a proper arena.

In Salem, however, Sewall's extensive family network again aided him. Here, he was befriended by a distant kinsman, John Higginson, whose comfortable position in the community rested on his country law practice. Higginson and his wife were hospitable to Sewall and treated him in their home to those small luxuries of beer, wine, and tea which he could not afford on his teacher's income. More importantly Higginson encouraged Sewall to explore the law.[14] Sewall became a frequent visitor in the older man's home, and Higginson gave him instruction, a patient ear to his queries, and access to a small legal library and collection of legal records.

For several years Sewall contented himself with teaching school and spending spare hours in the study of law. But a real legal apprenticeship required his full attention. Higginson understood this and in time took steps to help Sewall acquire the needed training.

In 1756 Higginson arranged a meeting between Sewall and Chambers Russell. Russell was not, like Higginson, a country lawyer. He was an active professional, a judge and an expert in maritime law. He was also Stephen Sewall's colleague on the Superior Court bench. Shortly after this meeting, Russell agreed to take Sewall into his home as his student, and to support him during the apprenticeship.

The advantages of Sewall's apprenticeship were enormous. Russell had an extensive legal library, a luxury in colonial America, and one that guaranteed Sewall a more sophisticated legal training than his country cousin had enjoyed. As Russell's student, Sewall had the rare opportunity to receive daily practical exposure to a full range of provincial legal actions, for Russell served as a Vice Admiralty judge as well as a justice of the province's Superior Court. The value of these academic and practical advantages was enhanced by the judge's astute commentary and his willingness to instruct his pupil.

Surely as important as the legal education Sewall received was the political education acquired in his year with Chambers Russell. During this apprenticeship Sewall gained his first glimpse of the political world of the province. Russell's home was an excellent vantage point: the judge was a man of considerable standing in Massachusetts, first in his class at Harvard, wealthy, and firmly ensconced as a Middlesex County political leader.[15] He held, in addition to his judicial posts, a near-permanent place in the General Court of the province. This legislative tenure was the result of almost 26 uninterrupted years as the representative from the area of Charlestown, Concord, and Lincoln. But perhaps most attractive about Russell's success was his comfortable position above the scramblings for petty office, and the removal from the ugly machinations of factional politics which his monopoly on local office and his judicial appointments assured him. The judge was, by all current measures of a man, a compelling model of success for Sewall.

When Russell died a decade later, Sewall's eulogy revealed the deep impression the older man had made upon his student. The eulogy paid tribute to Russell's personal qualities, to his intelligence, and to his devotion to family and friends. But Sewall's highest praise went to Russell in his role as community leader. The young lawyer saw in Russell's relationship with the community he virtually governed all the admirable qualities of the father-child relationship. The judge was responsible, concerned, protective; he kept a watchful eye out for the welfare of his fellow colonists. And, Sewall noted with satisfaction, the community showed their appreciation by respect for and deference to the judge.[16]

The eulogy's analogy to the paternal relationship was central to Jonathan Sewall's understanding and evaluation of the society in which he lived. He was still a young man when he praised Chambers Russell as a guardian of the lives of other men and women, but he never swayed from this conviction that the paternal care of the majority by a privileged but responsibility-laden minority was rational, necessary, and productive of social harmony.

The paternal analogy was equally compelling in Sewall's understanding of his personal life. The history of his youth, his young manhood—and perhaps even his maturity—could be traced in the series of strong involvements he was to have with older men. Sometimes these were antagonistic relationships, as with Jonathan Mayhew;

but more often they were sympathetic. Sewall's pattern of response to these relationships was already firmly set when he left Chambers Russell's home in 1757. He was intensely loyal to those older men who showed warmth or bestowed favor. He was stubbornly resistent to and resentful of those in positions of power who he believed abused him or slighted him.

Whatever their nature, these relationships with older men strongly influenced his public and personal life. In most cases there were positive practical results. By 1757, a succession of men like Stephen Sewall, John Higginson, and Chambers Russell had helped advance Sewall's career. But these relationships equally shaped his expectations of, and for, his personal behavior. In a subtle but important sense, men like Chambers Russell were deceptive models for Sewall to emulate. Sewall saw most of his patrons at their apogee—men well-established in their communities and their professions, the compromises and conflicts of their ascent safely behind them. He saw, therefore, none of their less admirable or more difficult moments. He seems to have unwisely concluded that in most cases such moments had not occurred, that a man could become powerful without ever sacrificing integrity or compromising principle. In this regard his year with Russell was especially misleading. This man, who more than all others Sewall had established as his model, was in 1756 a community leader: secure, respected, above the pettiness of politics, free from strains upon his integrity. If, in fact, such a consistently untroubled life had been possible for Chambers Russell—a man born to wealth and to social station—it was not to be for Jonathan Sewall.

CHAPTER TWO

The Life of the Provincial Lawyer
1757-1767

IN 1757 JONATHAN SEWALL left the Russell home to begin his own legal career. But if his apprenticeship was ended, his study of the law was not. Mastering his profession, he grudgingly conceded, was far more difficult than any young man might reasonably expect. In fact, after over a decade of legal study and practice, Jonathan Sewall would argue that the law

> is fathomable only by those intellects whose naturally squab-thick powers have been, as it were, wire-drawn to a sufficient longitude by diurnal & nocturnal porings, poundings, dreamings, sleepings, cursings, & swearings over codes, pandects, digests, institutes, abridgments, reports, entries, commentaries, actions, pleas, replications, rejoinders, surrejoinders, rebutters, surrebutters, etc. in infinitum. This is but a faint glimpse of the immense sea of legal—what shall I call it?—chaotical confusion of primary principals of abstract ratiocination, thro' which for the tedious space of 3 lives, or 21 years, we toil, tug, labour, plunge, paddle, scramble, wallow & from which, per varios casus, per tot discrimina rerum, we at length emerge with souls fitly enlarged & enlightened for assuming the guardianship of the lives, liberties, & properties of our ignorant fellow man.[1]

This elaborate description of the law and the lawyer's education was given, only half in jest, in 1771. But its emphasis on the mysteries and complexities of Sewall's profession was in itself a comment on the changes in law his generation had witnessed. For law in Massachusetts had undergone a metamorphosis that closely paralleled in time his own personal career.[2] It had not, as Sewall knew, always been so filled with the formalities of "rejoinders" and "surrejoinders," but had progressed from a simple and flexible agrarian law to a sophisticated code requiring trained professionals to interpret it to their fellow colonists.

Sewall had set up practice in 1757. But had he begun his career when his mentor, Chambers Russell, was young, he would have found the courtrooms filled exclusively with gentlemen judges and amateur lawyers, none of whom expected to make their fortunes—or even their livelihood—from the "chaotic confusions" of the law.[3] No diurnal and nocturnal porings would have been necessary to master the bastardized version of English law that governed Massachusetts for over a century. From its blend of frontier practices, local and borough customs of England, the common law of royal courts, and strong doses of Mosaic law, a simple and flexible legal structure, which suited an agrarian community,[4] had emerged. This law was often practiced by the colonists themselves, who had little awe of the courtroom or of its judges. Ordinary men and women were comfortable in courts that "frequently rise in the middle of a cause, if they are hungry at noon, or sleepy at night, and let the jury wander where they please, without taking the verdicts in those cases which they have gone through."[5]

What paid practice there was in Massachusetts was, in modern parlance, a sideline. The sheriff who served a writ would, for a fee, also draw it. The tavernkeeper, whose law office was conveniently located behind the bar, would proffer his legal services as well as his ale to the tavern's patrons. Merchants, apothecaries, and tailors could all supplement their income by mastering and practicing the strange mixture called law in Massachusetts.[6] Usually, however, even these amateurs did not carry the case to court. Local disputants chose to bypass the aid of others entirely, and argued their own cases before the bench. Their presentations were uninhibited, although their frequent flights of oratory and of fancy were finally constrained in 1656 by a wearied General Court.[7]

But the long reign of the part-time lawyer and self-pleaded case was ending in 1757 as Sewall was sworn before the bar. Major changes were prompted by internal as well as external pressures upon the colony's legal system and its apparatus. As the size and complexity of Massachusetts' commercial life increased, and particularly as the demands made upon it by the empire's trade legalities multiplied, the need for a more sophisticated manipulation of English law was felt. The colony's expanding mercantile enterprises required legal procedures more uniform with English practices. And in Massachusetts, as in the mother country, the differentiation of functions within business organizations ended the era of the omnicompetent merchant, able to serve as his own attorney. These businessmen would look for specialists to handle their conflicts and compromises with British navigation law and imperial commercial regulations. Finally, the Crown's interest in the judicial and political machinery of the province, which had been steadily growing during the eighteenth century, created a need for the services of a staff of qualified Crown lawyers and judges.[8]

Thus the young full-time lawyer of the 1750s and 1760s came to pore over the complex English law. But if colonial law was growing ever more uniform with England's, the structure of the legal profession remained distinctly American. Sewall faced no discrimination within the bar between barrister and solicitor. This rigid differentiation within the English legal system never took root in Massachusetts.* Nor could any American lawyer, young or established, ever hope to enjoy the luxury of a specialized practice. Jeremiah Gridley, one of the leading lights of the bar when Sewall's career began, was fond of reminding his proteges that a colonial lawyer was a jack-of-all-legal-trades, who "must study common law, and civil law, and natural law, and admiralty law; and must do the duty of a counsellor, a lawyer, an attorney, a solicitor, and even a scrivener." [9]

---

* By the 1760s the bar had established ranks within the profession. A three-year clerkship, and two years of practice in the inferior courts of the province, made a young lawyer a "counsellor." Two additional years of practice were necessary before he received the title "barrister." But these were gradations on a continuum, not sharp and unbreachable divisions of labor. Counsellor and barrister served a client interchangeably.

Although the new professional lawyer enjoyed a steadily rising status in the province, he still found it necessary in the 1750s and 1760s to wage warfare on the amateur and the unlicensed "pettifogger" who practiced outside Boston in rural Massachusetts. Within his own county of Middlesex, for example, Sewall had few legitimate legal rivals, but he faced competition for local clients nevertheless. Like that of any other full-time lawyer in this period of transition, Sewall's livelihood depended upon his ability to persuade the ordinary citizens that their legal affairs required the services of a member of the bar.

It was this necessity that made of Sewall and his colleagues "wandering attornies." For one means of accustoming the country people to the use of professional services was for bar members to be present at every county sitting of the Superior Court. Thus four times a year "following the court" busied young and old lawyer alike.[10]

Some lawyers found the back-road travel, the crowded evening accommodations, and the courtroom-door soliciting a heavy price to pay for the continuing increase in their profession's prestige and profitability. But in his younger days at least Sewall considered circuit riding a social event as much as a professional necessity. He relished making plans for these junkets. "Dear Guillaum," he wrote fellow-lawyer William Cushing with typical enthusiasm, "I hoped to have seen you Face to Face this term at Boston, and there to have settled the necessary preliminarys of the Worcester Campaign this season; such as, whether we should sup on bak'd apples and milk at Judge Russell's three times or five times on our way?"[11]

Whether or not Cushing's optimism matched Sewall's, most of Sewall's colleagues did acknowledge the importance, if not the pleasures, of these trips with the court around the province. They not only educated the litigants of Barnstable, Worcester, and York on these tours; they also educated themselves. For these swings around the province brought together lawyers from all over Massachusetts, solidifying their sense of community and creating—in a world of expensive and difficult to acquire law books—the possibility of shared information. This meant an increased uniformity of practice and an upgrading

of practice everywhere. Also, the court trips offered the younger lawyers exposure to the greatest legal and juristic minds of their province:
men like Jeremiah Gridley, James Otis, and Edmund Trowbridge.

At these circuit sittings, young lawyers like Jonathan Sewall fed off
the scraps left by their profession's stars. Had Sewall depended upon
the circuit to make his fortune, he would have been in dire straits, for
volume was all-important in court cases. No single case profited the
lawyer greatly, for the court set a standard legal fee, no matter what
the value of the suit itself. The lawyer who won his case could expect
to receive about £3, including travel expenses, and the cost of drawing the writ.[12]

Those cases Sewall did handle in his first years following the court
were usually affirmations, actions in the Superior Court taken to seal
original, lower court rulings. For these routine requests, it seems, even
the novice lawyer could be trusted. Though unchallenging—and tedious—these affirmations formed the bulk of Sewall's Superior Court
business in the fifties and the early sixties. Even these were heavily
concentrated in his own home county of Middlesex, where Chambers
Russell had generously turned over to him a portion of his own well-
established practice at Charlestown. Of 52 Superior Court affirmations
between 1762 and 1765, 40 were entered by Sewall in his own baili-
wick.[13] Idle as this may have left him in the courts of Barnstable,
Essex, or York, this concentration was an encouraging sign of his success in Middlesex. For, more than likely, these affirmations represented cases he had handled in the local inferior courts.*

Neither the tedium of affirmations nor the problems of making ends
meet diminished Sewall's enthusiasm for the law. It was this obvious
affection for his profession that precipitated and cemented an otherwise highly unlikely friendship. No two young men seemed less des-
tined to be close friends than John Adams and Jonathan Sewall. Sewall was, on the surface at least, lighthearted, fond of indulging in
pleasures, always ready for a practical joke, his wit sharp and his natural powers of parody—even self-parody—irrepressible. Adams was

* The records of the inferior or county courts of Massachusetts for the pre-Revolutionary
period have not survived.

doggedly serious about himself and others, self-critical, introspective, driven by an ambition for fame Sewall could only faintly comprehend. But these two young men shared an interest in and a talent for the law which overrode all other considerations.

They began a correspondence in 1759, out of which a close and enduring intimacy developed. Sewall "always called me John, and I him Jonathan," Adams recalled in 1819, "and often [I] said to him, I wish my name were David." [14] In their early years, when both struggled as legal neophytes, their letters offered encouragement to flagging spirits, and recorded each man's despair at real or imagined inadequacies. Adams poured out his desire for fame to his sympathetic colleague:

> I expect to be totally forgotten within seventy years from the present hour, unless the insertion of my name in the college catalogue should luckily preserve it longer. . . . Yet, though I have very few hopes, I am not ashamed to own that a prospect of an immortality in the memories of all the worthy, to the end of time, would be a high gratification to my wishes.[15]

Sewall, whose ambition was more materialistic and thus more practical, nevertheless recommended inner satisfaction as an anodyne to Adams's despair: "What think you my Friend of the inward pleasure & Satisfaction which the human Mind recieveth from the Acquisition of Knowledge?" he asked Adams. But if fame were Adams's heart's delight, Sewall wished him a miraculous development in history:

> But if in the Estimation of the World, a Man's Worth riseth in proportion to the Greatness of his Country, who knows but in future Ages, when New England shall have risen to its intended Grandeur, it shall be as carefully recorded among the Registers of the Literati, that *Adams* flourished in the second Century after the exode of its first Settlers from Great Britain, as it is now that Cicero was born in the six Hundred & Forty Seventh Year after the Building of Rome? [16]

Their letters were often philosophical, occupied with arranging and rearranging the hierarchy of knowledge, always in such a way that Law stood supreme. Sewall wrote:

Law is a sublime study, and what more sublime! what more worthy the indefatigable Labour & pursuit of a reasonable Man! than that Science by which Mankind raise themselves from the forlorn helpless State in which Nature leave's them, to the full Enjoyment of all the inestimable Blessings of Social Union, & by which, they (if you will allow the Expression) triumph over the Frailty & Imperfections of Humanity? [17]

Despite the enthusiasm given full expression in these letters, Sewall was not blind to the often cosmic difference between the Law and the legal practice of the provincial lawyer. On the level most frequently encountered by the provincial lawyer, the law was a tedious routine of wranglings and writ drawings. Justice was the resolution of petty disputes between neighbors, the granting of divorce, or the adjustment of a sailor's wages. The lawyer's craft was an exercise in proper phrasing and double-checked punctuation in writs and special pleadings; it was the regular application of memorized form and procedure to the repeated problems of local merchants and farmers. Law on this level was only livelihood, and the lawyer only practitioner.

Sewall showed a genuine appreciation for the craftsmanship necessary on this practical level. But the self-conscious plier of his craft was a tailor-made target for his satiric eye. His apparent irreverence must surely have irritated Adams, who insisted on a solemn deference to his profession, and to himself. Sewall, on the other hand, was always ready to add his own touches to that still-prevalent caricature of the lawyer as pettifogger, a caricature Adams struggled so desperately to erase from the minds of the province.

Sewall spared Adams his critique of the lawyer as a would-be conjuror, calling up the mysterious but fickle powers of the law. This description he sketched for his cousin, the merchant Thomas Robie. For if Adams was Sewall's professional alter ego, Robie was Sewall's fellow spirit in pleasure. It was with Robie that Sewall executed hoaxes on ministers or practical jokes, or exchanged riddles and musical puzzles.[18] It was for Robie that Sewall had written, in 1771, his elaborate description of the unfathomable law.

If Sewall was amused by the life of the lawyer, he was equally en-

tertained by the plight of the client. When Robie found himself involved in a £10 legal imbroglio with a bricklayer named Loring,
Sewall could show no sympathy for his cousin's frustration-driven
tirades against the legal process and its practitioners. For Sewall the
complex process of the Court and its law became foolish and troublesome precisely because it was applied to foolish personal squabbles,
and employed for matters adult and reasonable men ought to resolve
outside the courtroom. It was the quality of the dispute that made the
law and the legal process either regal or comic. If Robie now discovered himself upon a battlefield with weapons and rules of war he could
not understand, he must silently bear it and not complain. "At the
present," his cousin ordered, "be content silently to adore it as an in-
comprehensible mystery, too profound to be fathom'd by . . . the *lay
gens.*" [19]

Once the legal mechanism was set in motion, Robie would have to
wait for the slow grinding out of justice. Justice would be served,
Sewall cheerfully informed him, "in the course of a few years, before
the end of our present century, if the writ don't abate by the death of
either party."

The result of Robie's several months in court proved Sewall's con-
tentions. The case, which Sewall reluctantly handled for his cousin,
ended in a compromise settlement, slightly favoring Loring. When
Robie complained of his opponent's victory in receiving from him the
costs of the suit, his lawyer consoled him. The triumphant bricklayer
was no richer for the £2.14.8 in costs Robie had paid; the court clerk,
the sheriff who executed the writ, and Loring's own lawyer had got it
all, and probably an equal sum from Loring himself. Such was legal
justice in Massachusetts.

Petty or no, contests like this between Loring and Robie were the
bread and butter of a colonial legal practice. Sewall's own practice,
despite the growing number of important mercantile interests he represented, always retained the flavor of his cousin's struggle with the
bricklayer. The conflicts and jealousies of the countryside most often
busied him, and the court cases that resulted from these squabbles over

land, money, and livestock, or real and imagined insults to honor and reputation, were variations on the Loring-Robie dispute.

The case of Thomas Perkins, his wife, and three other York County couples who came to Sewall for help in filing a trespass complaint was typical. These four couples had, by pooling their funds and rotating their attendance in church, purchased a choice pew in the local meeting house—"one of the highest and best" by their own account. Their good fortune, and perhaps their pride in it, had apparently provoked a fellow York husbandman, Obediah Merrell, to set fire to the Meeting House in order to reduce their "convenient and Comfortable Scituation" to ashes. Sewall filed the complaint, argued the case, and won a favorable verdict for his clients. In the end, however, he could only hope the couples' private satisfaction was great, for their monetary compensation was not. Although the pew had cost them £20, the court awarded them only 40 shillings for its loss.[20]

Country jealousies did not always provoke crimes as serious as arson. Sewall became familiar with more common forms of revenge like false accusation and slander. The practice of "contriving to ruin a good name" brought Sewall clients like Samuel Winchell, a yeoman of Topsham, who found himself in court after publicly labelling cabinetmaker Hugh Wilson "a damned thief." Wilson, it appeared, "found"—and sold—some hay Winchell claimed to be his own. Winchell had boasted that he could prove his accusation of theft, but in 1764 the first jury at the Falmouth Superior Court session judged otherwise. Winchell's display of temper cost him £11.0.6.[21]

Lost property was a serious problem in rural Massachusetts, especially when much valuable property could—unlike Winchell's and Wilson's disputed hay—move of its own volition. Cows, calves, rams, sheep, and favorite horses frequently strayed away. It was not, however, the losing but the finding that drew lawyers into the affair. Trespass charges were entered by livestock owners against other husbandmen and yeomen who used as their own the stray animals that they found. Many of Sewall's clients insisted that the lucky finder knew perfectly well to whom that "sorrel horse" or "white ram" belonged.[22] Others were willing to concede the finder's ignorance and sue only for damages and losses.

The fine line between finding and using and stealing and using was a more serious problem for jury and lawyers alike. In October 1765 Sewall was retained by John Oliver and Michael Nagail, two men indicted for what Sewall termed "the ignominious narrow-soul'd Crime of Sheep-Stealing." [23] Their case was to come before the Bristol Superior Court that term, but Sewall had business at the Boston Court which prevented him from attending the country sitting. He believed the men innocent, and wanted to see their defense well handled. Thus, on October 5, he wrote a letter to his friend John Adams, asking him to take the case. As Sewall understood it, the case against his clients rested on the accusation by a Colonel Northrop that at or near the time Nagail and Oliver passed his farm with their herd, he lost some 50 sheep. Northrop's charge that the two men took his sheep was circumstantially corroborated by a second farmer, Ezekial Gardner, who swore that he had seen Northrop's sheep in the Nagail-Oliver herd. As the two men passed his farm, Gardner said, he lost 15 sheep. He pursued Nagail and Oliver, found his sheep among theirs, and as they were delivering these sheep to him, he "saw a Number of Sheep in their Drove with Colo Northrop's mark."

Sewall recommended that Adams rest his defense on "these two points which [Nagail and Oliver] prove; namely, that they, bona fide, bought and paid for as many Sheep as were ever seen in their Drove, and that some of them were mark'd with the same mark as Colo Northrop's, whose they are charged with stealing." But even if Adams could not successfully prove these points, the case need not be lost. "Even if our Clients shod [sic] fail in their proof," Sewall reasoned, "if it be considered with Attention how difficult it is, when passing thro' the Country with a Drove, to prevent other Sheep from mixing with them; when the Drove are frequently jumping over into pastures, and the Sheep in Inclosures jumping into the Road when they hear the bleating of a large Drove, how easily others mark'd precisely, or nearly, in the same Manner may get among them unobserved by the

Drovers; and if it be considered that the Intention constitute's the *Crime*.—These Things being attended to, I say, the Jury ought to have clear proof of an Intention to steal, before they can declare them guilty.''

When Sewall completed this apparent thinking out loud, he apologized to his friend. ''I hint these Things to you not because I think *my* Head is better than *yours,* but because *two* Heads are better than *one.''*

Sewall's defense strategy reflected his knowledge of the realities of country life. Sheep did, of course, wander, herds were difficult to keep separate, and unmended pasture fences probably accounted for many instances of apparent theft. Theft of property remained, however, the most frequent charge in Sewall's criminal cases. Almost every court session he filed—or responded to—pleas of trespass arising from the breaking into, entering, and theft from one man's close (or woodlot) by another. Local juries compensated his clients like James Fowle of Woburn or Nathan Taylor of Upton for loss of rye or timber.[24] But there were acquittals that give some evidence that the vagueness of property lines between neighbors rather than malice or greed accounted for a trespass. In these cases the judge and jury helped to settle boundary disputes and to prevent two neighbors from returning to court.

If theft, slander, arson, and even stark instances of assault and battery were familiar entries in Sewall's record books, the major portion of his courtroom activities revolved around matters of debt. The colony's inadequate system of informal banking was based on promissory notes and personal bondings. Not surprisingly the court served as a referee in the continual bickerings between men with personal financial transactions. Because promissory notes were a form of tender, cases like that between Jonathan Brewer and Sewall's client Joseph Waite were common. Brewer, a wealthy Framingham man, endorsed to Waite a promissory note he held from a third party, Phineas Atherton. Atherton, however, never honored his note; in fact, when the case finally came to court in September of 1765, Atherton was missing from the scene entirely. Waite, a gentleman from Brookfield, called upon Brewer to make good the promissory note, but Brewer refused. The Worcester inferior court upheld Brewer's refusal, but at the September sitting of the Superior Court Sewall won a reversal of the judgment for his client.[25] In cases simpler than the Brewer-Waite dispute, where one party sued a second party for payment on his own promissory note, the legal suit was actually no more than a dunning measure.

Such was the anatomy of the colonial lawyer's practice. But acquiring that practice was less simple than mastering the legal skills required to sustain it. In establishing himself, the young lawyer found the patronage of the profession's elder statesmen more important than his own individual talents. Sewall knew this well, for his own start had been eased by Chambers Russell's gift of the Charlestown practice. In fact, however, Russell's generosity had far greater importance than simply providing Sewall with an initial clientele. By it Russell had decisively influenced the direction of Sewall's career. Because of Russell's bequest, Sewall did not, like many young lawyers, succumb to the lure of Boston, where competition was acknowledged to be tougher, but opportunities for income and fame appeared to be greater.

One of the admitted attractions of Boston was, of course, the presence there of many of the leading lights of the profession. Their patronage, if it could be won, guaranteed success. But these urban leaders did have their country counterparts. And by virtue of their almost undisturbed local monopolies, these rural patriarchs could be equally helpful in securing a young lawyer's future. In Sewall's vicinity such a man was Edmund Trowbridge, the undisputed ruler of the Middlesex and Worcester bar.

"Old Goffe," as Trowbridge was called behind his back,* was a crotchety, gloomy man, more skilled in the intricacies of legal form than in his courtroom presentation. Despite this lackluster courtroom style he had served ably as Attorney General of the province since

---

* Edmund Trowbridge had for a time adopted the surname of his maternal uncle, Colonel Edmund Goffe, whose adopted child and heir he was. He later resumed his paternal name.

1749, and precisely because of his knowledge of legal technicalities "Goffe" became an invaluable advisor to his close friend, Thomas Hutchinson, the legal novice who became Chief Justice in 1761.

Trowbridge's power over the legal profession and its spoils in the two counties was virtually unchallenged. "He had," John Adams wrote with grudging respect, "power to crush, by his frown or his nod, any young lawyer in his county." [26] It was Trowbridge who took up where Chambers Russell had left off the supervision and guidance of Sewall's future. A close professional relationship developed quickly between the old and the young man, and by the early 1760s Sewall had become an informal junior partner in Trowbridge's extensive practice. In 22 of the 45 Superior Court cases Sewall participated in between 1762 and 1765, he was acting as Trowbridge's associate.

Although he was based in Middlesex and Worcester, Trowbridge had province-wide connections. Through him, Sewall gained the acquaintance and the legal loyalties of important mercantile families like the Goulds of Boston, the Tyngs, and the Hunts.[27] Added to what elite clientele Russell had passed on with his Charlestown practice, these wealthy families formed the core of Sewall's future blue-ribbon practice. But Sewall's association with Trowbridge yielded more than clients. From it came experience in the courtroom, exposure to the legal forms and procedures in a wide variety of cases, and the opportunity to work with the man legal historian Charles Warren called "perhaps the most profound lawyer of New England before the Revolution." [28]

Trowbridge's original interest in Sewall may well have stemmed from Russell's personal endorsement, or from Sewall's family connection with Justice Stephen Sewall. But "Goffe" would not for long have wasted his patronage on a mediocre lawyer, no matter how well recommended he came. It was Sewall's performance that insured Trowbridge's continuing interest. Sewall was talented, and he had a special aptitude for mastering legal intricacies, which the learned Trowbridge reveled in and enjoyed developing. His powers of logic were exceptional. And in the courtroom he was smooth, eloquent, and subtle—qualities Goffe admired perhaps the more because he lacked them himself. John Adams, never overly generous with praise for competitors, conceded that Sewall had as much power over a jury "as any lawyer ought ever to possess." [29]

CHAPTER THREE

The Rewards of Loyalty
1763-1768

IN THE SUMMER of 1760, while Sewall pored over "codes, pandects, digests, institutes . . . etc. in infinitum" in his Charlestown home, a series of events in Boston were about to draw him deeply into provincial politics.

That summer an influenza epidemic struck Boston. One of its most deeply mourned victims was Jonathan Sewall's uncle, provincial Chief Justice Stephen Sewall, who died in September. Sewall had been a popular figure in Massachusetts politics and law, and the people of Boston paid their respects in the longest funeral procession Massachusetts had ever witnessed. Jonathan Sewall's old adversary, Jonathan Mayhew, never sparing with his words, offered a fittingly effusive eulogy.[1]

But the judge's death was a political as well as a public event. A heated competition for the Superior Court vacancy quickly ensued, and the Massachusetts political world, which had been temporarily united by the new administration of Francis Bernard, once again dissolved into personality-based factions.

The two leading candidates for the bench were Lieutenant Governor Thomas Hutchinson and James Otis Sr. Hutchinson was the choice of the Court itself. Though he had no legal training, the Lieutenant Governor had the requisite social standing. And, Hutchinson had judicial experience. He enjoyed, simultaneously with his executive position and his seat in the Council, bench appointments as Judge of Probate in Boston and Judge of the Suffolk Inferior Court of Common Pleas. His appointment to the Superior Court would create an embarrassment of political riches certain to draw resentment in a province where applicants were many and political plums few.

Leaders in the legislature lobbied for James Otis Sr., then Speaker of the House. Otis was a qualified and experienced lawyer, but his claim to the office was built as much upon broken promises and disappointments as it was upon his legal credentials. For the truth was that the elder Otis's career was marred by his long history of failure to ascend to the Superior Court Bench. An opening left by Paul Dudley in 1749 had been filled two years later by Chambers Russell. It was widely rumored that Otis had both sought and expected this place on the bench. In 1755 a vacancy was created when Richard Saltonstall stepped down. Again Otis was passed over, this time for Peter Oliver. Governor Shirley assuaged the angry Otis with pledges that the next vacancy would be his. Now Otis came to collect his office, for he obviously felt one governor's pledge would and should be binding on another.[2]

While Otis actively lobbied, Hutchinson coyly hung back. He permitted himself to be drafted by the Governor for the office, and when the offer was made he heightened the appearance of reluctance by warning Francis Bernard to reconsider. Only when Bernard had assured Hutchinson that Otis would in no case be the recipient of the office did the Lieutenant Governor acquiesce.[3]

Whether Bernard was fully aware of the political consequences of his appointment is uncertain; perhaps he had not had time enough in his new office to acquaint himself with the political idiosyncrasies of Massachusetts. He was soon to feel the weight of his decision, however, for it brought down upon him the lasting and active antipathy of the two Otises (both of whom were rich in political power and talents) and the charges of abuse of patronage that would haunt him through his decade as Governor.

Bernard's own needs as a new governor had probably weighed

heavily in his choice. He had heeded the wishes of his Superior Court judges, hoping no doubt to insure what would be an asset to any provincial executive: a loyal, and thus predictable, judiciary. He had also acted with an eye toward further securing the affections and loyalty of his second in command. Supporters of Otis, however, viewed the choice in a different light. They insisted that the Hutchinson appointment was not only an abuse of patronage, but also a purposeful packing of the Court to insure the outcome of a major struggle between the Crown enforcement agency, the Customs, and local merchants. This matter was scheduled to reach the Court soon. The merchants were challenging the constitutionality of the general writs of assistance. As it was Hutchinson himself who had introduced the use of these general writs in 1756, he was certain to uphold their legitimacy. Thus his appointment precluded the trial's outcome. This interpretation cast the new Governor as an opponent of merchant interests and as an outsider antagonistic to the rights of the province.*

The events of the following month seemed to support the Otis faction's interpretation. Thomas Hutchinson took office in January 1761; a month later the arguments for and against the writs of assistance began. James Otis Jr. resigned his office as Advocate General to argue the merchants' case.

Years later, when the Tories tried to understand and explain the Revolution, they would look to James Otis Sr.'s thwarted judicial hopes as the spark that set Massachusetts aflame. From the father's disappointed ambitions sprang the son's determination to do battle with the government. The first blow in this battle was struck in the writs of assistance case. The Tory interpretation of the Revolution's origins was, of course, as much an unintentional tribute to the Otises' talents and leadership as it was the myopic conclusion of a challenged political elite. It was true, however, that one could see per-

* John Adams later wrote that Thomas Hutchinson was appointed Chief Justice to decide in favor of the writs of assistance in 1761, in order that tyrants might "Conquer the English colonies, and subject them to the unlimited authority of Parliament."
(John Adams to William Tudor, March 29, 1817, *WJA,* 246–47.)

sonified in the bitter struggles between Otis and Hutchinson the evolving struggle between assembly and executive.

The enmity and division in the political sphere gave new importance to the personal loyalties of men like Johathan Sewall. Although many of his younger colleagues were inclined to support the popular faction of the Otis family, Sewall continued to cast his lot with those men who had nurtured his career. Both Chambers Russell and Edmund Trowbridge were intimate friends of Thomas Hutchinson, and both were firm in their support of Governor Bernard. Sewall had himself already sampled the Governor's benevolence: in the fall of 1760, Bernard had commissioned Sewall as a Justice of the Peace for Middlesex County.* Thus, if Sewall had little reason to disturb the course his career was taking under Trowbridge and Russell's gentle management before the Hutchinson appointment, he had even less reason to do so now. To move to Otis's camp would be to lose his patrons; to remain loyal would deepen their attachment to him. And, surrounded by enemies, Bernard would be certain to take more immediate note of a talented young friend.

Sewall's personal experience with the Otis family over that same winter reinforced his disinclination to alter his loyalties. Simultaneously with the battle over the writs of assistance, Sewall had waged his own war with the popularly elected branch of the legislature. As executor of his uncle's estate, Sewall quickly discovered that the judge had died as penniless as he was popular. Jonathan Sewall realized that sizable debts would remain unhonored if extraordinary measures were not taken. These measures, he believed, should be taken by the province itself. To this end, he decided to petition the Assembly for a grant to settle the Chief Justice's accounts. He turned to the elder Otis for the sponsorship and management of his petition.

Sewall was probably naive in believing that Massachusetts Bay would willingly translate affection into dollars. Perhaps, on the other hand, his choice of the Speaker of the House as the bill's sponsor shows that Sewall anticipated the difficulties ahead. Whatever his ex-

* The commission is dated November 20, 1761.

pectations, the suspense on the matter was short-lived. On March 28 the Assembly refused Sewall's petition.[4]

John Adams, who was much given to the theory of great and sudden turning points in public and private histories, believed the rejection of the petition worked a reversal in loyalties in Sewall analogous to the recent, more spectacular conversion of the Otises.

> [Sewall] had been as ardent an American and as explicitly for resistance to Great Britain, in arms, as I ever had been or ever have been. . . . but Colonel Otis, of Barnstable and his son, the great Boston orator, states-man, and patriot, had not supported his petition with as much zeal as he wished, and his resentment of their *nonchalance* became bitter. Hutchin-son, Trowbridge, and Bernard soon perceived his ill humor, and immedi-ately held out to him prospects of honor, promotion, and wealth.[5]

This interpretation, true to Adams's shrewd understanding of Sewall's temperament, was marred by political anachronism and distorted by political moralizing. Of Sewall's anger there could be no doubt. Even had he understood clearly the slim chance of his petition's success, the defeat would sting. Sewall was a man particularly apt to carry a grudge against those in authority who insulted him or thwarted his desires. He would angrily blame Otis for neglect, and the Assembly for ingratitude to his uncle. But these were personal and emotional judgments rather than political ones. At stake was family reputation, not American resistance to British policy. The petition affair provided Sewall with an emotional confirmation of a practical decision to sup-port the administration: an administration that had *already* shown its interest in him. Sewall's decision did not carry, in 1761, that commit-ment to Toryism which such a choice would carry in 1774. Adams speaks unhistorically when he portrays his friend as casting off his "Americanism." Sewall had simply chosen with reference to his own career, in a situation whose political consequences were not yet known as Revolution.

Yet, Sewall's choice would lead most logically to the Loyalist op-tion. "The die," as Adams was so fond of saying, "was cast." An appointive government career was now more than ever a likely consequence of Sewall's connections and loyalties. His ambitions would surely lead him to take advantage of opportunities to serve the men in power who favored him. And, in so far as personal and practical loyalties took on ideological significance, Sewall's public support and defense of Bernard and Hutchinson would become an apology for imperial status quo.

Sewall's own value to Bernard's now beleaguered administration did not become apparent until 1763. Early that year he enhanced his position with his debut as a political essayist in a newspaper skirmish between government and antigovernment factions. Sewall was a novice at this particularly popular provincial art form, but he immediately revealed his potential worth to the administration as a propagandist and apologist.

The newspaper battle revolved around a wartime measure of 1762. In September of that year, Governor Bernard used his executive powers to increase the armament and manpower of the provincial gunship, which he had sent to protect the New England fishery off the coast of Newfoundland. The Governor reported his action to the Assembly in a message dated September 16. The Assembly raised no protest over the expenditure itself, which was insignificant, but the Governor's independent action raised serious constitutional issues in the elder James Otis's mind. Otis saw the Governor's appropriation of provincial funds "without the knowledge of the House and . . . without their privity or consent" as a usurpation of the Assembly's historical role. In a response to Bernard, drafted by Otis Jr., the Assembly reminded the Governor that "No necessity can be sufficient to justify a House of Representatives in giving up such a privilege; for it would be of little consequence to the people, whether they were subject to George, or Lewis, the King of Great Britain, or the French King, if both were arbitrary, as both would be, if both could levy taxes without Parliament." [6]

The Governor returned Otis's handiwork to the Assembly, declaring it disrespectful to King and Government, and totally unacceptable as an official communication from the House. But the Assembly, after some debate, sent the unaltered address back to the Governor. The Governor ceased all efforts to have the offending correspondence corrected, and contented himself with having the last official word in the affair: He addressed to the Legislature a lengthy vindication of his conduct regarding the military appropriations.[7]

Otis would not, however, let the matter end here. In a move that anticipated the most successful of the later propaganda techniques, Otis took the dispute to the public through the newspapers. In November 1762 he published ''Vindication of the conduct of the House of Representatives of the Province of the Massachusetts Bay: more particularly in the last session of the General Assembly.'' The ''Vindication'' included a full account of the exchange between Assembly and Governor, all the pertinent documents that passed between the two branches of government on the matter, and Otis's own extended commentary on the constitutional issues he believed raised by the Governor's independent action.

The ''Vindication'' triggered a general antiadministration attack that continued through the winter months of 1762–63. As the attack widened Thomas Hutchinson became a particular target in the press, for a conflict of will between Hutchinson and Otis had developed regarding instructions to the provincial agent, Jasper Mauduit.*

Sewall entered this newspaper fray in February 1763. Under the pseudonym ''J'' he produced an extended series of satirical political essays designed to expose and discredit the motives of the government's opposition.[8] On the whole, these essays bore the heavy-handed touch of the amateur. Sewall dubbed Otis ''Bluster'' and characterized him as a man driven by mental derangement and disappointed ambitions. With an organized cabal of fellow malcontents, Bluster had worked through the press to undermine legitimate authority in Mas-

---

* Otis' behavior during the Mauduit dispute did little to shake the Tories' firm belief that personal antipathy to Hutchinson guided Otis's political behavior. In the middle of the debate in the Assembly over instructions to the provincial agent, Otis shouted: ''Damn the letter and D—— Mr Maudit [sic] I don't care a farthing for either but I hate the L-G- should prevail in anything.'' (Freiberg, ''Prelude,'' pp. 46–47.)

sachusetts. This cabal, who held "their nocturnal assemblies, and with senatorial wisdom consult, debate, project, write, drink, & smoke," [9] had sought to ruin the reputations of honorable men, and to harm the province by raising false cries of danger to liberties.

Sewall's rather ungentlemanly exposure of Otis's emotional difficulties and his attack on the "Vindication" did little to stem his opponent's rising popularity. The younger Otis was in his prime; his leadership in the challenge to the Bernard administration won him the powerful position of Boston town moderator that year. His election revealed both Otis's popularity and the expanding powers of the Boston Caucus Club, the political machine that masterminded that election. [10] On accepting the office Otis gratified his audience with a speech on British tyranny. On March 29, the local newspapers carried Sewall's response to that speech: a labored, unsuccessful parody, in verse. [11]

As the battles continued the issues expanded. Oxenbridge Thacher, Otis's legal partner in the writs of assistance case, had long cast a disapproving eye on Lieutenant Governor Hutchinson's propensity to collect offices. Now Thacher made public his concern that holding office in all three branches of Government was an abuse of British safeguards, which demanded separation of powers. His anti-Hutchinson article urged that the Lieutenant Governor, and the Superior Court judges as well, be barred from seats in the upper house of the Legislature. The article's appearance was timely, for elections were to be held in May for the Council seats.

Thacher's concern over monopoly of office was not wholly public-spirited. There was an edge of jealousy to his complaint that "a multiplicity of public trusts . . . was indeed a practice in the *infancy* of the country; but there might be a necessity for it then . . . that gentlemen of education and ability could not be found at that time to fill up every place in government; but through kind providence the case is very much alter'd now." [12]

Sewall's response to this attack, printed in the May 23 supplement of the *Boston Evening Post,* was superior to his other essays because it

shifted away from the earlier *ad hominem* arguments. He
began this essay with a philosophical discussion on liberty, which he
believed crucial to the rebuttal of Thacher's charge. The tension between the law and liberty, he wrote, was the essential dilemma of any
society. The British government was the best in human history precisely
because it had created a workable and admirable balance between the
impulse to personal gratification and the need of the larger society for
order. This balance, however, was achieved by the redefinition of liberty, or, as Sewall put it, the distillation of moral impulse from mere
craving for license. The society in which liberty and law were in equilibrium was one in which its people understood and accepted Montesquieu's definition of liberty: "in societies directed by laws, liberty
can consist only in the power of doing what we ought to will and in
not being constrained to do what we ought not to will. We must have
continually present in our minds the difference between independence
and liberty." Liberty was a right to do whatever the laws "permit."
Thus liberty—"rightly understood"—was the greatest of God's blessings. Its paradoxical fulfillment through submission preserved the
very social organization which man's impulse for rational freedoms
had created.*

The delicacy of the balance achieved by the British constitution
made innovation and tampering indisputably dangerous. The system
did, Sewall conceded, require constant surveillance, for men who administered the law might abuse their power and tyranny result. But all
self-appointed and self-declared watchdogs must themselves be
watched. The loudest declaimers for liberty were not always its truest
friends: Rome had its Catiline; Massachusetts, its Bluster. In the end,
Sewall cautioned, liberty and society could be preserved only if the individual citizen did not "give implicit credit to the turbulent
harrangues of every bold, disaffected, popular disclaimer," but judged

* There is, of course, strong similarity in Sewall's definitions and Burke's. Of liberty,
Burke wrote: "the Liberty I mean is *social* freedom. It is that state of things in which
Liberty is secured by the equality of Restraint." (Quoted in Connor Cruise O'Brien,
ed., *Burke's Reflections on the Revolution in France* [Baltimore, 1968], p. 15.)

for himself the health of his society. Precisely because it was so difficult to discern the true patriot from the false, and true danger to liberty from false accusation, men should move for any change with enormous caution. The consequences of a misguided action would be irreparable—and usually tragic. British society stood like a house of cards; the slightest dislodgement of one seemingly insignificant piece could bring the whole structure down.

Fortunately, Sewall explained, the system was substantially self-regulating. Were men in authority to abuse their powers dangerously, the abuse could not be hidden. The threat would be immediately and universally felt. For this very reason, the scattered and nonuniversal alarms being sounded in public assemblies and private caucuses against the administration of the law must be suspect.

Thus far, Sewall's argument had been carefully and brilliantly developed. He espoused liberty, then redefined it in its most conservative form. He endorsed the vigilance of the citizen against tyranny, but reversed the direction from which that tyranny threatened society. Having thus justified his suspicions of the antiadministration forces he at last began a long, point-by-point refutation of the specific charges against Hutchinson.

The major accusation against Hutchinson was that his service in legislative, judicial, and executive capacities would threaten public liberty. This charge, Sewall argued, arose from his opponents' misreading of their revered Montesquieu's maxim on separation of powers. Montesquieu, as Sewall understood him, saw no danger in the individual man serving in dual or multiple capacities. The philosopher, an admirer of the British system of government, was warning against the threat of liberty engendered in the overlap of a majority of one branch with the majority of a second branch of government. Montesquieu's maxim was, after all, based upon the successful organization of the British system, and in that system, a Lord, made a chancellor or a judge, was not required to give up his seat in Parliament. "If my argument is conclusive with respect to England," Sewall said, "it is so, *a fortiori* in regard to this province, because our Board of

Councellors is not the Supream [*sic*] Court of Judicature here, as the House of Lords is there.''

To dispel concern over Hutchinson's dual services in executive and legislative capacities, Sewall drew upon the example of the King himself. The supreme executive, through a renunciation of his *control* of Parliament, was assured an essential *share* in the legislative branch. Thus, the necessary separation of powers was secured by the independence of the legislative majority from the Executive.

Sewall capped his rebuttal with an assurance of security which was to prove overwhelmingly ironic in light of political developments in the next decade. He noted that this specter of arbitrary power, raised by critics of Bernard and Hutchinson, was nothing more than a phantom. For ''we are a dependent state, under the control and protection of Great Britain,'' and if Massachusetts were to be weak enough to suspect the Lieutenant Governor of a wicked design to enslave his country, surely she must be weak indeed to fear him, ''unless we can also suppose the King, Lords, and Commons of Great Britain, to be in combination with him.''

Sewall's confidence in the benevolence and integrity of those in power was the obvious thread of his philosophical cloth. Within his own experience this had been true. Yet there were others who saw Sewall's loyalty in a less flattering light. Although the newspaper battle ended in May, the August papers carried an interesting postscript to the debate. This essay, entitled ''On Self Delusion,'' [13] was more than an attempt to have the last word in the now slumbering debate. It was intended as a sobering criticism of ''J,'' his motivations and his ambitions. This angry, scolding piece was the work of John Adams. Adams saw his friend as a party man, and nothing more, ''enlisted under the banners of a faction.''

A thousand reprimands from Adams could do little to silence Sewall. But while others flocked to the ''banners of a faction'' in the debates that followed news of the Sugar Act, Sewall did rest his pen. Nor did he take a public stand on that flurry of political activity in 1764 which included both the first Committee of Correspondence and the first nonimportation agreement. For Jonathan Sewall, the year's major event was decidedly domestic. His long-delayed marriage to Esther Quincy, daughter of Massachusetts squire Edmund Quincy, at last took place.

Sewall met Esther in 1759, on a boating party. He was immediately infatuated, and wrote a long and lavish account of the moment.

> When I first cast my Eyes on [Esther], she appeared to me in the rank of Agreeables; & I viewed her with that unruffled pleasure, with which I consider a fine painting; being asked to sing, she readily performed her part with such unaffected Modesty & with so nice a Judgment (joined to as musical a Voice as ever Nature gave) as commanded my whole attention, & added insensibly to the pleasure which I before received from gazing on her; in her whole Behavior she discovered the utmost pleasantness & good-Humour; in short to real good Sense was joined, such Delicacy of Manners & such becoming Modesty as effected in me the disorder of which these are some of the Symptoms.

Sewall's symptoms were highly romantic. When Esther wandered from his sight, he found his eyes "roving and wandering about, without fixing on any one Object seeming as it were at a loss where to point till she appeared again." Whenever the opportunity arose, Sewall placed himself beside her, and "when she changed her Seat, my Mind presently suggested some Excuse for rising & walking about till I could seat myself by her again." [14]

Their courtship began immediately. Each weekend Sewall rode to the Quincy residence in Braintree where he enjoyed not only Esther's company but, coincidentally, the companionship and conversation of John Adams, who was seriously courting Hannah Quincy at the time. Though Adams privately judged Esther less intelligent than her sister Hannah, he nevertheless approved the match. Yet despite Esther's willingness and Sewall's commitment, the courtship dragged on for five years. The delay was a matter of practicality. Marriage was still as much an economic as a romantic institution, and an early union would do little to assist Sewall's fortunes, or Esther's. He was still a struggling lawyer, and her father was teetering on the brink of a temporary

financial ruin in June 1759. By November of that year Edmund
Quincy had filed a petition of bankruptcy in the Assembly.[15] Not until
January 1764 did the wedding take place.

Thus the year of the Sugar Act was one without overt political activity for Sewall. He seemed equally careful not to commit himself publicly in the dramatic debates over the Stamp Act in 1765. But his
silence in this instance did not reflect approval of imperial taxation
policy; Sewall, like his radical friends, opposed the Stamp Act and its
precedent-setting direct taxation. The opposition to the Act was in fact
almost universal, and it united in sentiment if not action such unlikely
political bedfellows as Otis and Hutchinson, Bernard and Sam Adams.
But the public expression of protest was firmly in the hands of the antigovernment leaders, which limited the options available to Sewall for
expression of his own opposition. The antigovernment faction saw as
one issue the passage of and the enforcement of the Stamp Act; thus
protest of the taxation was as fiercely antiadministration as anti-
Parliament. The very organizations that executed the protest tactics
were in themselves challenges to the established authority in the province. Therefore, a public declaration by Sewall might well be read as
an antiadministration stance.

The career consideration was not the only cause for silence. A genuine disagreement over tactics existed between government men and
popular leaders: the humble petition to Parliament, conceived as proper
by Thomas Hutchinson, was in striking contrast to the direct action of
intimidation of stamp collectors, so acceptable to Sam Adams. Beneath
the tactical difference lay an even deeper ideological split. Though
Thomas Hutchinson and Francis Bernard sought repeal as honestly as
Sam Adams and James Otis, the former petitioned for it as a matter of
favor, and the latter demanded it as a matter of right. Sewall, like
Hutchinson, would prefer submission to the tax to the unlawful resistance waged by Otis and Adams.[16]

The Stamp Act was repealed in March 1766, and protest against imperial policy quieted. Not so protest directed against local administration. In the wake of repeal, and before the election of the Council,

recriminations against Bernard and Hutchinson were vocal. The election of James Otis Jr. as Speaker of the House revealed the strength of the antiadministration party; but that strength was more strikingly revealed when Francis Bernard exercised his veto power against Otis. The price of this challenge to the popular party was the defeat of the Lieutenant Governor, the Provincial Secretary, a Superior Court Justice, and Attorney General Trowbridge in their candidacy for the Council.[17] The Governor had, by his defiance of the Otis faction, learned the full extent of his opponent's power. He had lost control of the upper House.* When Bernard made especial mention of the omission of these men from the list of Councillors, the House responded facetiously that their exclusion would leave these gentlemen more time to study law and discharge their various offices.[18]

It was clear that antiadministration forces had grown bold in the wake of a tax repeal they attributed to their own protest. In rapid succession, they forced the government into a humiliating compromise over compensation for victims of the Stamp Act riots,[19] and then followed with a frontal attack on Francis Bernard's record as Governor. Sam Adams and Joseph Warren, as "A" and "Paskelos," set the pace of this newspaper exposé, accusing the Governor of abuse of powers and personal avarice, both of which must perforce contribute to the erosion of provincial liberties. The newspaper challenge to Governor Bernard produced a situation tailor-made for Sewall's reentry into politics.[20] His skills lay in the persuasive powers of logic and style. And, this assault on authority was clearly divorced from the larger and more ambiguous issue of imperial taxation. On December 1, 1766, Sewall, as "Philanthrop," began a lengthy defense of the executive.

He devoted his opening essay to the establishment of a philosophic framework. This was not an idle indulgence of his own interest in po-

---

* The election of James Bowdoin as Chairman of the Council in lieu of the vetoed James Otis marked the beginnings of the Council's effective unity with the House. Bowdoin, a Harvard graduate, was the son of one of the richest merchants in New England, and by 1766 a devoted member of the Otis-Adams faction.

litical theory. For his purposes, he believed that it was essential first to prove the superior virtues of social man over natural man. Succeeding in this, he would then analyze the essential components of social man's organization of society. If he could prove authority, and respect for authority, to be crucial to the maintenance of society, then he would vindicate Francis Bernard and justify his own defense of the Governor.

Sewall believed that the virtues of society were readily apparent to all men. True, man in nature was unrestrained in his pursuit of self-gratification; but this liberty, Sewall argued, drew man to an immediate and therefore infantile range of pursuits, leaving his rational capacities undeveloped. Furthermore, the possibilities for this self-gratification were always endangered by individual man's helplessness in the face of nature's more hostile creatures. In short, man in nature was weak, insecure, and childish. Men combined in society, however, were a species transformed. They were "lords of the lower world" of beasts by virtue of the ascendency of reason, which the formation of society both required and assured. Society protected and preserved mankind; it fulfilled God's intention that man become a rational creature.

This joining together of individual men produced a collective individual: society. All legitimate actions taken for the preservation of that collective individual must therefore be oriented toward the common good over—and if necessary at the expense of—the individual good. In short the whole was not only more than the sum of its parts; it also operated on an entirely new moral level.

In his "J" series Sewall had discussed the tension between individual and social will, and had shown the threat "natural liberty" posed to "social liberty." The protection of that social liberty he called the law. He reconciled the conflict, and justified the creation of law by redefining liberty. Now, as "Philanthrop," he introduced a second instance of imperative redefinition. For a second sacrifice was required of men in their move from nature to society: "the natural state of equality (in which all men are born)" must be exchanged for an "artificial state of *preheminence* [*sic*] and *subordination.*" This artificial arrangement was called government. Government was a social division of labor, by which some administered the law so that all might obey it. This arrangement was essential to society, regardless of the form it might take; no man could destroy it without substituting a better form.

Sewall had drawn a kind of metaphysical balance sheet: man in nature had total freedom and equality but limited possibilities; man in society gave up individual liberty and individual equality in exchange for safety, security, and the opportunity to develop his higher powers. The cost of the exchange could not be reduced or bargained, but was absolute. Both sacrifices must be maintained, for the power "of doing what we ought to will" (social liberty) is dependent solely upon the acceptance of subordination.

Having established the importance of the unequal or authority relationship, Sewall now began to discuss the problem of its maintenance. In a free society such as Great Britain the authority relationship rested upon a voluntary acceptance of subordination. This noncoercive condition added to the fragility of Britain's government. In British society, therefore, a man might destroy the state simply by persuading the citizens that voluntary submission was unnecessary. Such a traitor could also attack the subordinate-preeminent relationship by an *ad hominem* attack on the preeminent. "Reviling the ruler" became treason, because what undermines the person usually undermines the office as well. For the majority of citizens, Sewall wrote, "a contempt of the former, and a *veneration* for the latter, are totally incompatible."

Of course Sewall places the usual eighteenth-century limitations on the authority relationship: "I am not endorsing unlimited passive obedience and non-resistance." Men in authority are to be honored and obeyed only as long as they "steadily pursue the sole end of their creation, the good of the community." But as long as they pursue this end, though they err or flounder, their authority is inviolate.

Thus, the stage was set for the vindication of Bernard by proving the purity of his intentions. Sewall could concede that on occasion the Governor had erred, yet could condemn those who had subjected his person and office to "rude savage treatment."

This formulation of the problem was essential, for Sewall understood the nature of the attack on Bernard. The antiadministration men were only secondarily concerned with the specific charges they had leveled against the Governor. Their accusations were not, for example, grounded sufficiently in fact to serve as a basis for impeachment procedures, or for any legal examination into the Governor's behavior. Most charges relied heavily upon insinuation, or upon implications of guilt by association. In many instances, they were based on gross distortion of facts. The primary goal of these opponents was, as Sewall suggested in this first essay, to arouse general suspicion of Bernard the man, Bernard the Governor, and finally, of the executive office itself. Thus a barrage of accusation, covering the widest ranges of personal and professional morality, could produce the desired effect: Sewall could win all his battles but lose his war. Hence, he must create his own framework within which the vindication of the Governor on specific charges would expose and indict the motives of his enemies. The Governor's innocence must reflect upon his accusers as well as upon himself.

Sewall had a wealth of anonymous opponents to choose among. As he put it, "A's, AA's, and B's, in short almost the whole alphabet is conjured up" in the attack upon the Governor.[21] Despite the plentitude of contributors,* the three major themes, greed, abuse of power, and violation of provincial rights, remained constant.

Most of the illustrative charges could be disproved or sufficiently challenged to neutralize them. In some instances Sewall needed only to muster available facts to dispel the accusation. Where fact was more open to interpretation, or less readily accessible, Sewall proved adroit in shifting the burden of proof back upon his opponents. It was, however, in his handling of the Governor's role vis-à-vis the Stamp Act

---

* There were over 21 articles attacking Bernard in the *Boston Gazette and Country Journal* alone between January and May, 1767. (Philip Davidson, *Propaganda and the American Revolution, 1763–1783* [Chapel Hill, 1941], p. 145).

that Sewall was revealed at both his best and his worst. The Stamp Act discussion demonstrated his ability to redefine the questions at stake to his own advantage, and his ability to lead readers to draw conclusions of his own choosing. At the same time, the Stamp Act discussion was the most difficult for him, not because of the subject matter, but because the strongest argument in Bernard's defense required Sewall to contradict one of his own philosophical tenets.

The antiadministration writers charged Bernard with supporting the Stamp Act. They could produce sufficient proof of his explicit action in support of the Act, such as the commandeering of Castle William for the storage of the stamped paper. But they made their case even more cogent by denying the Governor the defense of neutrality. They did this by characterizing the Stamp Act crisis as a political moment of absolute polarity. This polarization eliminated the possibility of a neutral stance. In short, one was compelled by circumstance to be for or against the enforcement of the Stamp Act. Attempted neutrality in this circumstance was seen as support for British policy, for where united resistance by the weaker group is a prerequisite for success against a stronger force, any neutrality always serves the stronger force. Thus the Governor could fairly be faulted not only for what he did do, but also for what he failed to do.

Sewall recast the entire debate. He chose to deemphasize the effects of Bernard's actions or inaction, and stressed instead the Governor's motives. He shifted the reader's attention away from external consequences and focused on the Governor's internal personal dilemma: the conflict between duty and conviction. This dilemma could arise only if Bernard was wholeheartedly opposed to the Stamp Act. Its existence, then, was proof of Bernard's loyalty to the province. Yet as governor he was bound by his oath to uphold and enforce the law. To do otherwise would be to discredit himself with the people he served. Sewall's tactic was a gamble: there was a thin line between eliciting sympathy for the Governor's cross-pressured existence and exposing him as an ambitious hypocrite.

The crux of Sewall's defense of Bernard was that Bernard could be, and was, personally opposed to the Stamp Act, but was publicly obliged to enforce it. The request for understanding of and sympathy for this contradiction between act and thought worked a curious reversal of one of Sewall's own convictions. He had earlier insisted that personal criticism of Bernard and Hutchinson be silenced because the man and his office were inseparable in the unsophisticated popular mind. He now pleaded with the popular mind to appreciate this very distinction between man and office. But a people subtle enough to make the distinction he required must surely be sophisticated enough to deal with any criticism leveled by Bernard's opponents.

Sewall reinforced his argument that Bernard was opposed to the Stamp Act by publishing excerpts from the correspondence of English politicians and merchants in his March 2, 1767, essay. The notables quoted included Pownall, Shelburne, and provincial agent Jasper Mauduit. All praised Bernard for his effective lobbying for repeal and for the cogency of his written arguments against the taxation. Most touched upon the Governor's own good character and his dedication to the interests of the province he governed. And there was poignant mention of the Governor's tragic position as law enforcer: ''While the people were for destroying him, he was saving the Province,'' a London gentleman wrote. Pownall, who might have been expected to understand Bernard's dilemma, praised him: ''All sides here have approved your conduct; first in so fairly giving your Opinion against the Stamp Act, and next in so honorably supporting the Law when it was enacted.''

Sewall's defense of Bernard and Hutchinson was founded in fact. The Governor and the Lieutenant Governor had actively opposed the Stamp Act. Bernard's second in command, excoriated as harshly as the Governor himself, had personally provided Isaac Barré with the most persuasive arguments for repeal.[22] However, proof of Bernard's opposition to the act was not sufficient to end the attack upon him. It was true that so long as provincials accepted the legitimacy of Bernard's official obligations, then the necessity of fulfilling those duties would mitigate public condemnation. But the more successful the radicals were to become in showing the polarity of Crown and provincial interests, the more readily this governor, or any governor, could be condemned for loyalties shown to Crown rather than province. In the end an impossible choice of loyalties would face a governor: obedience to the will of the established sovereign or obedience to the will of the local popular sovereignty.

It was difficult to judge the victor in this newspaper war, but the Governor and his officers appear to have been pleased with his champion.[23] Bernard wanted to reward Sewall, but no appropriate opportunity seemed to present itself. True, March was to be a month of office changings within the judicial and legal branches of the government. The vacancy on the Superior Court, resulting from Andrew Oliver's death, raised Edmund Trowbridge to the bench and thus freed the Attorney Generalship. But Trowbridge's contemporary and fellow elder statesman at the bar, Jeremiah Gridley, was slated for this office. There was, in short, a paucity of dispensable favors at the Governor's hand.

But, if all existing offices were filled or promised, a new office could be created. On March 25 Sewall was commissioned as Special Attorney General, to serve "in all matters and causes whereto Jeremiah Gridley Esquire shall be prevented attending." [24] There was of course some faint justification for the creation of Sewall's post. Gridley was 67 when he took over as Attorney General, and it was entirely possible that the required travel with the Court might prove too much for him.* Nevertheless the sour odor of political reward hung over the affair. It was no secret that the new Special Attorney, for all his legal talents, was also a prolific and "philanthropic" essayist.

The appointment was clearly impolitic and unnecessary, for only two months later the Governor granted Sewall a second, and legiti-

---

* Jonathan Sewall did, in fact, serve as Attorney General at the Middlesex (Charlestown) Superior Court, whose term opened on April 14, 1767, and at the Suffolk (Boston) Superior Court, opening on April 13, 1767. But this evidence does not necessarily support the special attorney appointment. Few Attorney Generals, including Sewall, served the King at every Court session.

mate, commission as Advocate General of the Vice-Admiralty Court
of Massachusetts.[25] In June Bernard made an effort to cover the original mistake by abolishing the offending Special Attorney status and
recommissioning Sewall as "Solicitor General, Council at Law, and
Special Attorney." This no less extraordinary appointment was fortunately short-lived. On September 10, 1767, Gridley succumbed
to "a rising of the lights," a mysterious but fatal eighteenth-century
illness.[26] On November 18 Sewall's status within the Government
was at last regularized by his commission as Attorney General.[27]

CHAPTER FOUR

Conflicting Loyalties, New Demands: The Struggle with the Government 1768-1769

SEWALL'S APPOINTMENTS to the Advocate's and the Attorney General's office gave him a position of importance in Massachusetts beyond his expectations, and perhaps even his ambitions. At forty, he had suddenly emerged a key figure in provincial politics.

But for Sewall, there were unexpected consequences to this success. For the political stage on which he had now moved front and center was a battleground between Crown and provincial interests. Sewall had never perceived his own loyalty to Crown and province as holding any inherent contradiction, but it was soon readily apparent that others disagreed. His choice of loyalties was of considerable importance to these political combatants: he held two important posts whose powers could, if properly manipulated, tip the balance for either side in many of their battles.

Pressure to this kind of partisanship came almost immediately. That it surprised and annoyed Sewall exposed his political inexperience. He had, of course, been partisan throughout the 1760s; it was his defense of the Crown interests which had carried him to the offices he now enjoyed. But until his ascendency into political office his partisan activities had been voluntary expressions of an ideological loyalty to the

British imperial system and of personal loyalties to its individual administrators. He was ready to continue to express this private commitment, publicly, whenever called upon. But he had never been called upon to demonstrate loyalty through the subordination of professional integrity and personal judgment to political considerations. He had never, that is, compromised the execution of professional responsibilities to satisfy political obligations. This was exactly what was expected of him in 1768.

Nor did the demand for partisan exploitation of his offices arise only from the Crown's representatives. Sewall had sensed that his new, active role in the provincial government had not placed him at the head of his provincial community—an honor Chambers Russell had enjoyed—but somewhat outside and apart from that community. His performance in office was surely to be seen as a test of his commitment to the general welfare of his fellow colonials.

Such circumstances as Sewall found himself in as he took office in 1768 would have placed a strain on any man. If there were to be any hope of retaining the good favor of both sides in the local struggle, considerable political finesse would be necessary; but even if Sewall had the political sophistication and skill needed—which he did not—he would have refused to employ them. For he had his own deeply personal investment in the disinterested execution of his legal duties. He was determined to acquit himself honorably in his offices, as he was certain the true heir to Chambers Russell must.

Sewall's first taste of the confrontations to come was with the government. Here the situation he faced was aggravated by a rivalry between customs officers and the executive, most sharply felt by Sewall in his capacity as Advocate General.[1]

As Advocate, Sewall was bound, by logic if not by law, to a loyalty to Customs House policies and to the new Customs Commissioners. Yet his actual bureaucratic superior was Governor Bernard, to whom Sewall owed both official and personal fealty. Unfortunately for him, the Governor and the customs agency were often at odds; vigorous customs enforcement usually required a supportive control over the public peace that the beleaguered Bernard could rarely provide. Thus, while the new customs commissioners threatened strict law enforcement, Bernard hoped to avoid any confrontation of major proportions with the Boston mercantile opposition.

These tensions between the civil and customs agencies were exacerbated by a long history of personal feuds. For several years the Governor and John Temple, head of the customs operations in Massachusetts until 1767, had struggled for control of the customs patronage apparatus. The Temple-Bernard feud dated back to 1764, when Temple, as Surveyor General of the northern revenue district, sought to establish his reputation in England by a show of activity and a semblance of enforcement success. The era of salutary neglect was ending, and Temple intended to present himself as the agent of its demise. Locally, Temple wasted no time in executing a plan to wrest exclusive control of the customs appointments. He did not hesitate to wage open war with his one rival, Francis Bernard. In 1764 Temple suspended one of the Governor's proteges, James Cockle; Cockle was charged with accepting bribes, neglect of duties, and attempting to bribe the Surveyor General.[2]

In justifying the suspension, Temple took every opportunity to link Bernard with the hapless Cockle, and to condemn the Governor for his interference in customs operations. In his letters to the Commissioners of Customs and to influential friends in London, Temple painted Bernard as a man driven to arbitrary and shady acts by his insatiable avarice.* The attack on Bernard continued throughout 1765 and 1766, with Temple hammering away at Bernard's remaining customs appointees and driving out of the service any officer so foolish as to attempt neutrality.[3]

At the same time Temple took care to establish a favorable image of

---

* There is no doubt Bernard took advantage of his control over certain customs offices for the profits in bribes and compoundings which accrued. But Bernard also fought for control over these offices as a means of exerting influence on customs policy; that is, he hoped to determine the intensity and manner of customs enforcement through a control of personnel. Bernard did not want an honest customs agency; he wanted a quiet one.

himself in the eyes of the local populace. He portrayed himself as an honest law enforcer; he painted Bernard as greedy, unscrupulous, and unpredictable. Through this comparison, Temple emerged a moderate. His marriage to the daughter of James Bowdoin, a leading Boston merchant, solidified the Surveyor General's position. There is no doubt that Temple outmaneuvered Bernard on both sides of the Atlantic, presenting himself abroad as the eager watchdog of the King's interests, and locally as the mediating force between the legitimate application of customs laws and their misapplication by the avaricious governor.

Fortunately for the Governor, Temple's control was greatly diminished in 1767, when the Townshend Acts ushered in what were to be the last reforms of the customs service. In an effort to increase the effective enforcement of the laws, Townshend centralized the operations of the customs service in America. An American Customs Board, made up of five Commissioners, was established at Boston, and to it were delegated all powers of supervision previously exercised in London by the English Board.

The care with which the new Board was chosen reflected the British government's genuine desire for customs reform. Four Commissioners—Henry Hulton, Charles Paxton, John Temple, and John Robinson—were experienced customs officials. Hulton, the senior Commissioner, had served as plantation clerk to the London Board since 1763, and had gained his practical experience in the customs houses of the West Indies. Robinson was the long-suffering victim of Rhode Island's wrath, diligent though unsuccessful in his efforts to enforce the trade regulations in that province since 1764. Paxton was a native of Massachusetts, Surveyor and Searcher of Boston under Temple's supervision, and probably the man responsible for the idea of an American Board. Temple had, of course, served as Surveyor General. Only the fifth Commissioner, William Burch, came to the Board without previous experience. Care was also taken to insure that the office of Commissioner carried prestige. Each man received an annual salary of £500, and there were excellent possibilities for added income through seizures and libels.[4]

But the appointment of John Temple to the Board guaranteed that the feud would continue, and expand. The potential dissolution of his private fiefdom, occasioned by the new five-man rule, now provided Temple with two enemies: his traditional foe, Governor Bernard, and his fellow Commissioners, who immediately began to challenge his monopoly of patronage within their jurisdiction.

The strains were thus multiplied: the Board as a whole threatened the Governor; Temple was antipathetic to both Bernard and the rest of the Board; and both agencies faced a hostile and well-organized public opposition. The only factor promoting cooperation was the occasional, natural alignment of the four new Commissioners and the Governor against Temple, a bureaucratic accommodation based upon the principle that the enemy of my enemy is my friend.[5]

Sewall almost immediately came into conflict with the Customs Board. Although he was willing to uphold British laws and British policy he proved singularly unwilling to rubber-stamp their irregular application for political or personal ends. His customs superiors, however, required the manipulation of his powers as Advocate and Attorney General in their efforts to crush mercantile opposition.

As Attorney General Sewall represented the highest provincial authority in the interpretation of the revenue laws. The rubber-stamping of the Board's application of these laws would give them the freedom of action they desired. As Advocate General, his cooperation meant the easy manipulation of the legal apparatus for purposes of lucrative law enforcement and strategic reprisals against the local mercantile opposition. However Sewall, who approached his offices as a lawyer rather than as a political figure, failed to satisfy their expectations. He quickly alienated the Board with a series of disinterested legal opinions on matters that affected the commissioners' pocketbooks as well as their authority. These decisions were the products of Sewall's first major assignment as Attorney General: the clarification of Townshend's new customs regulations and the resolution of disputes between merchants and customs men over ambiguous clauses within these new laws. These disputes were hardly academic, as a great amount of money hung in the balance. The customs men would find every new technicality of the law in their interest, for the complexities of procedure were fertile ground for seizures and libels.

Sewall repeatedly disappointed the customs men. In January 1768 he set down a liberal interpretation of a new law covering loading procedure, which favored the merchants:

> Where a rigid adherence to the strict Letter of an Act of Parliament will expose the subject to great Hardships & Inconveniences, is not necessary to answer the evident purposes of the Act, it is safest & most consonant to the principles of Law & Reason, to give a Liberal Construction to the act, rather than to go beyond the plain design of it, thro Fear of transgressing the Letter; for in such Cases, *Qui haret in Litera, haret in cortice*.[6]

Such fair-minded rulings were appreciated neither by the Commissioners nor their staff. By February 1768 the Board was requesting the English Attorney General to reverse some of Sewall's decisions.[7] And only six months after the Board began to function at its headquarters in Boston, a major confrontation between Sewall and the Commissioners took place. The confrontation grew out of the Board's first major assault on its local mercantile and shipping opposition. In April 1768 the Commissioners decided to take advantage of an incident involving John Hancock in order to make a show of strength. Early that month John Hancock's brigantine *Lydia* returned to her home port after a voyage to London. No sooner had she docked than customs men appeared to watch the vessel's unloading. When Hancock asked these officials their business, they replied they were there to prevent the clandestine running of any prohibited goods. Politely, Hancock permitted them the freedom of the deck; but he ordered his Captain not to allow any tidesman below. Despite this prohibition, however, customs man Owen Richards sneaked into steerage that evening. Learning of this, Hancock came immediately to the *Lydia*. He demanded the intruder come topside, but Richards refused. Hancock next demanded to know if Richards carried a writ of assistance. When Richards admitted he had none, the merchant ordered his mate and boatswain to forcibly return the unwelcome visitor to the deck. Hancock continued his interrogation when Richards was topside. Did the customs man want to *search* the *Lydia?* Richards said no. This questioning by Hancock was not a matter of random curiosity: tidesmen were legally allowed on board vessels either to search or to watch for running of prohibited goods. If they intended a search, they were allowed below deck, but no such permission held for watching. Rumming, it was assumed, could be detected from topside. Thus Hancock was satisfied he had remained within the law.[8]

As might be expected, the Customs Board viewed the episode in a different light. On April 15 Sewall received a letter from the secretary of the Board, detailing Hancock's resistance to the officers of the port of Boston, and requesting that Sewall instigate legal procedings immediately.[9] The ordinary procedure would be the presentation of the case before the next grand jury; the Board, however, specifically instructed the Attorney General to bypass this procedure in favor of the speedier and more certain indictment by "information." An information could be filed directly by the Attorney General and approved by the courts without any grand jury action, and in the hostile atmosphere of Boston the Board hoped to avoid the whims of a local jury. Sewall was familiar enough with the information procedure, for he made frequent use of it, as the King's attorney, in clear-cut criminal cases. In those instances speedy justice was the obvious intent. But Sewall recognized that the Board's major concern was the avoidance of the grand jury in a revenue case, and he ruled against the application of the information in the *Lydia* affair. He considered this innovation in usage to be dangerously open-ended: dangerous, that is, as a legal precedent. Further, he felt that the *Lydia* case was a legally unsound test for this novel use of the information. Thus Sewall was also passing judgment on the merits of the case against Hancock. In refusing to file the information he chose his words carefully to include both points:

tho it is my Resolution at all times to perform faithfully and impartially the duty of my office in aiding and protecting the King's Officers in the due Execution of the Revenue Laws; yet considering the present Case in all its Circumstances & Consequences I could not think it expedient in so

doubtful a matter, to go out of the common course, and commence a
criminal prosecution, which as it appears to me, might probably in the
End be rather prejudicial than advantageous to the Crown.[10]

Sewall's refusal to file the information squashed the action. Although his decision was founded on sound law, the customs officers
were infuriated. His negative was publicly, and therefore politically, a
blow to their authority in the province. It was a clear reminder to revenue officers and smugglers alike that the Board had few resources for
executing their commissions in Massachusetts, and that even the fee-
ble but badly needed executive arm Sewall represented was not wholly
reliable. Against their archfoe John Hancock, the leading merchant of
Boston and the most open flaunter of Customs power and dignity, they
had suffered a serious public defeat.

The real blame, of course, rested not upon Sewall but upon the
Board's poorly conceived and executed attack: they had seized too
hastily upon an opportunity to punish Hancock, and their case was too
flimsy to have succeeded in any but the most prejudiced court. Indeed
Sewall had done the Commissioners a favor they hardly deserved
when he crushed the case before its legal inadequacies could be made
matters of official record. It was, after all, *their* man, not Hancock,
who had breached the law. To search, as the Commissioners themselves knew, was not to watch. Or as Hiller Zobel put it: "It was one
thing to detect a ship owner in the act of landing undeclared cargo; it
was quite another to rummage through a vessel's contents to discover
such goods. The law recognized the distinction, and so did Hancock." [11]

But the Customs Commissioners were angered and frustrated by
Sewall's interference. Fearful of Home government displeasure, the
Board sought to link the *Lydia* decision with its obvious difficulties in
the execution of its office. On May 12 the Commissioners wrote to the
Lords of Treasury, asking for the reversal of Sewall's ruling in the
Lydia case. They insisted that the precedent set by Sewall in this in-
stance would serve as an open invitation to local merchants to step up
their criminal activities. If Sewall's strict interpretation of the law

were affirmed, no customs officer could function effectively under his commission as it presently stood, and it would be necessary "that our officers should have further powers, otherwise the service cannot, by reason of the severity of the [political] climate in this country, be carried into effect." [12] The Commissioners were vague as to what these increased powers should be, but they were clear as to their present dilemma: if they could not stretch the punitive powers of the law, they could not hope to control the widespread resistance to their agency.

The Commissioners capped their memorial with a thinly disguised criticism of Sewall's general performance as a Crown officer.

> While the Crown Lawyers in this Country remain without some certain Salaries, they dare not exert themselves in the service of the Revenue, as they look to the people for their support, and not to Government; In the present state of this Country every officer or person employed in the service of the Crown is certain to be obnoxious to the people if he executed the duty required of him, and therefore it is not to be expected that an Attorney General should be sollicitious for the interest of the Revenue, seeing that Mr. Auchmuty Judge of the Court of Admiralty remains without a salary, or the least Emolument, though he exerted himself upon every occasion, even in the worst of times, when he acted as a Lawyer in behalf of the Crown, with a becoming Zeal and Fortitude, and is deserving of every Favour from Government. [13]

In discussing the absence of an independent civil list the Commissioners had touched on a central weakness in the colonial government structure. But the main thrust of their comments was to Sewall's particular dispirited performance.* Their praise for Auchmuty served to set Sewall's record in an unfavorable light.

The Commissioners stopped short of calling for Sewall's dismissal.

---

* A second letter followed on June 7, 1768, from the Board's secretary, Samuel Venner, to Thomas Bradshaw, the English Secretary of Customs. Though less explicit than the memorial, this communication served to support the memorial's complaint: "The Commissioners being dissatisfied with the Opinions of the Attorney General here . . . upon some points of the utmost importance to the Revenue . . . two cases are herewith sent for the Opinion of the Attorney General in England." (Samuel Venner to Thomas Bradshaw, June 7 1768, PRO, T/1, 465, p. 138.)

There were, after all, the niceties of protocol to be considered: even in his capacity of Advocate General, Sewall was subject to the Governor's authority and not the Board's. Any overt move to have Sewall superseded might bring the Commissioners into an embarrassing conflict with the Governor, whose especial patronage Sewall had secured through his newspaper activities in Bernard's behalf. And, for his own reputation if not for Sewall's, the Governor would be obliged to defend his protege.[14] Only John Temple would rejoice in such an embarrassing development, one that would raise dissension between his co-Commissioners and the executive.

Sewall remained ignorant of the May 12 memorial for several weeks. Nevertheless, through rumors carried to him by concerned friends, he was aware of the Commissioners' anger. For the moment, however, he did nothing in his own defense. He waited until an opportunity arose to learn the full extent of the Commissioners' actions against him.

In the meantime, the Customs war with John Hancock was renewed. On June 10 the Collector of the Port of Boston discovered several infractions of the law aboard the *Liberty*. The Hancock vessel was seized.[15]

This seizure offered the province's radicals their best propaganda opportunity since the Stamp Act.[16] The radical faction had long recognized the central role the customs apparatus played in the real struggle between provincial and imperial interests. But they also recognized the agency's vulnerability as a propaganda target. For the customs service operated as an autonomous unit within the province, an *imperium in imperio,* and it was therefore a most visible example of imperial imposition on the province's self-rule.[17] Its symbolic value to the opposition faction was strengthened by the existence of the very real economic foundations for mercantile grievances.

The seizure of the *Liberty* dramatized perfectly for the radicals' purposes the dangers inherent in the customs agency's autonomy. Radical propaganda could focus on the threat of an increased use of arbitrary power, evidenced by the Commissioners' readiness to manipulate legal technicalities in the interest of political and personal goals.[18] But in organizing their June protest the radicals chose a direct physical attack on the Customs Commissioners rather than a verbal assault on the customs agency. The first victims of the "spontaneous outrage" of local citizenry were Collectors Harrison and Hallowell, who escaped bruised and beaten from the June 10 riot that followed the seizure.[19] In the days that followed, mobs encircled the homes of the customs officers,[20] and a steady barrage of threats to the personal safety of the Board sufficed in place of further violence.[21] The message of the opposition was clear: though Massachusetts could not eliminate the customs laws, it could, as with the Stamp masters, eliminate their executioners. On July 11 the four unpopular commissioners fled Boston aboard the gunship *Romney*. They were delivered to Castle William, where they and their families remained until November 1768.

From the Commissioners' point of view the Board had every right, and in fact a pressing obligation, to enforce the revenue laws. In this light, their attacks on Hancock, though risky, were tactically sound. John Hancock was a symbol to both sides, and not merely the *bête noire* of the Customs Board. As long as he remained unchallenged the smaller shipping interests would continue their resistance. Hancock's conviction for smuggling would go far in squelching the open resistance both to the revenue laws and to the authority of the revenue officers. The *Liberty* seizure, like the abortive *Lydia* episode, was a test case for law enforcement.

The Board did have a legitimate case against Hancock's vessel, and this time it was determined to prosecute despite the threats to the members' personal safety. The members were probably emboldened by the presence of the gunship *Romney,* which had assisted in the seizure on June 10. The present moment seemed as opportune a one as they had yet enjoyed to take their stand in the hostile town of Boston.

The Commissioners intended to file two actions against Hancock. The first was the usual *in rem* proceeding against the vessel itself and the cargo of oil and tar aboard her at the time of the seizure. This proceeding rested on the vessel's infraction of clause XXIX of the Sugar

Act. Sewall was called upon to enter this libel, which he did in behalf of Collector Joseph Harrison on June 22.* The second suit was an *in personam* libel against Hancock and several alleged coconspirators for allegedly smuggling wine off the *Liberty* on May 9, 1768.[22] This was a bolder action, and posed a far greater risk to the Commissioners' continued health and safety. Prudently, they decided to postpone this latter action, for to arrest Hancock while public opinion was so aroused would have brought the mob down upon themselves.

The new Hancock suit drew attention once again to Sewall's relationship with the Board. As Advocate General he would have to act as their agent in bringing the case to court. To him would fall the duties of composing the interrogatories, examining the evidence, and researching and constructing the courtroom arguments. His performance as prosecutor, especially in the *in personam* libels, would be closely monitored. The Board had, in fact, directed its own solicitor, David Lisle, to assist Sewall, and to bring into the case a third lawyer of the Board's choosing, Samuel Fitch.[23]

Sewall probably had no qualms about the *in rem* proceeding, but as a good lawyer his attitude toward the *in personam* action would be one of caution and reluctance. The Commissioners' evidence was slim, and the Boston community almost unanimously hostile to the investigation. The case rested solely on the testimony of one far from reputable tidesman, Thomas Kirk, who claimed that he had been forced into the cabin of the *Liberty* and kept prisoner there for three hours while "many people upon Deck [were] at work hoisting out goods." † The Commissioners, however, intended to prosecute, and had gone over Sewall's head for approval of their *in personam* proceeding. The Board wrote to English Attorney General De Grey for a

* On August 17, 1768, Judge of Admiralty Robert Auchmuty declared the *Liberty* forfeited, but the oil and tar were released. Sewall had argued this case as Advocate General (LPJA, II, 177).

† Originally, Kirk had reported that nothing irregular had occurred that evening (Zobel, *Massacre,* p. 74).

ruling on the legality of their case. The decision to prosecute or not was thus taken out of Sewall's hands.*

The Board members' behavior seemed to confirm the rumors of their displeasure with their Advocate. And by June these rumors had begun to take a more definite shape. From various friendly sources Sewall learned that written complaints against him had been sent by the Commissioners to the Treasury.[24]

Sewall's response to this attempted political knifing reflected the unresolved tensions of his new political role. Foreseeing the conflict between personal judgment and professional obligation that would arise in the upcoming Hancock cases, and angry at the refusal of the Commissioners to recognize his right to impartiality, Sewall reacted hastily and heatedly to the news of their ctiticism. His course of action proved a strange combination of defeatism and stubborn resistance.

He went immediately to the Governor and tendered his resignation from both offices. His motivation for this dramatic gesture was a mixture of frustration and exaggerated personal pride; yet the gesture showed a measure of practical political sense. The Commissioners *could,* after all, damage Sewall's reputation; and in a system of office-holding based on patronage, the alienation of the Home government's goodwill and the removal of its support could mean political death. A man must of necessity look to his reputation. But Sewall's indignation caused him to exaggerate the real threat to his career posed by the Board's criticism. The carping and blame-passing of the May memorial were commonplace elements in government correspondence. As long as Bernard continued to support Sewall, he had little to fear from the Commissioners' dissatisfaction. Thus, when Bernard immediately reassured Sewall as to his own patronage, and urged him to put the matter out of his mind, Sewall should have let his complaint die

* De Grey's response, dated July 25, 1768, gave a cautious approval to the Commissioners. He recommended prosecution if "sufficient proof could be mustered" ("Mr Attorney General's Opinion concerning the Seizure of a Ship in Boston in New England," 25 July 1768, PRO/T1-463, pp. 85–86 [Original]; in PRO/T/64–188 [copy]).

there. Instead, he continued to pressure Bernard. He was compelled by a need for personal vindication. Believing his record in office to be fair and judicious, Sewall saw the Commissioners' unfounded criticism as an insult. Bernard's refusal to assist in punishing or reprimanding Sewall's accusers provoked the Attorney General as well.

Bernard resisted Sewall's demands, which would, of course, have required a confrontation with the Commissioners. In fact, Sewall's visit to the Governor came at a most inopportune time. In July 1768 the always-beleaguered Bernard was locked in a struggle with the provincial assembly over the rescinding of the Massachusetts Circular letter. He·was harassed by the growing threat of a legislative rebellion,* by street riots, and by rumblings of new nonimportation arrangements. Not the least of his troubles was the increasingly vocal complaint by Commissioner Hulton and his three fellow Board members that the Governor was incompetent to protect his Majesty's agents within the province.[25] It was clearly no time for the despairing Bernard to be faced with the resignation of a key officer or with the near impossible task of restaffing. But the alternative, a confrontation with the already irate Customs Board, was no more attractive. Furthermore, as Bernard well knew, intragovernmental incidents like this were unpredictable in their consequences. The spectre of the hostile John Temple hung over Bernard's head. Any effort to resolve this problem quietly, without embarrassment to the imperial government in Massachusetts as a whole, was certain to fail. The Governor was understandably annoyed.

Bernard tried initially to convince Sewall that the rumors of Board criticism were groundless, and rested on the idle gossip of troublemakers.[26] But Sewall left this first interview with the Governor unsatisfied and unpersuaded. He spent the next several weeks in search of some concrete evidence against the Commissioners that he might use to force the Governor's assistance in his defense.

His first success came on July 18. While working with David Lisle

* In fact, the Assembly did refuse to rescind the letter, voting 92–17 against compliance with the Home government's orders.

on the *Liberty* investigation Sewall confronted the Solicitor with the rumors. Lisle pleaded ignorance; he explained that he had no access to the Board's correspondence, and thus he knew nothing of the matter. He did volunteer the information, however, that the Board's secretary, Samuel Venner, who knew the contents of all the department's correspondence, could resolve the matter. When Lisle then agreed to arrange a meeting between the two men, Sewall promptly invited both customs men to his Cambridge home for the evening of July 20, following the Commencement Day festivities at Harvard.[27]

On the designated evening the Solicitor and the Secretary joined Sewall's other guests for dinner. The two customs officials must have been conspicuous that night, for most of their colleagues in the upper ranks of the service had found it necessary to flee to Castle William. Only John Temple and his supporters within the customs service remained safely in the town.*

After dinner Sewall's other guests remained inside while the host and his two new acquaintances held a private conversation outside. In the midst of pleasantries, Lisle rather abruptly came to the point. He supposed, he said to Venner, that the Secretary was ready to answer any questions Mr. Sewall might put to him. Sewall then made a gentlemanly gesture: he would ask Venner nothing if the Secretary felt his own reputation as a civil officer would be harmed by the conversation. Venner waived Sewall's concern aside. He was perfectly willing to answer the Attorney General's questions.

Venner's willingness to reveal the Board's secrets was not difficult to understand; Samuel Venner was Temple's protege. The Secretary proceeded to confirm Sewall's worst fears. Yes, the Commissioners had written against Sewall on several occasions since the year began. Two memorials especially came to Venner's mind. Sewall had been

---

* Robert Hallowell testified before the Board of Treasury that only John Temple and Samuel Venner were safe in the city of Boston after the *Liberty* seizure. (Robert Hallowell's testimony to the Board of Treasury, July 21, 1768, PRO/T/1–468.) The radical press insisted that the Commissioners' safety was never endangered. See for example, "Journal of the Times" *Boston Gazette and Country Journal,* January 25, 1769.

represented as "too much attached to the people and unfaithful in his office," and in the Board's judgment Sewall's partiality to the local interests crippled his usefulness to the Crown. The Board's memorials suggested that Sewall wanted to be relieved from his Advocate's office.

In essence, Venner was presenting the May memorial in its worst light. Although technically a distortion—the memorial had been far less direct than Venner's rendering of it—the Secretary's account was true enough to its intent.[28]

Sewall now had the reliable witnesses and specific information for which he had been searching. Armed with this, he returned to Governor Bernard. He shared the fruits of his investigation with the reluctant Bernard and again urged vindication or resignation. Sewall also went to Lieutenant Governor Hutchinson and to Robert Auchmuty, Judge of the Admiralty. With both he pleaded open support in his behalf, or assistance in persuading Bernard to approve his resignation.

Sewall's strategy proved effective at last. Bernard bowed to the inevitable, and promised he would take appropriate action to resolve the affair. The Governor had little choice: he could not afford to lose Sewall's talents for the Crown, and he could not permit Sewall's resignation to magnify in the public eye the already obvious internal dissension within the government.

Almost simultaneous with Bernard's capitulation the Commissioners were learning of Sewall's complaints from their own solicitor. In an effort to explain the unsatisfactory progress of the *Liberty* investigation, which he said was "not conducted with that Vigor & Spirit which the Service required," the solicitor mentioned Sewall's dissatisfaction with the Board's conduct toward him. Lisle detailed his own conversations with Sewall and Venner's role on the evening of the 20th.[29]

It is difficult to understand Lisle's motivation for this self-incriminating confession. Had he felt pressured when called upon to make his report on Sewall's handling of the Hancock case? This role as watchdog was, of course, the major reason for his collaboration in the *Liberty* investigations. Or perhaps he had hoped to curry favor by reporting the problem to the Board. Most likely, Lisle had collapsed under the pressure from Commissioners Henry Hulton and William Burch to tell what he knew of the affair. These gentlemen had already been alerted by Bernard, unofficially, and by Hutchinson as well.[30]

The complicated episode now posed a multiplicity of problems for Governor and Commissioners alike. Bernard knew that Sewall must be placated, and if the Board had in fact overstepped its powers by calling for Sewall's dismissal, it would be best to reassert his control over the Advocate's office. For his own reputation in England as much as Sewall's he must make it clear that no further criticism would be tolerated. At the same time, he must take care not to openly offend the Board, thereby exacerbating official relations in the process. Bernard's ideal tactic would be one that allowed the Commissioners some face-saving explanation but would get his point across. The Commissioners, of course, must exonerate themselves in the light of Sewall's challenge. Finally, it was necessary for both agencies to look to their public image, locally and at home.

The matter was handled rather skillfully. Both the Commissioners and the Governor presented the dilemma as the outgrowth of a plot to divide and publicly embarrass the two government agencies. By focusing on the necessity for the two agencies to cooperate in the face of sabotage, the blow of the Governor's implicit reprimand was cushioned. In this context of a third-party conspiracy, the actual issue of the Board's relationship with Sewall could be resolved as a token concession to the resolution of the crisis. In other words, the reassurance of Board support for Sewall would be a gesture of good faith. In return, the Governor and his staff would accept the Commissioners' innocence in the affair. The conspiracy explanation would be more convincing of course if culprits could be found. Some heads might have to roll—and Venner and Lisle were the obvious candidates.*

* I am not suggesting this strategy was the result of actual and explicit consultation between the Governor and the Commissioners, although I do not rule out this possibility. It is sufficient to suppose that both sides felt out the most beneficial tactic naturally, in

The only stumbling block to the execution of this scheme proved to be Sewall himself. He insisted on viewing the affair as an investigation into the Board's guilt or innocence. Thus he refused to cooperate with the Commissioners by naming his informers, and he embarrassed both the Board and the Governor by demanding any copies of the Board's official correspondence that mentioned his name.[31] Only after he had seen the correspondence, and could judge Venner and Lisle's guilt for himself, would he make any charges against them. Any other course of action would jeopardize his honor.[32]

Not surprisingly, the Commissioners were hesitant to comply with Sewall's request. They suggested a compromise arrangement. The Board would show the correspondence to the Governor, the Lieutenant Governor, and Robert Auchmuty. If these men found Sewall's fears groundless, then the Attorney General could cooperate in naming his informers.[33] They backed their proposal up with a letter from their clerk, Richard Reeves, attesting that no accusations against Sewall could be found in the Board's records.[34]

Sewall continued to resist. He demanded a personal reading of the documents in question. He did not discover in Reeves's testimonial any *"express* assurances of the untruth of my information."[35] He was insulted by, and suspicious of, the fact that the Commissioners had not declared their innocence to him "in writing, under their hand." He continued to threaten resignation through unsolicited assurances to the Board that the public service would not suffer "during the short time that I expect to be connected with [you] by my office of Advocate-General."

On August 22, the Board showed to Hutchinson and Auchmuty its May 12 memorial, and two letters from its secretary to Thomas Bradshaw, his English counterpart, dated May 12 and June 7, 1768.* Both

---

the manner of the politically astute. On the Governor's side, it is likely that Thomas Hutchinson, more talented in strategy than the bumbling Bernard, was the architect of the Government's part in this solution.

* The May 12 letter to Bradshaw was probably the official statement of the *Lydia* case and the request for its reversal. It has not been found among the Treasury or the Customs Board records.

Auchmuty and Hutchinson interpreted the May memorial as positively favorable to Sewall. Auchmuty declared:

> The reports made to Mr. Sewall, and from him to me, of your Representations to Government at home against him are materially different from those you have made of that Gentleman, the former being virulent and vastly prejudicial to his Character, the latter, accroding to my construction founded rather on a desire of promoting his Interest in Connection with the Crown; by acquainting Government how vain it is to expect an Officer in the Law department to exert himself at the Loss of his time and risk of his Bread merely for the honor of an office. [36]

Both men solemnly conceded, however, that a distortion of the May memorial could serve as the basis of the story told to Sewall.

The Judge and the Lieutenant Governor gave their assurances to Sewall that the Commissioners had not maligned him. Sewall promptly responded that the two gentlemen had been tricked, and "Memorials . . . very different from those copies" they had just seen had been sent to England. [37]

The Board continued throughout August to send reassurances to Sewall through Richard Reeves that these three documents were, in fact, the only pieces of correspondence relating to him.* Sewall's only reported comment was that this was "the most Mysterious Unaccountable affair that he had ever met with." [38] Nevertheless, his continued refusal to name his informers made it very clear that he was unconvinced of the Commissioners' innocence. He understood that the Board intended to portray him as the dupe of Venner. Realizing that he could not prevent this, Sewall all the more doggedly withheld his cooperation.

Tempers were obviously growing short. The four Commissioners (Burch, Hulton, Paxton, and Robinson) were anxious to hang the affair on Lisle, and more especially on Venner, whom they now suggested had been put up to his actions by John Temple. Here, then, was the conspiracy, and for that matter, not so unlikely a one, considering Temple's mastery of intrigue and dissension-sowing. On September 13

---

* These were not, of course, the only documents relating to Sewall. See the February 15, 1768 resolution of the Board, note 7.

Hulton and his three fellow commissioners appealed to the Governor, Hutchinson, and Auchmuty to come to their assistance. All appeals to Sewall had failed; would one of these gentlemen please officially charge Venner and Lisle as informers.[39]

Over a month passed while Hutchinson pressured Sewall to come forward; but he remained silent. On October 29, the same day Sewall filed the Hancock information, Hutchinson took the matter into his own hands. Lamely excusing Sewall's failure to give the Board the information by reference to Sewall's busy schedule in court, Hutchinson continued:

> As you are of Opinion that the Public Service will be prejudiced by any further delay I can no longer refuse or forbear to communicate to you the names of the Persons mentioned to me by Mr. Sewall as the Authors of the Reports to him. The first notice given him he informed me was by Mr. Venner, the Secretary of your Board & he afterwards received a further account from Mr. Venner & Mr. Lisle together but what part of the Reports were from one and what from the others I cannot remember.[40]

Though Hutchinson's information was slightly confused as to sequence, the Commissioners now had a written complaint on which to act. They moved quickly. On Thursday, November 3, both Lisle and Venner were called to the Board to respond to the accusation. Lisle asked permission to express himself in writing, and was excused to do so. Venner, more astute than the Solicitor, refused to respond at all until the exact charges against him appeared in writing.[41] The Commissioners obliged Venner: on Tuesday, November 15, formal charges were drawn up.

Lisle replied on November 18; he denied that he had told Sewall anything, since, as he had said before, he had nothing to tell.[42] Venner was again more cautious than Lisle. First he asked to see all the correspondence related to the affair.[43] Then, on November 21, he respectfully declined to respond to any charges since Jonathan Sewall had made no official declaration against him.[44] A little more than a week later the Board called Venner in for a verbal interrogation. Again he refused to answer. Over Temple's objection the Board next drew up a set of written interrogatories and demanded Venner's co-operation.[45] Finally, on December 15, the Board received Venner's answers to the written questions, and these answers were read into the records.

Venner had denied leaking any information to Sewall. According to his version of the July 20 conversation, he had told Sewall "he knew Nothing more of the Matter" than that he had heard the Attorney General's name mentioned once or twice in the Board's correspondence.

Hulton, Burch, and Robinson immediately wrote to Sewall of Venner's denial, hoping to persuade the Attorney General to come forward at last. But Sewall never answered. The Board was forced to proceed with its trial of Venner and Lisle on information supplied by Bernard and Hutchinson.[46] Finally on Friday, January 13, 1769, Sewall appeared before the full Board. He was shown the May 12 memorial, and Francis Bernard's long personal account of the affair, written to the Board on January 6.[47] This account gave the proper sequence of events regarding Sewall's dealings with Lisle and Venner. Did Sewall have any objections to the letter as it stood? the Commissioners asked. Sewall said no. This was as far as he would go in assisting the Board.

Venner was convicted on the spot.* On January 23, Venner's suspension was signed, despite John Temple's objections.[48] Three days later the hapless Lisle was declared "unequal to the Duty of his Office" and his removal was requested.[49]

Thus the affair ended on this side of the Atlantic. The four Commissioners, with the Governor's help, had succeeded in making stick an official version of the affair which cast Sewall as an innocent tool of the wily Venner. The whole episode, according to the Board's report, had been part of a plot to subvert intra-governmental harmony. Yet, no sooner had the report gone to London than an inevitable next round

---

* The Commissioners rather facetiously noted that their Secretary would not be charged with treason since the information he spread was not true. Instead his crime was the spreading of false rumor "with a malicious intention to sow discord between the Commissioners and the Attorney-General, thereby to embarras [sic] & distress the Board, & to injure the Service" (*MINUTES*, January 13, 1769).

of accusations began. The four Commissioners made clear that they held John Temple responsible for the affair. Henry Hulton, for instance, insisted that Temple "endeavored to make a dissention between the Commissioners & Mr. Sewal [*sic*] . . . & drew the little Secretary of the Board to be aiding in that dark transaction." [50] For his part, Temple threw his whole support behind Venner in the secretary's bid for vindication, indicating thereby his contempt for the transparent tactic of scapegoating. Later in 1769 Venner was exonerated by a committee of inquiry under the Duke of Grafton; his salvation, one suspects, was due not to the merits of his case but to the power of John Temple's connections. [51]

Temple requested his own removal from the Board and the four Commissioners cooperated in seeing that request granted. [52] Their triumph at his departure was dampened by new fears that Temple, now closer to the ears of their superiors, might spread criticism of them in the Treasury circles.*

Turning his back on the whole matter, Bernard returned triumphantly to England, a baronet. There he was accidentally drawn into a new contest with Temple, for the latter had been seeking the very customs post Bernard was awarded. [53] Temple fared well enough, however. He received a profitable appointment as Surveyor General of Customs in England, with £600 a year and 40 shillings per diem traveling expenses. And his role in American politics, though interrupted, was far from over. [54]

Sewall's gains in this Byzantine affair were almost perfectly balanced by his losses. He had won a measure of independence from the Commissioners, but his one remaining obligation to them, the Hancock trial, was to damage him far more directly than all their complaints against him, real or imagined, had done. Bernard had proved indulgent and loyal to Sewall, and had fostered his protege's career

---

* John Robinson sought leave to go Home in November 1769. His troubles with James Otis were the major impetus to his request for a change of scene (see chapter 6), but fear of Temple's effect on Home government opinion was a second consideration (John Robinson to Thomas Hutchinson, November 1, 1769, TH Mss, XXVI, 335–36).

even in the midst of this embarrassing episode Sewall alone had provoked: he secured for Sewall the coveted appointment to the new Vice-Admiralty Court at Halifax. But this victory could not compensate emotionally for Sewall's dissatisfaction at the affair's outcome. He believed his own reputation had been compromised in the interest of government harmony. His critics rather than he had been officially vindicated, while he had been labelled the tool of a petty officeholder. He ignored completely the political lesson offered by the affair's resolution: a man's personal standards of integrity and honor mean less than what is expected of him in office. Neither Governor nor Commissioners were sympathetic to Sewall's conflict of loyalties and his attempts through impartiality to resolve them. The community of Massachusetts would prove no more understanding.

CHAPTER FIVE

Conflicting Loyalties, New Demands:
The Struggle with the Community
1768-1769

FEW PEOPLE OUTSIDE Government circles concerned themselves with the Venner imbroglio, although it was to reach the newspapers that winter. Yet many paid close attention to a concurrent affair: the trial of John Hancock for the smuggling of wine. For his role in this courtroom fiasco, Sewall was to win the enmity of many of his fellow provincials.

The Commissioners had postponed this trial for several months, until in September of 1768 the arrival of military reinforcements at Boston spurred them to file their complaint against Hancock.[1] By November the troops were settled in the city, and their presence emboldened the Commissioners still further. On November 8, the four officials ended a five-month retreat to Castle Island and returned to Boston.[2] In anticipation of their return, the Board had set the prosecution in motion.

On October 29 Sewall had filed informations in the Admiralty court against Hancock and five others, including the Master of the *Liberty*, Nathaniel Barnard, and that perennial troublemaker, Daniel Malcolm.* The sums demanded were impressive, £9000 sterling of

---

* Daniel Malcolm, who had resisted a warehouse search in 1766, was also being sued in the fall of 1768 for illegal running of the cargo on board the sloop *Friendship*. (MIN-

each man—a high price for the smuggling of one hundred £30 pipes of wine. In effect, the Commissioners were calling for a treble-value penalty from each of the alleged conspirators.* On November 3 Arodi Thayer, Marshal of the Admiralty Court, served notice of the libel on John Hancock. Thayer went through the formal motions of arrest, and demanded a bail of £3000 sterling.[3] With some difficulties, Hancock satisfied the £3000 surety and thus freed himself until the trial opened on November 7.

Although this show of authority may have gratified the much abused egos of the Commissioners, their victory was short-lived. John Hancock was instantly made a hero by the press. The *Boston Evening Post*'s "Journal of the Times," a propaganda brainchild of Sam Adams, carried the daily story of the trial, with Hancock as protagonist and the administration and customs service as the unscrupulous villains. The loyalties of the "Journal" were of course predictable, but its success in stamping this heroic interpretation on the public mind undercut the Commissioners' hopes of restoring their own dignity and authority.[4]

The conduct of the trial itself contributed little to the Commissioners' cause, or to Jonathan Sewall's reputation. For five months Boston was witness to a trial marred by irregular proceedings and an openly biased bench, its courtroom tempo set by the prosecution's feverish attempts to build a case on hearsay evidence. The Commissioners, intent on convicting Hancock, made serious blunders. Their resort to bribery and threat was ill-concealed, and rumors were widespread that the Board had guaranteed government posts to any Hancock employee willing to testify for the Crown. These rumors were

UTES p. 107.) In September of 1768, when indictments for the Liberty riots were attempted before a Superior Court grand jury, Malcolm was a Boston-elected juryman. Bernard was justifiably frustrated by Malcolm's election, since it was widely known that Malcolm had led the riots. (Francis Bernard to the Earl of Hillsborough, September 9, 1768, FB Mss.)

* Although Dickerson cites this treble value as outrageous, Zobel argues that the sum was necessarily high because no lesser sum would be punitive for a man as wealthy as Hancock. (Dickerson, "John Hancock"; LPJA, II, 187.)

given credence when several witnesses were indicted for perjury. Among those so indicted was a former Hancock employee whose services aboard a government cutter prevented his presence at his perjury trial.[5]

As the months passed, the Commissioners began to rely heavily upon Robert Auchmuty's judicial favors. In January the Judge ordered the trial into closed sessions, a procedure, one critic noted, reminiscent of Star Chamber.[6] Later, the bench set aside the scheduled closing arguments to permit the Commissioners a last-minute effort to shore up their case. Even with such obvious assistance from the bench, the Commissioners and their attorney could do little to substantiate the charges. By January 30, 1769, the "Journal of the Times" felt confident enough to predict that the Advocate General had not produced, and would not be able to produce, any valid testimony to support the Crown's case. The entire affair, the "Journal" suggested, had been designed "to harrass [*sic*] and distress a most amiable and useful member of society, and in hopes that some evidence would be *fished up* in the course of a lengthy trial." [7] While one's opinion on the prosecution's motivation hinged upon one's political and economic position in the struggle between Crown and merchant, the point taken by the "Journal" regarding the "fishing for evidence" seems warranted. The prosecution had stalled for time, hoping to turn up, by various legal and illegal means, supportive testimony. All these efforts, however, had proved fruitless. The libel rested in March, as it had in November, on the testimony of the self-proclaimed perjurer, tidesman Thomas Kirk, who had originally claimed there were no irregularities in the unloading.[8] On March 25, the Commissioners at last bowed to the realities and permitted Sewall to drop the charges.*

* In their discussion of the *Liberty* case, Zobel and Wroth offer several possible reasons for its being dropped. First they suggest that the arrival of the Vice-Admiralty commissions for Auchmuty and Sewall assured Sewall a fixed salary and allowed him to forego the fight against Hancock which would bring him one-third the forfeiture if the Crown were successful. In the same vein, they suggest that Sewall's commission gave him an independence from the Commissioners which emboldened him to drop the case. Thirdly they point out that an admission of insufficient evidence might lead the Crown to stop

To Sewall this ending to the trial must have come as a great relief. His own role in the case had been degrading. In the courtroom he had not been his own man, for the Commissioners, not the Advocate General, had managed the case. Sewall had been made a party to trickery and sham through the frantic efforts of the Board to manufacture evidence where none could be found. Undoubtedly he shared the Board's belief that Hancock was guilty of the smuggling charge, and that there had indeed been witnesses to the incident. But in the courtroom Sewall rejected the philosophy of ends and means; he would not have substituted plausible but false testimony, purchased or cajoled, for the missing genuine evidence. Nothing in his career as a Crown attorney would suggest such a voluntary deceit by Sewall.

The political legacy of the five-month trial was bitter; it had produced only negative results for the Crown's cause. Sewall, Auchmuty, and the four Commissioners had served the opposition well as easy and visible targets for criticism, and had unwittingly aided the radicals in their tactic of focusing anti-imperial sentiment on key personalities.[9] Throughout the months the "Journal" had woven into one seamless piece the Hancock trial, the military occupation of Boston, and the personal betrayal of the province's interests by its own sons, those "Little creatures of the Court," Jonathan Sewall, Robert Auchmuty, and Charles Paxton.[10]

The closing of the Hancock trial provided Sewall with no respite from public criticism. The newspaper attack against him continued, for the radicals had also set Sewall up as a major target for their antimilitary propaganda. This was not without logic, for Sewall, as Attorney General, handled the flood of cases arising between soldiers and Boston citizens. These cases reflected the understandable tensions of military occupation, and the natural concern of Bostonians for their

---

prosecution (*LPJA*, II, 183–84). The first two suggestions seem untenable since Sewall probably knew of his commisssion in October 1768, and news of his appointment had been carried in the newspapers as early as November 29, 1768, one day after the trial actually began (Dickerson, *BUMR*, p. 28). The third proposal is the simplest and most likely explanation.

civil rights. The Whig newspapers, however, did much to fan rather
than extinguish the flames of conflict. Sam Adams's "Journal," in
particular, turned its attention to this delicate matter of coexistence between army and populace. Throughout its many accounts of real—or
imagined—incidents ran the disturbing theme of the ever-present
dangers in military occupation.

In truth it could be argued that the soldiers fared worse than the civilians.[11] They were harassed by a resentful populace and could expect little chance for redress from Boston's partisan Justices of the
Peace. The partiality of the local courts increased rather than curbed
the resorts to violence in the confrontations between soldiers and civilians. This absence of any neutral and effective agency willing to serve
both sides equitably would produce, finally, a situation that Crown
officers could not control.

As Attorney General, Sewall was called upon to handle most of the
legal cases arising from the occupation. Many of the charges brought
against the military were, in Sewall's judgment, nothing more than
legal harassment. He was especially indignant of what he saw as
trumped-up accusations of assault made against sentries on duty. Any
sentry who challenged passersby to identify themselves could, it appeared, find himself facing a criminal charge for assault against the
peace. Sewall was determined to put a stop to these transparent abuses
of the law. When on January 9, 1769, a Suffolk grand jury sought his
help in drawing an indictment against two soldiers, he would not assist
them. The sentry's rightful execution of his duties, Sewall insisted,
was not subject to criminal prosecution. The "Journal," in reporting
the incident, viewed Sewall's opinion as a virtual invitation for the
military harassment of local citizens. The Attorney General's position
was, as the "Journal" saw it, that "if a soldier should with his fixed
bayonet at the breast of an inhabitant stop and detain him two hours, it
would not in law be adjudged an assault." [12]

Despite the newspaper criticisms Sewall persisted in his efforts to
thwart what he believed were harassments of the military and abuse of
the law. He used his powers of *nolle prosequi* to cushion the effects of

local hostility against the soldiers. Throughout these months he could not fail to see the irony of the situation created by the military occupation. Bernard had called regular forces in to prevent the further embarrassment of civil authorities, yet their presence had only worsened the relationship of Government to populace.* The situation between troops and town was inherently explosive, and at times the judges and Sewall must have felt that they, and not Gage's troops, were the peacekeeping force. In 1770 John Adams would sum up the folly of military occupation to the Government. "Soldiers quartered in a populous town," he said, "will always occasion two mobs, where they prevent one. They are wretched conservators of the peace." [13]

The "Journal" was as persistent in its attack on Sewall as was he in his attack on the abuse of law. Their judgment was that his prejudiced behavior followed naturally from his relationship with Bernard. "The behavior of the K-g's Att-y while attending the jury," the "Journal" said in March, 1769, "was . . . no other than might be expected from one who has lately received so many lucrative court favors through the instrumentality of a G-r to whose views he had for some years past rendered himself quite subservient." Sewall was, in short, a lackey to Bernard. [14]

Thus, in an almost simultaneous attack, Government men had accused Sewall of a partiality to the people which prejudiced his performance as a Servant of the Crown and popular leaders had labelled him guilty of biased behavior in the interest of tyrannical government. Sewall's vulnerability to criticism seemed unavoidable, caught as he was between the expectations of Crown and colony. Yet he continued to pursue a narrowing middle path between two increasingly hostile interests. Committed to his own career and economic advancement, eager to enjoy the respect of his superiors, Sewall battled for his proper place among the office-holding elite. Their criticisms threat-

---

* This is not to say that the army failed to give Crown supporters a sense of security. During the occupation parties and other social events flourished, and the Commissioners of Customs paraded the streets of Boston with an air of confidence. Nevertheless, the presence of troops aggravated rather than eased the difficulties of the local government.

ened his material well-being as well as his ego, and in his struggle with them he was under constant pressure to decide when to compromise and when to resist. Popular criticism, on the other hand, threatened to alienate the community from him, and thus to deprive him of that popular appreciation for his services which his mentor Chambers Russell had enjoyed in more peaceful times. This approval constituted more than the observance of established gestures of respect, for these he continued to receive throughout the years of political turbulence; the approval he sought was no less than the open affection which confirmed a man's value within his society. Sewall wanted, in short, to be accepted and appreciated by both interests, to be excused his compromises, valued as an individual, and respected for his adherence to an openly self-defined integrity.

Despite Sewall's regrets at his popular image, his own social and political ideology restrained him from wooing public favor, or from appreciating the changes in attitude that caused him discomfort and disappointment. He was thoroughly conservative in his commitment to a paternalistic society. Thus he rejected what he felt was required of a man in the 1760s and 1770s who sought the affections as well as the formal respect of the people; he would not pander to what he believed were their misguided wishes or do them a disservice by using them as pawns in a political battle. The idea of men in office serving as spokesmen for popular opinion had no place within his political philosophy. He believed that one class of men was designated to govern other men, serving the governed's best interests as a parent serves a child. The obligations of those who governed were serious and numerous, but they included a resistance to the fickleness of the mass will. If the result of the Whigs' political rhetoric and organization was to be the legitimation of an active role in politics for the general populace, Sewall could never acknowledge such a political revolution. The concept of an active voice in the decision-making process by the governed, as opposed to their one, single, and original assent which had created their society, could not be made to fit into the hierarchical structure that Sewall believed served society best. Viewing the world as he did, he could only judge the popular adoration in which a James Otis or a Sam Adams basked as unseemly, and as a sign of unprincipled ambitions in the men who enjoyed and courted this popularity.

In fact, Sewall never viewed the radical opposition's leaders as spokesmen for the people, but as political rivals of his own class. For him, the troubles in Massachusetts were the result of a political struggle for office and power among the elite in which one faction employed novel and unprincipled techniques of mass organization. He recognized that the people could be used effectively to achieve political ends, for he had seen this to be true in Massachusetts. But because he could not accept the notion that popular will, *active* popular will, ought to play a legitimate role in shaping policy and governance, he would never acknowledge the general populace as a legitimate political base. The persistent Tory accusation that one disappointed man or one small group of ambitious men had produced the revolution in Massachusetts grew logically out of the conservatives' refusal to accept popular will as a legitimate political force. While Sewall astutely analyzed the variety of factors that made it possible for the people to respond to the urgings of the radicals, he always returned to the ambitions of the radical leaders as the genuine impetus and directive force behind the events leading to the Revolution.

Despite the alienation of popular affection engendered by Whig propaganda and criticism, Sewall's private relationship with Whig leaders remained unchanged. Until the alternative of revolution and independence became a political reality, leaders in Massachusetts continued to be highly discriminating in personal loyalties and relationships. Only when the political polarization of 1774–1775 forced men to define themselves narrowly by political loyalties did the ties of marriage, class, profession, and friendship lose their centripetal power. Here then was a cushion to the growing sense of alienation Sewall suffered. He and John Adams continued as friends until late in 1774, despite Adams's violent public attacks on "Philanthrop," and Sewall could still dine comfortably in the home of his radical brother-in-law, Josiah Quincy. Perhaps even more indicative of the importance of ties of marriage and family was John Hancock's concern that the *Liberty* imbroglio not becloud the intimacy suitable to two prospective brothers-in-law. "I would rather wave all matter of altercation," Hancock said in 1772, "and . . . with real seriousness express my inclination and wish (putting all matters of politicks out of view) that a perfect harmony and friendship may be kept up between us, and wish rather more familiarity than the common shew of friendship expresses, considering the connection I have formed with the sister of your Lady." [15]

If Sewall's social contacts with Whig friends did taper off after his appointment to Crown office, the deciding factor was probably the social rather than the political implications of his advancement. His position in government had drawn him into the province's most elite inner circle, presided over by Bernard and Hutchinson.

These persistent, stable factors in Sewall's life served to soften the impact of political conflict. Further, despite the political division within the province, of which he believed himself an innocent victim, Sewall presaged no permanent upheaval in the world he knew. In 1769 Massachusetts showed no real disposition toward revolution. Sharp criticism of the royal government and its officers might increase, new political tactics might bring temporary injustices to men like himself, but there were as yet no signs that the province intended to topple the political and social structure in which Sewall had achieved such remarkable success. Only hindsight could reveal a steady and inevitable disintegration of the imperial structure. Thus Sewall continued to plan his future along the orthodox lines of a government career.

Even had Sewall contemplated a dangerous disruption of the status quo, he would have been confident of its return to equilibrium. In the end such confidence reposed on British military and naval strength. Although aware that drastic measures might be necessary, that difficult and tragic times might be ahead, Sewall would never doubt for an instant that the final outcome would be the preservation of the old order.

CHAPTER SIX

A Retreat from Conflict
1770

THE HANCOCK TRIAL and the military occupation were not the only problems preoccupying Sewall in March of 1769. His career had reached a delicate and troublesome juncture with his appointment to the Halifax Vice-Admiralty bench. The Chief Justice commission was the ripest plum of that career, but the new office—with its more than generous salary of £600 per annum and its great prestige—had a serious drawback: the judge was expected to reside in his jurisdiction. The comfortable habit of absentee office-holding was under attack from the Home government, and the residence requirement was part of the government's overall reform policy. Sewall's commission had spelled out the Government's intentions by requiring him to take his oath of office, at Halifax, within six months.

The commission had been issued in October 1768. Yet the following March found Jonathan Sewall still in Massachusetts. His six-month grace period was fast running out. For Sewall it was a difficult matter to resolve: he was not at all eager to exchange the comforts of his own provincial life for the physical and social barrenness of the Halifax region; but to forfeit this office was unthinkable.

Fortunately for Sewall, Francis Bernard took steps to resolve the dilemma. The Governor had no intention of losing Sewall's services through a promotion he had himself arranged. Bernard meant to keep Sewall in Massachusetts, and toward that end he hastily negotiated with the Home government for an open-ended leave of absence for the new Chief Justice. To the Secretary of the Admiralty, Philip Stephens, Bernard insisted that Sewall was "engaged . . . in some Crown Causes of great consequences which will be in Danger of failing, if they are not continued under his Conduct till they are concluded." [1] Bernard needed Sewall in Boston far more, he told Stephens, than the Admiralty needed him in Halifax. As to how long Sewall's assistance would be required, Bernard could not say. It was certain, however, that the Governor was "not ready to name fit Persons for either of [Sewall's] offices." Almost all the good lawyers, the Governor lamented, were aiders and abettors of that "Factious party" of Sam Adams and James Otis, and it would require great time and effort to find suitable replacements for the two legal offices Sewall held. The Governor was aware of the irregularity of his request. Sewall ought never to have been granted the joint Attorney-Advocate General appointment at all. Now Bernard wanted Stephens' consent to Sewall's holding three offices simultaneously, and to the creation of an absentee situation in the new Vice-Admiralty court for at least a year. Despite any qualms he might have had, the Secretary of Admiralty bowed to Bernard's wishes. Sewall appeared to have no qualms at all about the ethics of the arrangement.

All that now remained was for Sewall to pay a short visit to the northern province, swear his oath of office, and appoint a deputy to manage the court. Even this he delayed, however, until midsummer. Finally, on June 24, Sewall boarded the *Rose* for Halifax. His departure did not escape the notice of radical newspaperman Sam Adams. "In one of the men of war which sailed for Halifax," his "Journal" article reported,

> Jonathan Sewall, Esq; Judge of Admiralty for that province, embarked; it is said the design of his voyage is to appoint deputy Judges for Halifax and Quebec; after which he is to return to Boston, the present scene of action, for all who have listed under the banners of corruption; What benefit a province can reap from a nonresident salary of £600 per annum, when all his deputies can do the business for about the sixth part

of that sum divided among them, we leave to our economical Ministry to point out. Our province must however certainly esteem itself highly favoured, that this foreign judge has so long after his appointment acted among us in the several characters of Attorney General, Advocate-General &c and discerning people cannot but highly applaud the wisdom of our superiors in multiplying posts and pensions in America, and making the expence of Government in the new settlements and colonies, bear a goodly proportion to the civil establishment of the mother country.[2]

Sewall's business at Halifax took only six weeks, but during his absence a major, though not unexpected, change in command took place in the Bay Colony. On August 1—amid the insults of "bells ringing great joy to the people" and great bonfires burning on King Street and on Fort Hill—Francis Bernard took his leave of the Bay Colony.[3] Lieutenant-Governor Thomas Hutchinson took over as acting executive. The change in leadership, while depriving Sewall of the immediate presence of his benefactor, did not threaten his privileged arrangement vis-à-vis his many offices. In fact, the darkening political situation which Hutchinson inherited from Bernard appeared to increase the currency of all loyal officers like Sewall.

The new acting governor faced the everywhere-apparent erosion of government authority. The administration had lost its tenuous control over the legislative branch in the recent May elections, when a radical victory transformed the Council into "a minor replica of the House." [4] Thus, legislative government, as it was constituted in Massachusetts, had been conquered by the Opposition. Only an extensive alteration in government structure, imposed by England, could hope to redress this imbalance. Such structural changes, as Hutchinson knew, would represent no less than a revolution from the right. Coupled to this major victory for the Opposition, the radicals' extralegal threats to the Governor's authority had increased. Continuing soldier-citizen tensions not only undermined the security of Crown officers and supporters; they also raised the very practical question of who would control Boston, and how. An impending economic boycott, scheduled for January 1770, raised this same question. It was not nonimportation itself that most directly threatened Hutchinson's government. The challenge came from the effectiveness of a novel extralegal enforcement agency, created by merchants and radical leaders, whose continued existence could enforce the boycott and undermine the governor's control within the province.

Hutchinson could do little in these circumstances but maneuver from a defensive posture, acting to preserve areas not yet under radical control and attempting to reassert authority through the application of such remaining powers as the veto and his appointive privilege.

Although Sewall might sympathize with Hutchinson's dilemma, the Governor's problems worked to Sewall's personal advantage. For one of the areas of loyalty Hutchinson most vigorously sought to preserve was the judiciary, with its complement of legal offices Jonathan Sewall currently held. Hutchinson's problem was the staffing of this traditionally loyal branch of government. Throughout the 1760s judicial and legal officers had remained satellites of the executive, not only because of the Governor's nominating and appointive privileges, but also because of the personal loyalties of the appointees. By 1769, however, the continuing dependability of this branch of government was problematical. Hutchinson faced threatened resignations and retirements. If he hoped to retain judicial and legal support, he would have to persuade active judges to continue in office and devise some effective means of attracting competent and reliable new men. Until the Governor could solve these problems, Sewall had little cause to doubt his own multiple office-holding would continue.

Hutchinson sought to secure control over the judiciary by the institution of a civil list. This appeal for independent salaries was an echo of Governor Bernard's own urgent request during his years in the Bay Colony.[5] But while Bernard had hoped independent salaries would free a dependable judiciary from the legislative power of the purse, Hutchinson now hoped the civil list would attract needed personnel.

The source for new justices and legal officers was, of course, the Bar.* But fewer lawyers were attracted to Crown service in the late

* Ironically, it was Hutchinson himself who had narrowed the source of judges to members of the Massachusetts bar. As Chief Justice, this was one of the reforms

1760s than in the past. If once the aspiring lawyer had looked to appointive office for the respectability and prestige it would bestow, and for the private practice it might draw to him, now the private sector, with its increasing legal opposition to the Crown, offered greater income possibilities and opened prestigious elective rather than appointive political avenues to the young and ambitious lawyer. If the Crown had nurtured the fledgling profession, it had also provided it with an avenue of escape: the growth of Crown legal activity in Massachusetts since 1763 had created a corresponding need for legal services among the merchants and businessmen of the province. For every case in the Admiralty Court that Jonathan Sewall might prosecute, each defendant required the services of one or two attorneys. Thus when Bernard had written to Admiralty Secretary Stephens that *no* loyal lawyers could be found to replace Sewall in his offices, he was, with perhaps pardonable exaggeration, underscoring the changing orientation of the legal profession.*

There were, of course, qualified and loyal lawyers for bench and legal offices. The problem was not so much one of numbers as one of geography and finance. Many older conservative lawyers, already established in their profitable county legal practices, refused to remove to Boston without some guarantee of equivalent income. Young lawyers like John Adams, who had cast their lots with the opposition, might stand to gain much from a move to the city; but Tory gentlemen like William Pynchon and James Putnam would be forced to sacrifice the secure for the uncertain. To draw these older men into Crown service Hutchinson had to offer secure incomes; to attract younger men

---

Hutchinson instituted in his efforts to make peace with that part of the legal profession angered by his elevation to the Superior Court bench (see Murrin, "Anglicizing," pp. 234–41).

* Murrin indirectly confirms this analysis in his discussion of the Loyalist and Patriot breakdown among Massachusetts lawyers. Most lawyers under thirty in 1776 were Patriots; that is, these were the men whose maturity coincided with the expanding possibilities for the lawyer away from the Crown's sheltering wing. Other Massachusetts lawyers, Murrin says, "could not reconcile systematic opposition to royal government with their own devotion to English law acquired in a lifetime's practice in sympathetic royal courts" (Murrin, "Anglicizing," pp. 247–48).

he had to hold out promises at least equal to those offered by Sam Adams and John Hancock.* Hutchinson summed up his problem in January of 1770: "You know how much we stand in need of good Crown Lawyers. (If the Judges' places in the Superior Court were made more respectable it would encourage our Young Gentlemen to endeavor to qualify themselves for it.)'' [6]

Sewall used the borrowed time that Hutchinson's difficulties provided him to reevaluate his new appointment to the Vice-Admiralty bench. He was plagued by serious doubts. His visit to Halifax had done little to whet his appetite for a life in the northern province. Though the Admiralty office removed him from the cross-pressures of loyalties under which he suffered as Advocate and Attorney General, it also placed him among strangers. Even more to the point, Sewall feared the new court might fail to justify its existence. In January 1770 there had not been a single appeal to his bench.[7] What business there was in his district was dispatched by a provincial court, established in the interim between Judge Spry's original Supreme Vice Admiralty court and Sewall's district court.[8] If this district court remained inactive, Sewall's salary would have to be siphoned off from the monies taken in by the other, more productive courts. Such a circumstance would be certain to prompt a reevaluation of the court's usefulness by the Treasury. Sewall had recognized the dangers of the situation almost immediately, and had made an effort to secure his post by urging the abolition of the interim inferior court.[9] His efforts proved abortive; the inferior court continued.

A bizarre event was to offer Sewall a possible solution to his problem. In September 1769 Customs Commissioner John Robinson and radical James Otis came to blows in a tavern brawl.[10] Although Otis had provoked the fight, Robinson bore the brunt of popular anger. Fol-

* Hutchinson's attempts to recruit Putnam for the Attorney Generalship were blocked by the absence of any independent salary for the office (see chapter 7). In March 1769 John Worthington of Springfield declined an offer to succeed Sewall in the Attorney General's office. He was, he said, too settled and too financially secure in Springfield to begin a new career in Boston (John Worthington to Thomas Hutchinson, March 24, 1769, TH Mss, XXVI, 304–5).

lowing the fracas, Robinson discreetly shipped off to England, leaving his new father-in-law, Elias Boutineau, to handle Otis's legal actions against him. The Commissioner was ill-disposed to return to his duties in Boston, and seized upon the idea of an exchange of offices with Sewall.

Boutineau acted as his son-in-law's agent with Sewall. The Robinson proposal amounted to a political round of musical chairs: the Commissioner would take the Halifax post, Benjamin Franklin's illegitimate son William would replace him on the Customs Board, and Sewall would remain in Boston as Attorney General with a fixed salary of £300, to be secured by Robinson's influence.

Sewall showed immediate interest in the plan. Privately he must have felt that a sacrifice of the judicial salary of £600 a year for the security of the Massachusetts office was a wise one.[11] Thus, with Sewall's approval, Boutineau next took the plan to Hutchinson, who forwarded the idea to Francis Bernard. Any exchange of offices remained academic, of course, unless the £300 salary could be settled upon the Attorney General's office. Thus the plan would lay in abeyance until Bernard or Robinson could successfully arrange this office's addition to the civil list.

Sewall waited comfortably in Massachusetts for news of his future. The relative peacefulness within the province must have reinforced his hopes for the success of the Robinson plan. He was, after all, anxious to remain in his native province. But in March of 1770 Sewall's placid expectations dissolved. The subsurface and surface tensions of Boston's military occupation exploded with the murder of Charles Seider and the alleged massacre of civilians on the evening of March 5.[12] Unexpectedly and more dramatically than ever before Sewall was made to feel the pressures of his provincial office.

It was Sewall's duty as Attorney General to prosecute Captain Preston and his men, a duty his personal convictions would not support. Sewall believed Preston and the soldiers to be completely innocent, and he placed full blame for the events of March 5 on Boston's radical faction. His own grudging intimacy with radical tactics of provocation, acquired through the innumerable soldier-citizen cases he had nol-prossed, made him firm in this opinion. No one believed more strongly that Otis and Sam Adams were behind these confrontations which climaxed in the tragic "massacre."

Sewall's own decision would surely have been to enter nolle prosequis in these criminal suits. Yet the pressures against such an action were overwhelming. In a unique harmony of interests, both the Crown and the radicals called for the trials. This was a political much more than a criminal issue, and one that Hutchinson's government would have to deal with successfully if it wished to restore political order. Thus a nolle prosequi would have provoked both parties to the dispute. There would be the danger of further violence from an infuriated populace, who believed a massacre had taken place. And Sewall's superiors would have quickly overridden his action, making it no more than a futile, and perhaps for his career fatal, gesture.*

Sewall might have sacrificed his office to his honor and resigned as Attorney General. But the price would have been the Robinson plan and all hopes of remaining in Massachusetts permanently. Yet as Attorney General he was unable to follow, or unwilling to accept the consequences of following, his own judgment. Sewall responded to his own apparent deadlock by flight: he simply withdrew from the scene of his dilemma and refused to play any role in the prosecution of the cases. He returned to his home in Middlesex, and declared a year's self-imposed exile from Boston and that city's political and legal chaos.

Sewall's response was as complex as it was unprecedented. He would neither defy nor submit to the pressures upon him. He had tried both responses in the past with little success. In personal terms, resolution seemed possible only through the act of withdrawal, a halfway

* Hiller Zobel points out that the jury itself could have indicted Preston and his soldiers without Sewall's assistance, thereby adding to the futility of a nolle prosequi action by Sewall (Zobel, *Boston Massacre,* p. 219). Zobel discusses Sewall's failure to prosecute the Massacre cases in his article "Jonathan Sewall," pp. 123–36. He does not, however, offer any interpretation of Sewall's personal motivations.

measure whose chief virtue was that it removed him from the conflict
entirely. Whatever the consequences of this decision, Sewall could
find solace in the fact that they would follow solely from this one act.
Had he stayed to prosecute the cases, an apparently endless series of
secondary decisions would have to be made, and their consequences
faced. A lackluster prosecution, for example, would have brought
post-trial criticisms, and perhaps public accusations of a courtroom
conspiracy to insure acquittal. These accusations would have added to
the government's displeasure with Sewall as well as the community's.
A vigorous prosecution would have required a series of courtroom
compromises from Sewall that would have been too reminiscent of the
Hancock trials. "Desertion," as John Adams baldly labelled it,
seemed preferable to Sewall.[13]

In the simplest sense, Sewall's decision was a gamble. And, in fact,
he seemed to have minimized both the real and psychic damage to
himself by this withdrawal from conflict. Sewall had one advantage
from the start: Hutchinson could not easily find a replacement for him
as Attorney General. In addition, his guaranteed income of £600 per
annum provided him with a buffer against the decrease in private legal
practice that might follow from popular anger. Furthermore, there was
no doubt that the momentary barrage of anger at Sewall's desertion,
no matter how intense, would be less taxing on reputation and ego
than the extended criticism of his conduct had he remained to prosecute the soldiers. Finally, Sewall may have anticipated his superiors'
indulgent response to his retreat, for indulgent they were.

The most likely explanation for his superiors' indulgence is that
Hutchinson did *not* want Sewall to prosecute the cases after all.
Hutchinson was wise in permitting Sewall's absence from the courtroom. As Attorney General, Sewall had nol prossed almost every case
brought against the soldiery. His reputation, spread by the Boston radical papers, as a man inimical to the province's safety was firmly established in the minds of the populace. To employ Sewall as prosecutor in these essentially political cases was to open the door to
charges of prejudicial prosecution, to cries of miscarriage of justice,

and to accusations that the Hutchinson government was engaging in a courtroom conspiracy. Crown officials, knowing of Sewall's genuine reluctance to try a soldiery he believed innocent, could not risk the possibility of a nonvigorous prosecution.

Thus Sewall took his year's retreat with full immunity. While the legal battles raged in the city, Sewall took shelter within the calm of his domestic circle, spending time with Esther, Jonathan Jr., Betsey, and a new son, Stephen, born that June.* He was not, however, professionally idle. He caught up on the work of his private practice in Middlesex County, and he made his customary journeys with the Superior Court as it traveled outside Suffolk County. While the October trial of Captain Preston occupied five of Sewall's fellow lawyers, he busied himself with the preparation of a more quietly controversial case, a bid for freedom by a Cambridge black woman. For a second time, Sewall aided this woman—known as Margaret—in her efforts to win her independence. The merits of this case, unlike those of the Boston Massacre affair, he could accept without moral reserve.†

Sewall's withdrawal from the conflicts raging in Boston proved salutory, but it was not truly a choice based on political—or emotional—acuity. This same course of action, or inaction, would be followed in the future with wholly destructive consequences. Thus the withdrawal in 1770 established a precedent for behavior that, although initially self-protective, would later prove self-defeating.

* The Sewalls' first child, named for Sewall's mother, Mary Payne, had died in infancy. A son, Jonathan Sewall Jr., was born on June 6, 1766. Elizabeth "Betsey" Sewall was born in 1768, and Stephen followed on June 8, 1770. A fifth child, named for Sewall's uncle Benjamin Sewall, was born on August 5, 1771, but died within two years.

† Sewall was notable for his defense of blacks in several cases. Perhaps the best known and most important of these was *James v. Lechmere* in 1769. Both this case and *Margaret v. Muzzy* are dealt with extensively in *LPJA,* I, lxiv, 26, 75; II,49–59; III, 333, 339; and in Zobel, "Jonathan Sewall."

CHAPTER SEVEN

In Defense of the Status Quo
1768-1772

SEWALL DID NOT entirely escape the Massacre trials, although his role was limited to the post-mortems of the press. On December 10 Sewall's old journalistic rival Sam Adams, writing as "Vindex," began the retrial of Preston and his men in the newspapers.[1] The innocence of those soldiers acquitted was transformed into guilt through the impassioned, persuasive writings of a man less troubled by fact or legal evidence than the Court had been.[2] As an antidote to Vindex, Sewall put forward the Crown's case.[3]

Vindex published three pieces on December 10, 17, and 24 before Sewall, as "Philanthrop," responded. The three essays offered a recapitulation of both the evidence sworn in the courtroom and the unverified eyewitness accounts printed in the local newspapers before the trials. Adams portrayed the soldiers as rash and hostile, at best foolhardy and at worst murderously conspiratorial. "One would think," Vindex wrote of Captain Preston's soldiers, "that they intended to assassinate." [4] In the course of his argument, Adams took potshots at other Crown supporters; in particular he challenged the competence of the Superior Court judges—"all well-stricken in years" and "laboring under infirmities of Body." * Nor did Adams hesitate to exploit the

---

* This attack was justified, of course, by the Bench's transparent use of illness as an excuse for postponement of the Preston trial.

anti-Catholic prejudices of his readers in his attempts to discredit the damaging testimony of one witness.[5]

Although Vindex's ethics were questionable, his effectiveness and persuasiveness were indisputable. Sewall's precision refutation, often point by laborious point, could not erase the overall impression of military brutality created by Adams or neutralize, as Thomas Hutchinson had hoped, the emotional charge of Adams's attack.[6] Of course Adams had the more responsive audience, and the advantage over an opponent who called for reason and impartiality in a time when strong emotions were aroused.

Of Sewall's essays, the most important did not deal specifically with the trial or with the events of March 5. Instead it was a paean to the British system of government and a call to responsible citizens to preserve rather than erode the rule of law. The essay repeated the themes of his earlier pieces, and was, on the whole, an orthodox presentation of that amalgam of Hobbes and Locke which served as a foundation for popular political thought in Massachusetts. In fact, the essay had an air of catechism about it. Few in Massachusetts would deny the virtues of civilization over Nature, the necessity for government, or the right of citizens to resist tyranny wherever they found it. What made this essay important, and gave it its peculiarly urgent tone, was Sewall's discussion of the absolute limitations of man and societies.

Human society, Sewall insisted, had only three political alternatives: anarchy, tyranny, and British constitutional government. The British system was unique in that it alone provided a genuine alternative to the two extremes. Most importantly, the British achievement in balance marked the absolute limits of man himself: human imperfection was expressed in the imperfection of Britain's mixed government. Sewall was struck by, and convinced of, the essential fragility of this sole civilized society, susceptible even in its most majestic moments to attacks of tyranny from above and anarchy from below. It was this fragility and the terrors of the political alternatives that explained the urgency of Sewall's plea for a cessation of the assault on authority. The immediate danger did not come from the authority above, for the

King, "Flesh of our flesh," threatened no tyranny. The true spectre was anarchy, for when "the minds of the multitude are disturbed and inflamed," their passions are "as a flood which knows no bounds when once the dikes are broken."

It was Sam Adams's attack on the character of the judges, in combination with the habitual disrespect for those who governed that the radical press encouraged, that "Philanthrop" feared would lead Massachusetts into the dissolution of society and the miseries of "licentious anarchy." Sewall's essay was an appeal to the radicals as true patriots and as reasonable men to remember that it was better that "small though *real* evils in government should subsist for a while" than that a "good constitution" be subverted by overhasty efforts to eradicate them.

Sam Adams would not, of course, deny the beauties of society or the privileged status of English society in particular. But while Sewall dwelt upon the dangers of anarchy Adams was preoccupied with the threat of tyranny. To preserve the British constitution Adams believed it was necessary to purge the nation of its high-ranking conspirators. From this analysis would emerge the notion that America could save the *spirit* of the British constitution only by separating herself from the cancerous *body* of the English government. But men like Sewall could not accept the notion that this spirit could be successfully severed from the material body of King and Parliament that gave it life. Nor would the English government let that empire over which the constitution held sway be destroyed. In the last analysis anarchy would be, and must be, defeated by armies.

The newspaper series allowed Sewall a platform for his views on the Massacre trials. His was a somewhat self-vindicatory exercise, designed to underscore the basis for his refusal to prosecute these cases. But the "Philanthrop" series was also a gesture of loyalty directed to Thomas Hutchinson. Although the Acting Governor needed Sewall as long as the Attorney General's office was unsalaried, Sewall had not yet cemented his personal relationship with Hutchinson. In fact, Hutchinson had been lukewarm toward the Robinson plan, which would of course establish Sewall as his permanent Attorney General.

Hutchinson's lack of enthusiasm for the plan was not motivated by personal considerations. He admired Sewall's talents and respected him as a polemicist of value to the Crown. Hutchinson, however, was hoping for a permanent appointment to the Governor's chair, and was thus understandably eager to build around him his own coterie of officeholders who owed their loyalty directly to him. Toward this end the Acting Governor had promised the Attorney General's office to the conservative lawyer, James Putnam, when and if a salary could be won for the post. Hutchinson recalled this promise to Bernard in the letter that carried news of the Robinson plan. Putnam, Hutchinson reminded the Governor, "has depended upon it and . . . would be of great service here." [7]

The offer to Putnam had of course presupposed Sewall's eventual departure for Halifax. With the introduction of the Robinson plan, Hutchinson felt the power of appointment slipping from his hands. Fortunately, a new development at the end of 1770 promised to answer the needs of both Hutchinson and Jonathan Sewall. From John Robinson came a second and more readily executed proposal: Sewall would exchange place for place with the Commissioner.

The new plan had the obvious virtue that salaries were already affixed to both offices, and the disadvantage to Sewall in income would be only £100. Upon hearing of Sewall's acquiescence in the plan, Hutchinson wrote to Bernard: "I am glad of it for they want a man of Sewall's knowledge in the law and other abilities." [8] Although he did not make a point of it to the Governor, Hutchinson's own satisfaction with the plan arose from the release of the Attorney General's office. The new arrangement, were it approved by the Home government, would enable him to secure not only Sewall's services in Boston but Putnam's as well.

Robinson's new proposal reflected his doubts that a salary could be won for the Attorney General's office. In this view he was supported by Bernard. [9] The two men proved only partially correct, for over the summer a small salary of £150 was at last attached to the office. This figure was inadequate for Sewall's purposes, but it did offer that other interested officeholder, William Franklin, a wedge in opening separate negotiations with Sewall. Robinson had discarded his original arrangements with Franklin when they had proved inconvenient; now Franklin sought Bernard's help in securing an exchange solely to his advantage with Sewall. This surprising turn of events provided Sewall with two options.

Franklin, as Lieutenant Governor of New Jersey, could not make a place-for-place offer to Sewall as Robinson had done. His only negotiable asset was money. Recognizing this, he offered Sewall a £200 annual income as compensation for the judge's post. This sum, added to the £150 from the Attorney General's office, would produce an adequate income for Sewall. The £200 compensation would be siphoned from the judge's salary of £600. That is, Franklin would settle for the Chief Justiceship and £400 per annum, paying Sewall a yearly "annuity" of one-third the post's value. The offer, highly irregular in modern terms, was common practice in Sewall's day. Franklin also promised to handle the essential bureaucratic details such as securing Lord Sandwich's approval of the arrangement.[10]

Bernard, now informed of both plans, simply communicated them to Hutchinson for Sewall's choice. Bernard added that Sewall need not hurry his decision since no further business would be done by Parliament in regard to offices in 1771. Hutchinson, however, pressured Sewall to make a speedy choice, suggesting that some "inconvenience might arise from the delay." What that inconvenience was he did not say, but his reference was obviously to the Putnam appointment.

Hutchinson personally believed Sewall would prefer the Franklin plan. Sewall carefully spelled out his preference in a letter to the Lieutenant Governor which the latter enclosed in his own note to Bernard on September 23, 1771. "I . . . have just received an answer from Mr Sewall which I shall enclose to you and which is so explicit that I need add nothing to it." It is unfortunate that the usually loquacious Hutchinson chose to be so cryptic, for Sewall's letter is lost. But Hutchinson's hunch was probably confirmed by that letter. Sewall had no love for the Board of Commissioners or for their tactics. Despite the pressures of the Attorney's office, the Customs appointment would bring him into even starker opposition with his community. And as long as the official salary for the Attorney's office remained a modest £150, Sewall would be secure in it. Thus, with the Franklin plan, he could enjoy the income of £350 (more than the original Robinson plan had offered) and the advantage of a permanent residence in Massachusetts.

In the end, however, Sewall's decision did not matter. For before any final arrangements could be made, both proposals were withdrawn. John Robinson, emboldened in 1772 by James Otis's generous legal pardon,* decided to return to his post as Commissioner of Customs. His long-standing offer of exchange with Sewall was abruptly dropped. The Franklin plan collapsed as well, ending in near disgrace for Sewall. Early in 1772 Sewall learned that the New Jersey politician had promised far more than he could actually deliver. He had implicated Sewall in a minor scandal, for, as was to become painfully obvious, Lord Hillsborough was not at all pleased with the annuity arrangement that Franklin and Bernard had once guaranteed. In fact, it seemed that Lord North as well as Hillsborough would be "displeased at the proposal." By a rapid turn of events, Sewall found himself suddenly in need of Hutchinson's help. His innocence in these Franklin negotiations required confirmation. In this Hutchinson complied. "I know Mr. Sewall not only would never have made such a proposal," he wrote to England, "but he never would have hearkened to it when made if he had not been assured he should give no offense." [11] Sewall would repay Hutchinson's favor in the coming years.

A final effort was made by the undaunted Bernard to secure a permanent joint appointment for Sewall as Solicitor to the Customs Board and Attorney General.[12] Sewall's opinion on this particular combina-

---

* Otis dropped all claim to the astronomical reparations awarded him by a sympathetic Massachusetts jury. He sacrificed this monetary satisfaction when Robinson agreed to make a public apology, through Boutineau, for his participation in the Tavern assault (Tudor, *Life of James Otis,* appendix, pp. 503–6).

tion of offices must have been unenthusiastic at best. This plan too came to nothing.

The matter was finally resolved with a simplicity that stands in sharp contrast to the maneuverings of almost four years: a flexible Home government simply permitted the status quo to continue. The pattern established during these years of abortive negotiations for place changing was, after all, one of absenteeism: Sewall remained in Boston while his deputy Joseph Gerrish managed the affairs of the Halifax court. Sewall's duties as Attorney General served in 1772, as before, as the official raison d'être for residence in Massachusetts. In the end, his chief benefactor proved to be the tolerance of the Home government for this absentee arrangement. As long as the Admiralty permitted the pattern to continue, Sewall could enjoy all the benefits to be derived from his promotion to the bench without any of its inconveniences.

CHAPTER EIGHT

Loyalty—Not Independence
1774

THE DISCONTENT and tension of almost a decade seemed spent in the Boston Massacre and its aftermath. A calm settled upon the Bay Colony in 1771, and men and women turned their thoughts to their private worlds of career, family, and friends.

For Jonathan Sewall, that private world held out the many satisfactions of wealth and social status. He was a member of the colony's most exclusive circle, and now lived, like many of this group, in one of the most elegant sections of Cambridge, itself one of Massachusetts' most elegant towns. This move in 1771 to Brattle Street gave perhaps unconscious testimony to the clustering of like-minded men, for Brattle Street, with its high concentration of conservatives, sat like a political statement in the midst of its community. It was nicknamed Tory Row.[1] Here, sheltered a bit from the outside world, Sewall and his family enjoyed the luxuries his success conferred: the elaborate coach for travel to and from the Anglican church, the household servants, the well-stocked wine cellar, and the country retreat in Lincolnshire where favorite horses could be kept.

Yet whenever possible Sewall used his wealth to bring him satisfactions that could not be measured in glasses of Madeira or acquisitions of new property. These were the satisfactions the role of benefactor held out to him. If he despaired of every achieving that paternal relationship with his community which Chambers Russell had enjoyed, he managed to find some of its pleasures by helping individual young men. He used his money and influence to do so. In Halifax, for example, he pressed for the appointment of an inexperienced applicant to the office of Marshal of his Vice Admiralty court. "He is," Sewall wrote by way of explaining his support, "of a worthy Family, who were among the first settlers at Halifax; but whose present Circumstances by the Death of his Father, are become such as induce me to wish the small profits arising from that office might fall to the Lott of this Family." [2]

But it was with Ward Chipman that Sewall most fully re-created his own fortunate relationship with Chambers Russell. Ward Chipman was the son of John Chipman, a fellow lawyer and friend to Sewall until his death in 1768. The older barrister's sudden death—of what eighteenth-century doctors diagnosed as apoplexy—left the fourteen-year-old "Chip" in embarrassing financial circumstances reminiscent of Sewall's own childhood. Sewall came immediately to the boy's aid. He kept Chip in school with contributions raised from other members of the Bar, and with large outlays from his own pocket. When Chip graduated from Harvard in 1770 Sewall took him into his home as a law student and as a member of the family.

Sewall was not unaware of empathy's role in his close relationship with Chip. In 1775, when Chipman left the Sewall household to open his own practice, the two men exchanged lengthy farewell letters. Chip's was an expression of gratitude; but Sewall's response was an autobiography. In the younger man's plight he had vividly seen his own past. "Our circumstances in early life have a striking resemblance," he wrote to Chip. "I recollect the time, when, under the like discouraging circumstances with which you were then embarrassed, I wish'd, tho in vain, for a friendly arm to lean on." [3] Sewall's strongest memories were of his own precarious social standing as a young man, and from these came his "ardent wish of saving from sinking into obscurity" the son of a respectable family. The ease with which the loss of a protecting father could force a man into obscurity, the insecurity of one's footing in the world without the benevolent assistance of an older man: these were the irrevocable lessons Sewall had selected to remember from his own past. It was this reconstruction of his past that served as an impetus for Sewall's kindness toward Chipman, but the relationship between the two men outlasted mere philanthropy. Sewall was correct when, in another and more practical context, he said: "I substituted myself in [your father's] room." [4]

The pleasure of Sewall's Brattle Street days was shaken suddenly in 1773 when the power struggle between opposition and Crown, never really dead, was revived. The radicals, maneuvering from a position of strength in the legislature, focused a new and intensified attack on the executive branch. Once again they reduced the struggle to a matter of individuals, this time by publishing some private letters of Thomas Hutchinson that allegedly proved his betrayal of provincial rights and liberties.

Hutchinson's letters, along with correspondence from leading provincial conservatives like Andrew Oliver, Charles Paxton, and Robert Auchmuty,* had reached Massachusetts by way of Benjamin Franklin, then in London. The circumstances of their acquisition were mysterious, for these letters, thirteen in all, were ostensibly the private property of English placeman Thomas Whately, to whom they had been written in 1768 and 1769. Nevertheless, Franklin had them at his disposal in 1772, and late that year he forwarded them to Thomas Cushing, Speaker of the Massachusetts Assembly. Franklin intended the letters for internal circulation only, and meant them to serve the province's radical leaders as examples of the private views of their conservative opponents in general, and Hutchinson in particular. Sam Adams proved loath, however, to let such an obvious propaganda opportunity slip by merely because of Franklin's gentlemanly restraint. In June 1773, Adams read the letters before a secret session of the entire Massachusetts Assembly.[5] He then saw to it that the correspondence was

* There were seven correspondents in all: Hutchinson, Oliver, Paxton, Auchmuty, Thomas Moffatt, Nathanael Rogers, and George Rome.

marketed in pamphlet form. Thus the purloined letters were made a matter for public consumption.[6]

The main thrust of the pamphlet was to show Hutchinson's responsibility for the military occupation of Massachusetts and for the ensuing bloodshed of the Boston Massacre. The radicals charged that Hutchinson had purposely distorted the state of affairs in Boston during June 1768, and that his prejudicial accounts had led Britain to take repressive military measures against the province. With this accusation, the radicals skillfully shifted the onus of misrule from the shoulders of the departed Francis Bernard to those of the current Governor, Thomas Hutchinson.

Even before the pamphlet reached the press, Hutchinson moved to deny these charges in a formal message to the Assembly.[7] But the pamphleteers dismissed the Governor's denials, confident that the "judicious reader will find within these letters the fatal source of the Confusion & Bloodshed . . . which threatened total Destruction to the Liberties of all Americans." In short, Hutchinson was certain to be damned by his own hand.

The brilliance of the pamphlet was, of course, its appeal to the populace through exposé and sensationalism. And its harsh judgment of Hutchinson was simultaneously echoed and reinforced in the legislature. There the radicals capped their propaganda victory by producing motions in both the Council and the Assembly calling for the removal of the Governor and the Lieutenant Governor.[8]

Sewall was now to prove his value to Hutchinson. As "Philalethes," he executed a series of seven articles in defense of the Governor.[9] The first appeared in the *Massachusetts Gazette* on June 18, 1773. In it, he took an audacious tack. Instead of attempting to neutralize the radicals' charges, Sewall proposed to stand them on their heads. By examining the same sources, Sewall discovered heroic rather than treacherous motives in the Governor's accounts of events, and a picture emerged of Hutchinson as protector rather than subverter of American liberties. The remarkable divergence between his and the radicals' interpretation of the same texts Sewall attributed to the difference in the objectives of the respective inquiries. The radicals' complete misreading of Hutchinson's intent was the natural consequence of the negative predisposition and prejudice they brought to bear upon the evidence; his own interpretation was founded on reason and impartiality.

Sewall's technique was simple. If the radicals accused Hutchinson of painting a dark and distorted picture of the *Liberty* affair, Sewall countered with the suggestion that Hutchinson's report was designed to vindicate the province. As proof Sewall drew attention to the Governor's careful and consistent distinction between "the mob," responsible for the lawless state of affairs, and "the people," innocent of any role in the riots or the drafting of rebellious declarations. This distinction, Sewall insisted, had preserved the reputation of the majority of Massachusetts' citizens. "True it is," Sewall conceded, "the Governor discovers [relates] his Disapprobation of Mobs & riotous Proceedings—and what good Member of Society can approve them?"— but it is precisely Hutchinson's "generous Tenderness to his Countrymen" that impels him to rush to England an impartial account of the affairs, which disassociates those countrymen from the mob.[10]

Although this tack was somewhat transparent, Sewall had few alternatives. He preferred not to undertake a sweeping defense of Hutchinson's entire political career or of Crown policy within the province, a strategy that if successful would have carried with it a vindication of the handling of the *Liberty* issue. But this would have been to open a political Pandora's box. Having chosen to stick closely to the specific charges at hand, Sewall gambled on an aggressive reinterpretation. The major weakness of this tack, of course, was that the Governor's guilt or glory was not a matter that could be convincingly proved or disproved. In the end only a few accusations could be tested against some objective evidence. In those few instances Sewall had little difficulty winning his point through the logical examination of fact. It was an easy matter, for example, to disprove the radicals' contention that Hutchinson's letter of August 1768 had brought the troops to Boston. Sewall had only to remind his readers of the extensive preparation necessary for a military operation of this type to be effected. A letter that began its trip across the Atlantic in August could not have produced a military occupation in September. Unfortunately, this kind of rebuttal could not be frequently employed, and the most controversial of Hutchinson's statements could only be defended by a resort to interpretative sleight of hand.

A most troublesome item appeared in Hutchinson's letter of January 20, 1769. In this rambling piece to Whately, the Governor had mused at length upon the state of affairs in Massachusetts. "This is most certainly a Crisis," he assured his correspondent. Regarding its remedy, Hutchinson added these thoughts:

> I really wish that there may not have been the least Degree of Severity beyond what is absolutely necessary to maintain, I think I may say to you, the Dependance which a Colony ought to have upon a Parent State; but if no Measures shall have been taken to secure this Dependance [*sic*], or nothing more than some declaratory Acts or Resolves, it is all over with us.

Hutchinson then wrote:

> I never think of the Measures necessary for the Peace and good Order of the Colonies, without Pain. There must be an Abridgment of, what are called, English Liberties. I relieve myself by considering that in a Remove from the State of Nature to the *most perfect* State of Government, there must be a great Restraint of natural Liberty. I doubt whether it is possible to project a System of Government, in which a Colony 3,000 Miles distant from the Parent State, shall enjoy *all* the Liberty of the Parent State. I am certain I have never yet seen the Projection. I wish the Good of the Colony when I wish to see some further Restraint of Liberty, rather than the Connexion with the Parent State should be broken; for I am sure such a Breach must prove the ruin of the Colony.

The Governor's mere mention of "an Abridgment of . . . Liberties" was enough to bring down the wrath of the province upon him.* Sewall recognized the compromising character both of the phrase and

---

* The Council made this paragraph on abridgment of liberties the subject of one of its nine resolutions regarding Hutchinson that led up to the appeal for his removal.

the letter itself, and he devoted his entire essay on August 5, 1773, to the task of defusing this political bomb.

The crux of his defense was to interpret the letter as philosophical rather than political. This he did by raising Hutchinson's observations from the particular to the general. In this context, the specific paragraph at issue does not refer to Massachusetts in 1768, or necessarily to Massachusetts at all. It is "plainly a *general* observation upon the State of *Colonies, indefinitely,* considering them in their *Esseance, Abstractly,* as they *really* and *necessarily* exist." Obviously Hutchinson is not recommending any innovation in policy; the "must" of "there must be an Abridgment" is not prescriptive but descriptive.

Arguments like these probably had less effect on public opinion than Hutchinson himself believed. In his *History of Massachusetts Bay,* the Governor attributes the "recovery of the people from the distemper" to the influence of "the same ingenious writer who had silenced, for a time, the calumniators of Governor Bernard." In the face of Sewall's "moderation, candour, and perspicuity," Hutchinson the historian observed, the radicals had retreated, permitting "the flame to die away." [11] It is far more likely that the complaints and charges against the Governor were simply eclipsed by Massachusetts' new preoccupation with tea.*

It was the destruction of the tea in Boston Harbor [12] that brought down upon Massachusetts those abrupt and radical changes in provincial government for which men like Andrew Oliver [13] and Francis Bernard had long wished.† The British determined not only to exact

* Hearings were held in England in January and February of 1774 on the accusations against Hutchinson. The Governor was completely vindicated, and the legislative petition for his removal was ordered ignored and dismissed (Hutchinson, *History,* III, 299.).

† Bernard had suggested several "radical" reforms in December of 1768 in a confidential letter to John Pownall. He urged that punitive actions against certain Boston selectmen be taken; a reform of the magistracy of Boston be undertaken by removing all Justices of the Peace who were Sons of Liberty or sympathizers with that organization; and he suggested that the form of government in Massachusetts be amended so that the Council be appointed by the King (Francis Bernard to John Pownall, December 23, 1768, FB Mss, VII, pp. 239–49).

punishment for the destruction of the tea by closing the Boston port; they also instituted, by way of the Massachusetts Government Act, sweeping governance reforms. These reforms had three objectives: to destroy the legislative unity of House and Council by which radicals controlled Massachusetts politics; to strengthen the executive power, primarily by reducing assembly controls rather than creating new powers for the Governor; and to check the growth and power of the radicals' political organization.

The radicals' control of legislative government was made possible by the structural relationship of Council to Assembly. Because under the unique charter of 1691 the Council membership was selected by the lower house, the party that controlled the Assembly also held the Council. The Governor could exercise no direct influence in the election of Councilmen. His only official power was the veto of House nominees. While this power could eliminate certain individuals from seats in the Council, the Governor could not replace these political enemies with political supporters. Furthermore, the House, in response to the veto, could refuse to nominate a replacement for the Council seat; as a result of this political struggle Council membership fluctuated from 20 to the established maximum of 28 during Hutchinson's administration. As long as the majority of those elected by the House were radicals, the Council, though reduced in number, retained its political strength as an ally of the House.[14]

The Massachusetts Government Act abolished this elective council and replaced it with a mandamus body, serving by appointment and at the pleasure of the Crown. This new council would function as the legislative arm of the Executive.

To increase and make more secure the executive power, the Crown eliminated the right of the legislature to withhold approval from all appointments to judicial and legal offices. As of July 1, 1774, commissions for Justice of the Peace, inferior court judges, sheriffs, and the Attorney General were issued at the Governor's pleasure. The King reserved only the right of approval over the Superior Court bench. This near-monopoly of appointive powers freed the Governor's hand in the selection of personnel and multiplied his own patronage possibilities.* This reform, coupled with a civil list, would hopefully serve to multiply the number of Crown supporters within the Government.

The final area of consideration was the radical political organization itself. To restrict the opposition party, the Massachusetts Government Act limited the radicals' local vehicle, the town meeting, to a simple elective function. Only one annual meeting would be necessary to satisfy this function of selecting town officers. Any extraordinary session would require the written consent of the Governor. By curbing the town's right to convene at will, the British intended an end to the opposition's successful manipulation of the town meeting for the airing of radical ideas or the legitimation of radical demands.

To oversee the transition in governance, the Crown replaced the civilian Governor, Thomas Hutchinson, with a military executive, General Thomas Gage.

These Crown innovations were, however, matched—and thwarted—by the radicals' own active expansion of their extralegal organizations. The well-established Committees of Correspondence provided Massachusetts radicals with the efficient communications link necessary to prevent the isolation and subjugation of the colony. The weakened legislative organization was bypassed through the establishment of a provincial congress, modeled on the provincial convention held in 1769. The merchants' committees organized in 1769 to police nonimportation provided the model and the experienced personnel for new agencies to enforce the Solemn League and Covenant against importation in 1774. The organized mob action, which had served the radicals well since 1765, provided them with an instrument for intimidation of Crown supporters. This intimidation reduced sharply the Crown's hopes of building an active and militant Loyalist buttress against the radicals.† Finally, the convening of a Continental

* This change also followed closely from Bernard's recommendations in December, 1768.

† For a discussion of the Loyalist Association to combat intimidation, see chapter 9.

Congress, set to meet in Philadelphia in September 1774, elevated the conflict between Crown and radicals from a local to an intercolonial one.

One outgrowth of these political developments in 1774 was a crisis of loyalty within the province. Resistance to the reorganization of the Massachusetts government had produced a network of organizations, which, taken together, constituted an opposition government.[15] Thus two authorities now vied with each other for the political allegiance of the provincial body politic. But the mere existence of a resistance government was not sufficient to create a conflict of allegiance; the institutional forms—congresses and provincial conventions—had existed before. What made the challenge ideologically legitimate was the suggestion, to a people wedded to the concept of compact government, that the Massachusetts Government Act was a violation of the original contract with English authority. If indeed the terms of that contract—which established the provincial structure of government—were substantially altered by Britain through the 1774 reforms, then she had relinquished her right to provincial loyalties and all old obligations were dissolved. Massachusetts was free to make a new compact of government as she saw fit. The existence of a viable political alternative, present in the form of a provincial congress and taking national shape with the Continental Congress, gave the now philosophically essential plebescite in Massachusetts a clear focus; Massachusetts could choose Parliamentary sovereignty, under the terms of the Massachusetts Government Act, or some form of home rule.

On a less abstract level, the English initiative had given a distinct psychological edge to the radicals. The Crown's reorganization of the Massachusetts government seemed to confirm the radical claim that there was a concerted conspiracy to curb provincial liberties. Equally important, the radicals could now appeal to the province to resist illegal innovations rather than to repudiate established authority. This appeal was consistent with English conservatism and its rhetoric of preservation. Like the revolutionaries of 1688 they could convincingly call for revolution not rebellion, a returning of the political wheel to its original position.[16] And to fill the vacuum created by a rejection of this innovation, they offered a new allegiance to a government built on established and traditional institutions like the town meeting, and upon the sovereign power of the townspeople so assembled. Thus the choice was no longer loyalty or disloyalty, government or void; opposition could be expressed in positive terms, by affirmation of a new allegiance.

This political polarization forced a realignment of personal loyalties as well. Friendships were put to the test, among them the friendship of John Adams and Jonathan Sewall. Despite a decade of political disagreement, the two men had never found cause to renounce their personal affections for each other. Now, however, both men struggled to readjust their lives to their new self-definitions. Sewall was a Tory; Adams a Whig. Adams was determined to represent Massachusetts in the Continental Congress; Sewall, to serve the new Governor and his new government. Their differences were no longer restricted to questions of the legitimate perimeters of resistance to British measures, as in the Stamp Act crisis, or to debates on the nature of the relationship between the executive and the provincial assembly. Adams rejected the imperial system; Sewall reaffirmed it.

Fittingly, in their final conversation at the Falmouth Court sitting, they strove to restore one another to political grace. "Mr. Sewall invited me to take a walk with him," Adams recalled many years later:

In the course of our rambles he very soon began to remonstrate against my going to Congress. He said "that Great Britain was determined on her system; her power was irresistible and would certainly be destructive to me, and to all those who should persevere in opposition to her designs." I answered, "that I knew Great Britain was determined on her system, and that very determination, determined me on mine; that he knew I had been constant and uniform in opposition to all her measures; that the die was now cast; I had passed the Rubicon; swim or sink, live or die, survive or perish with my country, was my unalterable determination." [17]

From the conversation it was clear that Sewall was equally determined to sink or swim, survive or perish, in upholding his opposing political views. No resolution of differences was possible and the two men parted. They did not speak to each other again until 1787, when the conflict that divided them had itself been resolved.

CHAPTER NINE

The Causes and Cure of Popular Madness

1775

WITHIN TWO MONTHS after Sewall and Adams said their farewells, the Sewalls were uprooted from their Cambridge home. With the rise of rural mobs, "vastly more vigilant & spirited" than their city counterparts,[1] a long-standing pattern was being quickly reversed: Loyalists were now fleeing their country residences to seek refuge in Gage's Boston. Such a country mob had surrounded the Sewall home on September 1, while the Attorney General was attending court in Boston. Frustrated by Sewall's absence, the crowd of some fifty men and boys had first smashed windows, then threatened the family, and finally struck a bargain with the frightened Mrs. Sewall which exchanged most of Sewall's wine cellar for the crowd's peaceful dispersal. Though he found his family safe when he returned to Cambridge the following day, Sewall refused to risk any recurrence of this midnight violence.[2] Within the week his family had joined the burgeoning ranks of Tory refugees in Boston. Sewall was never to see Cambridge again.

From Boston Sewall joined in the attempts made in late 1774 to organize other provincial Loyalists in their own defense. In perhaps unconscious imitation of the radicals' enforcement organizations, he assisted in drafting a Loyalist Association. "We the Subscribers," its preamble began,

> being fully sensible of the Blessings of good Government, on the one hand, & convinc'd on the other Hand, of the Evils & Calamities attending on Tyranny, in all Shapes, whether exercised by One, or by many; & having of late seen, with great Grief & Concern, the distressing Effects of a Dissolution of all Government; whereby our Lives, Liberties & Properties are rendered precarious, & no longer under the protection of the Law; & apprehending it to be our indispensable Duty to use all lawful Means of our power, for the Defence of our persons & property against all riotous & lawless Violence, & to recover & secure the Advantages which we are entitled to from the good & wholsome [sic] Laws of Government, do hereby associate and mutually covenant & engage to & with each other, as follows. . . .³

The six-point program that followed included armed vigilante protection for subscribers' property, and a united effort to guarantee one another's rights in "eating, drinking, buying, selling, and communing and acting" as they pleased. The association pledged resistance "at the risk of our Lives if need be," to the "pretended Authority of any Congresses, Committees of Correspondence, or other unconstitutional Assemblys of Men." * Gage himself worked with Loyalists to transform this statement of principles into an actual organization. But Loyalists, perhaps too fixed in their dependence upon the British army, could not be mobilized to protect themselves. Instead they sought the safety of Boston.

Throughout the winter and spring of 1775 the city's population swelled. The army commandeered the best lodgings that Boston had to offer and the Tory gentlemen secured what remained. Food was scarce and menus unvaried. "Pork and beans one day," cried John Andrews, "and beans and pork another." ⁴ Prices were astronomical. "We have

---

* This Association is similar in content and form to other Loyalist pledges drafted throughout the provinces. For example, in January 1775, Dutchess County (New York) Loyalists issued their Association, promising to support one another "in defense of life, liberty and property." (Peter Force, ed., *American Archives*, 4th series, Vol. I [Washington, 1837], p. 1164.)

now and then a carcase [*sic*] offer'd for sale in the market,'' Andrews recorded in April 1775, "which formerly we would not have picked up in the street; but bad as it is, it readily sells for eight pence Lawful money per lb., and a quarter of lamb when it makes its appearance, which is rarely once a week, sells for a dollar, weighing only three and a half pounds.'' [5]

By April of 1775, Boston had taken on the appearance of the besieged and isolated city that it was. [6] Smallpox threatened, and people died of dysentery every day. Sewall, luckily settled in a roomy home on School Street, observed the scene around him with unhappiness. To ward off his own despair and depression he resorted to humor and philosophy. But the philosophy was touched by cynicism, and the humor seemed more self-mockery than jest. When, for example, the funerals became so frequent that "for a month past you meet as many dead folks as live ones in Boston streets," and men viewed these dead with less interest than they did "a quarter of a poor half-starved Sheep," Sewall judged that "this is all natural eno', for when there is not a supply of victuals for all, the survivors will feel less regret at seeing the crowd thin off.* The whole experience of war, pestilence, famine was, he concluded, to be understood as "the best school of philosophy that ever was invented.'' [7]

Sewall spoke of the revolution that was beginning around him as a drama, a play, a performance in which he was not participant but observer. In this manner, he placed an artificial distance between himself and the events around him. To Thomas Robie, who had sought his own escape in Halifax, Sewall insisted that he had no desire to leave Boston yet. He wished, he said, carrying the illusion of his own aloofness from events to its fullest, to see the end of the play. "I assure you," he wrote in July, "I have never from the beginning felt the least disposition to cry. Everything I see is laughable, cursable, and

---

* Ten to thirty funeral processions made their way through the streets each day in July, and Gage, anxious not to let the American militiamen surrounding the city know its plight, refused to allow the death bells to toll (Moore, *Diary of the American Revolution* [New York and London, 1860], I, 110).

damnable; my pew in the church is converted into a pork tub; my house into a den of rebels, thieves & lice; my farm in the possession of the very worst of all god's creation; * my few debts all gone to the devil with my debtors." Yet he would not cry, for "All this is *right, says Doctor Pangloss, and this is the best of all possible worlds, and the garrison of Boston the best of all possible garrisons." "Be it so," he affirmed, "with all my heart." [8]

Sewall did what he could to be of help to Gage. He served the general as personal secretary and Attorney General. The rebels knew him to be a confident and aide to Gage, and this alone was sufficient to insure his infamy; but the radicals' particular animosity toward Sewall during the seige of Boston rested heavily upon his reputation as a political essayist. Beginning in December of 1774, the Massachusettensis letters were published, and radicals mistakenly attributed these essays on politics and government to Sewall. The error was in itself a compliment and showed how firmly his reputation was established within the province as the opposition's most formidable opponent. The very power and persuasiveness of the Massachusettensis series, the "great exultation" it produced among Tories and "gloomy apprehensions" among Whigs, led to an immediate identification of Jonathan Sewall as its author. [9]

John Adams, who returned from Congress in November of 1774 to find "Massachusettensis shining like the moon among the lesser stars," instantly thought him to be his old friend Sewall. [10] This opinion Adams maintained even after the true authorship was discovered. The actual author of these essays, Daniel Leonard, was a newcomer to political writings, and incidentally a newcomer to the Loyalist side.† Yet

* On July 6, 1775, the Provincial Congress had voted "that Mr. Fisk, who has the care of Jonathan Sewall's farm, have liberty to cut on said farm one ton of English hay and two tons of salt hay, and that Mr. David Sanger be directed accordingly" (William Lincoln, ed., *The Journals of Each Provincial Congress of Massachusetts in 1774 and 1775 and of the Committee of Safety* [Boston, 1838], p. 588).

† It was Ward Chipman who, years later, revealed Leonard's authorship. Chipman had personally copied the essays in a fair hand for Leonard before their publication (Edmund Quincy, *Life of Josiah Quincy of Massachusetts* [Boston, 1867]).

Adams and his radical friends were not entirely wrong in perceiving Sewall's touch in the essays. Extensive notes on taxation precedents, the very examples used in Leonard's twelfth essay, are found in Sewall's hand among his papers. If he was not the author, "the moon among the lesser stars" was in part Sewall's accomplishment.[11]

The belief that Sewall had authored the essays, added to his past and present role as Crown advisor, guaranteed for him a prominent place in a propaganda skirmish that flared between Gage and the radicals in June 1775. On June 12, Gage issued a proclamation offering pardons to all "who will forthwith lay down their arms, & return to their usual occupation." [12] Only Sam Adams and John Hancock were excepted. The Provincial Congress responded with their own offer of pardon to all those "who have fled to the town of Boston for refuge, and to other public offenders against the rights and liberties of this country." Excepted by name in this counteroffer were the naval and military commanders Graves and Gage, and Jonathan Sewall, Charles Paxton, and Benjamin Hallowell. These gentlemen's offenses were "of too flagitious a nature to admit of any other consideration than that of condign punishment." [13] The exceptions made by each side served only to enhance in their colleagues' eyes the stature of the parties mentioned.

Although Sewall had not entered the newspaper lists during his year in Boston, he did set down in print his ideas on the rebellion. These writings, both public and private, represent a synthesis of his political thought. One product of these musings on politics was an amateurish play, "A Cure for the Spleen, or Amusement for a Winter's Evening." "The Cure" was a stilted dramatization of the opposing views on Parliament's sovereignty over the colonies.[14] It is set in a local taproom, where several Massachusetts men debate the validity of an American call to arms against the alleged tyranny of Parliament. Innocent townspeople like the barber parrot radical rhetoric, while the hero of the tale, the sagacious, rational "Mr. Sharp," brings them to their senses through an impartial examination of British constitutional history. Lawyer that he was, Sewall reduced the ideological conflict of his day to a simple matter of legal precedent. Through Sharp, Sewall shows that the King had no legal authority to enter into any compact with a colony that might place it beyond Parliament's control. Such an act was contradictory to the British constitution. Thus the sovereignty of Parliament was supreme, and any rejection of it by a dissident colony would be treason. Having settled that point, Sewall's hero goes on to condemn those rabble-rousers who "have blown up a spark . . . into a raging conflagration." *

Sharp enjoyed an ideological victory over the radicals that was greatly at variance with the reality of American politics. Of this Sewall was painfully aware. He was certain too that he understood the cause of the conflict exploding around him. And, knowing its cause, he believed he could suggest its cure. In May 1775, he put aside playwriting to address a long and urgent letter on the political and military situation in America to his acquaintance and superior, General Haldimand, Governor of Canada.[15]

Sewall was concerned above all that the British authorities understand and acknowledge the serious nature of the American problem. The opposition's success throughout the colonies, he told Haldimand, was overwhelming. "A union," he pointed out, "is formed by a great majority, almost throughout this whole continent, for opposing the Supremacy, and even the lowest degree of legislative jurisdiction,—of the British Parliament, over the British Colonies . . . an absolute unlimited Independence is the Object in View."

At first observation, Sewall admitted, this determined resistance to the Mother Country seemed inexplicable. The American people, now organizing for war, were blessed with every advantage that the "Nature of human society admits." They had land, prosperity, and a benign protective parent nation. They enjoyed civil and religious liberty. They had, it was clear, no objective grievance.[16] Yet these people had

---

* Sewall's *Cure* is, in fact, a dramatization of Thomas Hutchinson's speeches to the House of Representatives and to the Council in 1773. Hutchinson's legal and historical argument for Parliamentary sovereignty is the same as Mr. Sharp's (see, Nelson, *The American Tory,* pp. 33–35).

been impelled on the road to revolution by one ambitious man, James Otis, a man who boasted "no Principle of public or private Virtue." The explanation for this strange reality must be looked for, Sewall said, deep within the nature and organization of American society itself. Some imperfections, inherent in the American social organization, made the colonists susceptible to this form of manipulation. Sewall had, he believed, discovered that imperfection: That "hidden Spring which causes so wonderful a movement in the Machine . . . is no other than the ancient, republican, independent Spirit, which the first Emigrants to America brought out with them; and which the Forms of Government, unhappily given to the New England Colonies, instead of checking, have served to cherish & keep alive."

Sewall was seeking to explain the grounds for the response of the masses to radical leadership and manipulation. The motivations of that radical leadership in joining their cause to James Otis's he treats as self-evident. The merchants, for example, sought a free and unrestrained trade, "the sure and easy means of arriving at a Superiority in Wealth." The liberal clergy acted "from a rooted Enmity against the Church of England." And those politicians who rushed to keep burning the fires Otis sparked acted from ambitions just as consuming as his own. These leadership groups, individually and then concertedly, "by the help of the single word, Liberty . . . conjured up the most horrid Phantoms in the minds of the Common People." It was thus the tradition of republicanism, with its emphasis on Liberty as a cornerstone of legitimate society, that the leaders employed to rouse a populace who had no genuine interest in the struggles of their superiors. Like Original Sin, this republican spirit lay quiescent within the body politic until called forth by political and economic ambitions. "The simple unmeaning mechanics, Peasants, and Labourers, who had really no Interest in the Matters of Controversy, hoodwink'd, inflamed, and goaded on by their spiritual Drivers, fancied they saw civil and religious Tyranny advancing with hasty Strides; and thus the Flame soon spread thro these Provinces, and by the help of Kindred Spirits on the other Side the Atlantic it has at length spread thro the Continent.'' *

Great Britain's error, Sewall added, lay in permitting an organization of government in New England which sustained and tolerated this republican spirit in her colonists. † England now must pay the price of her blindness and indulgence.

> Great Britain is at length reduced to this simple alternative; either to renounce her claim of supremacy over the colonies, or in support of it, to conquer them, and establish such a form of government for them as shall be, in itself a specific remedy for the inbred disease. She must now make her election; if she chooses to give up her colonies, the sooner she does it, the better it will be for herself, and for all the Kings' loyal subjects among them. If she resolves to maintain her supremacy, which I must suppose, she must exert herself with her native vigor.

It was lethargy on the part of England's leaders, or perhaps an ignorance of the true situation, that Sewall most feared. The British policy of leaving things to run their course and right themselves had allowed popular enthusiasm to be whipped to a frenzy. The people, as if in some bewitched state, were now "totally incapable of attending to the dictates of reason." The only remedy, Sewall insisted, was a dosage of fear. The spiraling insanity of rebellion could not be stopped by threat or by an appearance of force; only a genuine and overpowering

* Sewall's long-standing belief that the masses of people were deluded and deceived by their ambitious leaders was shared by Galloway, Inglis, and many lesser Tories as well. Tory correspondence carried references to this deception. For example, on May 30, 1776, Richard Lechmere of Cambridge, Massachusetts, wrote to London friends: "under the protection of General Gage we shall be able to speak our minds freely, and open the eyes of a deluded people, who have hitherto been deceiv'd by a sett [sic] of designing villains and bankrupts who have supported themselves at the expense of almost ruining the Town and Province" (*MHSP* 2d series, XVI [1902], 286).

† Galloway wholeheartedly agreed. He believed that the charter government of New England produced "so many pure democracies" that inevitably their principles "tended to erase every sentiment in favor of mixed monarchy." With these principles as a base, it was easy for the ambitious conspirators to start a revolution (Galloway, *Historical and Political Reflections on the Rise and Progress of the American Rebellion*).

application of force would restore America's political sanity. Like slapping the face of a hysteric, a speedy and ruthless military suppression of the insurrection would cause Americans to "pause, reflect, look back and look forward . . . examine . . . question . . . & Reason will again resume her Seat to direct and govern their Ideas and Actions."

Sewall had addressed his thoughts to a military man, and he followed the explication of his theory with a lengthy discussion of military matters. He had a clear sense of how many troops would be necessary to "strike Terror thro' the Continent." He wanted no small police force, no parade of two battalions in scattered cities; he proposed an army of 15,000 in Massachusetts and a secondary force of 10,000 at New York, supported by enough ships to blockade all northern ports. He was confident that an overwhelming force sent speedily to Massachusetts would end the rebellion in New England. And, to Sewall, the subjugation of New England was the subjugation of America. The army in New York was no more than a precautionary measure designed to keep that colony busy with thoughts of self-preservation, and thus to break links between New England and the rest of the colonies. In all his thinking on the revolution, Sewall exhibited the myopia of a Massachusetts conservative: he assumed that the rise and fall of the independence movement turned upon events in his native province.

Sewall emphasized speedy action. Delay, he believed, would increase the possibility of European intervention, an intervention that would turn an imperial concern into an international war. He feared as well the possibility of internal dissension over policy within the English government itself. Furthermore, swift military action would prevent the transformation of America's raw, unskilled fighting mobs and militants into disciplined soldiers. Finally, there was the question of Loyalist morale. Delay would bring despair to loyal subjects in each town and village, and drive them into opposition—or "sink them into a Stupid Disregard to Life."

It was into that "Stupid Disregard to Life" that Sewall had seen many of his own friends sink. Whigs boasted every day of the low morale of those "poor Dogs," the Loyalists, who sought to leave their homes but could find "no Country where a Sentiment worthy of a man is Entertained but detests them." [17] And Sewall's own depression had deepened. His despair was made more intolerable by his firm belief that the rebellion was unnecessary and that civil war would bring nothing but tragedy. "Oh! With what fine touches would . . . a pen describe the bewitching charms of the great goddess Liberty," he wrote,

> how would he paint her worshippers, some plunging themselves, their wives and children in certain poverty & destruction, quitting or wasting their substance, strolling about like pilgrims, not knowing whither they are bound; others plundering & destroying all around them, killing horses, stealing cattle, sheep, money, goods, burning houses, barns & hay—the whole troop rushing into the arms of Slavery, & all in honour of the afore-sd goddess Liberty, as Indians cut & mangle themselves to please the Devil. [18]

By June 1775, Sewall was anxious to leave America. Although he boasted of an eagerness to watch events unfold, he was in fact weary of all he saw and heard. He knew that to leave Massachusetts was an impropriety, for no official leave of absence from his office as Attorney General had been granted. Nevertheless, he could not stay. He had not fled the difficult decision of loyalties between King and colony, but he now chose to leave the scene of conflict between the two. Although Sewall was depressed and bitter, his departure from Boston was no simple psychological retreat. The realities of "musketry, bombs, great guns, redoubts, lines, batterys, enfilades, battles, sieges, murder, plague, pestilence, famine, rebellion, and the Devil" also shaped his decision. [19]

Sewall first planned to join Robie in Halifax, and there take up his Vice Admiralty court duties. But news of a smallpox epidemic in Canada dissuaded him. Instead he "consented, determined, bargained & agreed to quit America," and to transport "myself, my wife, children, manservant, and maid servant . . . to London." [20]

CHAPTER TEN

Waiting, London
1775-1778

THE SEWALLS ARRIVED in London on September 22, 1775. The voyage had placed both psychological and physical barriers between Sewall and Boston, and his anticipation of a reunion with friends and the exploration of London served to divert his mind from its recent concerns.

Sewall was greatly relieved to find his mood lighten. In the tensions of the past year he seemed to become aware for the first time of his own tendency toward deep depression and withdrawal. But he insisted upon seeing this as a new development in his personality, born in the extreme circumstances under which he and others like him had suffered for the sake of their loyalty. He particularly despised that tendency toward melancholia which he felt developing in the months in Boston. In a leave-taking letter to Ward Chipman he had admonished the younger man never to fall into that trap of passivity which was the inevitable result of depression.[1] Depression and despair, he wrote, "like wilful blindness" prevented a man from seeing the means to rectify or conquer his circumstances; it made him victim rather than victor.

It was as much a warning to himself as to Chip. Sewall feared his melancholia as some counterforce growing within him that would vanquish a "natural gaite de cour" he felt he possessed throughout his life, and especially in his youth. He believed, as he told Chip, that "throughout the course of my life, in the most dreary prospects, I don't know that I ever felt a disposition to despair." This natural optimism which he took as his hallmark had "perpetually prompted me to hope that things would be better tomorrow; and this enabled me to make light of present inconveniences, and to look out for and to embrace all the means of mending them within my reach." This was surely a selective recollection, drawn from a past which included not only the admirably cheerful acceptance of tiring circuit riding with the Courts but also the compulsive behavior of the Venner affair and the flight from the Boston Massacre trials. But Sewall fixed upon this resiliency and optimism as a reflection of his true self. Thus he created an internal struggle to recapture, and live up to, a standard of behavior that had never wholly been his.

Now in London, Sewall determined to reassert that resiliency and resourcefulness which he believed had marked his youth. He evaluated his circumstances and found them unsettling but not unfavorable. He had a secure income from his Vice Admiralty bench on which to subsist in what he felt would be a temporary exile from Massachusetts. This he knew placed him in a far more favorable situation than friends whose wealth remained behind in America. And a convivial social life seemed assured through a highly complimentary status accorded him among the exiles. Upon his arrival he had taken his place with ease among the elite ranks of Thomas Hutchinson's inner circles. The men of this circle, and especially Sewall—who maintained a warm and fatherly relationship with many of the younger, less established men *— were the leaders of the New England population in London.[2] When Sewall chose No. 1 Brompton Row, in Knightsbridge, as his residence

* Sewall's special relationship with the younger refugees can be seen in the pattern of socializing set by Hutchinson. As leader of the Massachusetts refugee group, Hutchinson was careful to greet each new arrival. An invitation to Hutchinson's residence was usually the first greeting each Loyalist, young or old, received. But only the select few—Sewall, Oliver, and other members of the elite—received a second audience with the ex-Governor. Sewall, on the other hand, moved with flexibility from circle to circle, entertained a wide variety of gentlemen, and took an interest in the lives and careers of the younger men.

in England, a virtual Massachusetts colony grew up around him. If he was in exile, at least he was not alone.

This visit to London might also be turned to good advantage, for his own career and for the career of his protege, Chipman. These anticipations were not unrealistic, for as a member of the earliest wave of refugees Sewall encountered a warm and open-handed ministry. The government seemed willing to demonstrate its faith to the Loyalists, and several appointments to be enjoyed "as soon as the rebellion is suppressed" had already been awarded. Sewall's friend, Jonathan Bliss, had won from Lord North an appointment as Solicitor to the Board of Customs.[3] To show his serious intent, North had ordered Bliss's salary to commence immediately. If Bliss had been this fortunate, Sewall's own hopes were justifiably high. His initial reception by Lords Dartmouth and North had been cordial, even warm, and his government connections now included Governors Gage and Haldimand as well as Francis Bernard and Thomas Hutchinson.*

But more than any other factor, the very strangeness and novelty of his circumstances enabled him to cast off his depression. He was in London, a city in which "everything is upon a scale so much above what I have ever seen, that my mind seems to be lost & confounded in infinity." [4]

After a brief period of limbo, when influenza confined him to his chambers, Sewall gave himself over with relief to the exploration of his new surroundings.[5] He was enthusiastic about all he saw. This enthusiasm was possible in large part because Sewall felt himself a visi-

---

* In these hopes Sewall, like most other Loyalists, was sadly mistaken. The initial reception given Loyalists in 1775 and early 1776 proved misleading. The government's largesse served to whet political appetites and to instill confidence in Britain's determination to make a speedy restoration of order in the colonies. However, as Mary Beth Norton has shown, this honeymoon between refugees and ministry was short-lived. As the war was prolonged the refugees' pensions were foreshortened, and most office-seeking was limited to military or military-related commissions. Sewall, then in his fifties, might be helpful to younger men like Chipman and Edward Winslow, both of whom returned to New York and the military service; but his own career could not be served during the war.

tor rather than an emigré in London. Like most of his fellow refugees, he refused to entertain the notion that his separation from America was permanent; it was because London was a temporary diversion that what he tasted seemed so sweet.

Sewall spent his days sightseeing with Hutchinson, Samuel Curwen, Francis Waldo, or his cousin, Sam Sewall.* His personal identification with English tradition and English institutions had been heightened by his recent commitment of political loyalty, and by its consequences. Thus, he was almost aggressively receptive to those monuments or institutions which reflected the continuity between provincial and national consciousness. And all he saw confirmed him in his belief that his loyalty was well founded. He felt confident of Britain's greatness and power, and her determination to retain sovereignty over her colonies. To see London was to be reassured that he would see Boston again.

While all Sewall saw reassured him, paradoxically it soon gave him pause. The greatness, wealth, and majesty of England would, after all, seem quite different were he forced to remain in that country. "Unless a gentleman can get his Share of [the wealth]," he wrote to Edward Winslow in New York, "he has no business here." Sewall's own salary, ample in America, was pitifully inadequate for a gentleman's life in London. " £600 per An. is but as a Drop in the Ocean," and a man living in England with only these meagre resources "Is Nothing—less than Nothing & Vanity—& his contemplation of his own Comparative Littleness, is Vexation of Spirit." [6] Sewall understood that this "Vexation of Spirit" arose not merely from an economic but from a social "littleness" as well. His observation struck at the core of the dilemma of most New England Loyalists. If circumstances compelled an American to make his permanent residence in England (which of course would not, could not be the case) where would he find a place for himself within this vastly different social structure, a place equivalent to

---

* The New England Loyalists did an inordinate amount of sightseeing and travelling, having little else to occupy their time. See Samuel Curwen's Journal for a vivid account of these refugees' daily activities.

the one he had forfeited? Sewall saw the dimensions of the necessary shift in social scale and recognized that no equivalent place could be found. The provincial elite who had come to England would, at best, be absorbed into the middling ranks of English society. They would be deprived of prestige and divested of any leadership role in the decision-making process. Integration into English society would demand a readjustment of the provincial's image of himself. For if it was true, as Sewall had observed, that American society was but a "Miniature Yankee puppet-show" in comparison with England, then his own accomplishments in Massachusetts were only a provincial imitation of success. As a citizen of England, Sewall would have to exchange his claims to prestige and power for the lesser position of local currency.*

This fuller understanding of his own stake in the outcome of the war soon broke down his optimism into a jumble of conflicting emotions. His anger at the American rebels was revived and intensified: "I declare that in my conscience I believe the plotters, instigators & cherishers of this most unnatural, causeless distructive [sic] rebellion to be the worst set of men that have ever lived from the days of Lot to this day . . . [they are] barbarous, inhuman, unchristian, & diabolical." [7]

Yet the mere possibility of a permanent separation from his native Massachusetts produced in him a premature homesickness: a melancholia he alternately indulged in and renounced. "I wish never to see [America] again," he wrote to Edward Winslow, "and would shun it as I would a country infested with the plague." Yet he confessed in an unsolicited letter to a rebel friend that he longed for "one peep at my house," and he pestered Thomas Robie and Ward Chipman for fish from American waters, newton pippins, and cranberries from home. [8]

His emotions were contradictory, but his preoccupation with America was constant. He renounced her; he was eager to return; he hoped for her decimation; he prayed for her safety. He followed little

---

* William Nelson summed up the Loyalists' anomie: "It was, of course, their loss of occupation and social standing, their loss of *place* [Nelson's italics] in society, that made the refugees miserable in spirit" (Nelson, *The American Tory,* p. 158).

in British politics but that which affected the war. He mixed with no one in London but fellow Americans, and with few who were not New Englanders. On Thursdays he met at the Adelphi Tavern with the New England Club, to share news of conditions in Boston, New York, and Philadelphia, or rumors and facts of troop movements.* When the New England Club disbanded in the summer of 1776, Sewall opened his own drawing room to American companions and the Brompton Row Tory Club, as these meetings were called, continued throughout the year.[9] These New England clubs served to preserve their members' American identities, even as they increased their sense of isolation from the society around them.[10]

The war itself was the focal point of Sewall's interest. His perception of events was shaped in large part by psychological necessities: to admit the possibility of American victory was to be forced to confront a loss of identity; thus, he maintained a complete and fanatical confidence in British success. The gap between British military performance and his expectation could have no other explanation therefore than stupidity, cowardice, or treason on the parts of admirals and generals. The failure to put a speedy end to the rebellion was an act of will by opposition politicians and military leaders like Admiral Samuel Graves.[11]

Sewall blamed Graves, for example, for the poor conditions in Boston and for the failure to pacify New England. "What excuse can be form'd for a British Admiral, who, with 30 or 40 Ships under his Command, Suffers a Garrison to starve, tho' surrounded with plenty of every Necessary within the reach of his Ships!" This tame and supine Admiral, he assured Edward Winslow, "is cursed as hard upon this Side of the Water, as he can be on yours." [12]

* Members of the New England Club were: Richard Clark, Joseph Green, Jonathan Bliss, Jonathan Sewall, Joseph Waldo, Samuel Sampson Blowers, Elisha Hutchinson, William Hutchinson, Samuel Sewall, Samuel Quincy, Isaac Smith, Harrison Gray, David Greene, Jonathan Clark, Thomas Flucker, Joseph Taylor, Daniel Silsbee, Thomas Brinley, William Cabot, John S. Copley, Nathaniel Coffin, Samuel Curwen, Samuel Porter, Thomas Hutchinson, Edward Oxnard, Benjamin Pickman, Jonathan Amory, Robert Auchmuty, and Edward Urquhart (JSC, p. 45).

Graves's inactivity Sewall next discussed with Chipman. "It re-
minds me of Voltair's [*sic*] Observation, in his Candid—viz, 'that the
English find it necessary to shoot an Admiral now and then, to make
the rest fight.' Sure I am this Admiral deserves shooting infinitely
more richly than poor Byng did, if the one half that is told of his un-
pardonable Neglect, be true." [13]

At the same time as he voiced these censorious sentiments, Sewall
spoke confidently to both friends of an offensive, which would be
launched that summer. This attack would prove decisive: "I verily
believe your Sufferings are drawing near a period—you will undoubtedly have, early in the Spring, an army of 40,000 & a Fleet of up-
wards of 70 Ships, & then the Mettle of the Rebels will be try'd—
hitherto their Successes have been owing to their having none to op-
pose them—the poor infatuated Wretches, as yet, know Nothing of
war." [14]

Similar predictions followed in the summer of 1777. Sewall, not
content to share his expectations of victory with fellow Loyalists,
wrote to Whigs in America as well. In these letters he adopted the tone
of a Jeremiah, and urged friends like John Foxcroft and John Lowell
to repent. "Depend on it," he told Lowell in 1777, "a dreadful storm
is gathered, and is approaching towards you; a terrible summer is
before you; and a day of strict reckoning hastening on." [15]

A cycle of despair and anger followed by great confidence seemed
to replace the seasonal marking of his year. In his fall and winter low
periods he cursed Americans; when his confident springs and summers
came, he hoped that British anger would be tempered with forgive-
ness. He came increasingly to see the war through the metaphor of the
Old Testament God and His errant children of Israel.

Sewall was not atypical of the Loyalists in the quasi-religious cast
he gave to the war, or in his rigid belief that British victory was inevitable.[16] His tendency to blame incompetence or political conspiracy
for the failure of the British forces to quickly conquer America was almost universal among the New England refugees. Their interpretation,

though jaundiced, had much plausibility. The rivalry between military and naval commanders made the necessary coordination of action almost impossible; the traditional independence of commanders made a centralized strategy unthinkable. And the persistent British military attitude toward preserving their trained and disciplined troops from danger did make Howe and his fellow officers hesitant to risk battle. These real failures in organization and attitude must surely have appeared to the nonmilitary eye of the refugee as incompetence or treason.[17]

Sewall's seasonal optimism was also shared by his friends. This optimism was keenest in 1777, when Burgoyne's army began its march through northern New York.[18] At the same time General Howe moved with an army of 15,000 from the British stronghold at New York toward the rebels' government headquarters in Philadelphia. Loyalists in England and America were jubilant. "It seems to be the critical time," James Putnam wrote confidently to Sewall from New York.[19]

As the autumn began, Chipman, serving as assistant muster-master to the army at New York, undertook to record the year's military events for Sewall. His reportage is the Loyalist view of the war writ small. It typifies the wild fluctuation in emotion which resulted from an eagerness on the Tories' parts to believe any rumor that implied victory. On September 11, Chipman wrote to Sewall: "The Campaign tho'opened late will, I conceive, prove compleatly decisive. Destruction seems now to await [the rebels] from every Quarter, and nothing but the most unfortunate and improbable accidents, or the worst criminal Neglect and Delays on the part of the King's armies, neither of which it is to be hoped will intervene, can [prevent] the suppression of this romantic rebellion." On the third page of this letter, Chip reported a march on Philadelphia by Howe which "excedes all our Expectations." Congress had tried to flee, Chip heard, and only the Philadelphia militia had prevented their disgraceful departure. Burgoyne, he told Sewall, had masterfully managed his northern campaign thus far, taking the American army by surprise near Albany. Yet two days later, in an addendum to this same letter, Chip conceded "the story respecting the Congress, is I fear premature." The information on Burgoyne's successes, however, could be depended upon.

A second postscript followed on September 20. "This whole week we have had no confirmation of accounts from General Burgoyne," Chip now confessed. Yet if the absence of news "makes us doubt everything," at the same time it allows us to "hope all things." [20] Then, on November 7, Chip wrote once again. "The particulars of the misfortunes of the northern army you will see long before this reaches you." He referred, of course, to Burgoyne's defeat at Saratoga. This defeat, Chip conceded, lay heavily upon Loyalists in America. "Our present situation is so gloomy that I can give you no Idea of the uneasiness which every where may be discovered." For once, there was no optimistic prediction of victory.[21]

The same despair spread over Loyalists in England when news of the "mortifying capitulation" reached them in December.[22] The defeat of Gentleman Johnny meant an end to all hopes of a speedy return home. The spectre of a French and Spanish alliance with the colonists was raised, and soon England might face an international as well as a civil war. There would be, Loyalists knew, a shift in military emphasis if war with France broke out. Vigorous efforts to reduce America would be superseded by the necessity of national defense.

By the spring of 1778 the New England Loyalists had deserted London. In their exodus they had bowed to the realities of protracted exile. Sewall chose as his provincial retreat the city of Bristol. "I shall set out next Monday, bag and baggage for Bristol," he told his kinswoman Mehitabel Higginson on April 1, "there to remain til the restoration of peace, and perhaps till the restoration of all things." [23]

Sewall probably had few regrets at leaving London. The city had proved too expensive and too large for his provincial means and tastes. And it carried bitter memories, for Sewall had buried his only daughter, Betsey, in November 1776.[24]

CHAPTER ELEVEN

More Waiting, Bristol
1778-1783

SEWALL'S NEW RESIDENCE was a busy seaport at the western entry to England, across the River Severn from the Welsh town of Cardiff. He had visited here in the summer of 1777, on an explorative outing with his cousin Sam and Samuel Curwen. Curwen thought little of the city; he found the Bristolians nosey, rude, and driven in all things by commercial motives. He recorded for its epigram the popular proverb that "One Jew is equal to two Genoese, one Bristolian to two Jews." [1] Yet Sewall shared the impression of other New Englanders that Bristol was as like Boston as any English town could be. And although the city's population was sympathetic to the rebels, in 1778 a New England colony sprang up within its borders. [2]

Sewall's first years in Bristol passed quietly and without incident. He took lodgings in Orchard Street with family and footman and the company of several New England bachelors. He enrolled his sons in boarding school across the street, and for 7/6 per week each boy could spend an occasional seven days with his parents. His own days were spent at backgammon, cards, reading, and letter writing. To his correspondents in Canada and America Sewall presented a cheerful optimistic mood, despite an occasional flare of anger against "those sanctified hypocrites," those "damned fanatical, republican, New England, rebellious, ungenerous, ungrateful sons of bitches," [3] whose Proscrip-

tion Act in September 1778 barred him from his own home,* and an
occasional harangue against the incompetence of the army and navy.

His health, Sewall insisted to friends, had improved with the move
to the provinces. He admitted that even now, in Bristol, periodic bouts
with illness confined him to his bed, and drove him to "spirited reme-
dies." [4] Yet he saw himself on the mend. His boast was important,
for Sewall took his physical condition to be a barometer of his state of
mind. His health was poor, he noted, when he was depressed; his constitution fit, or growing fit, in periods of optimism.

He managed, by subtle alterations in his expectations, to maintain
his confidence in a British victory, a victory that would render the
"diabolical Massachusetts act" of proscription ineffectual. Throughout 1778 and 1779 he looked to events for some catalyst to spur England to vigorous action. Though he shared his friends' belief that the
Carlisle peace offer would be rejected, he took heart from this by
projecting as its consequence that "the Haughtiness of the Congress
will rouse Britons to Vengeance." [5] Simultaneously, he looked for an
end to the war through the collapse of the American army and the
American government. He greeted as fact any rumor that confirmed
these hopes. "I cannot help giving Credit to the late Advices from
America," he wrote Isaac Smith in May 1778, "respecting the miserable State of the rebel Army, the Distractions in their public councils
and the universal Distress which prevails throughout the Land." [6] In
this vein, he hailed the American alliance with France as the certain
spur to internal rebellion in America. The American Protestants
would, he was certain, reject the government that had formed this unnatural friendship with a Catholic nation. Surely descendants of English Puritans and Protestants would recoil from those "French ways"
which prompted rebel leaders in Massachusetts "to ride through the
streets of *Holy* Boston, at Noon day, with *kept-Mistresses!* aye faith,
with kept mistresses." [7]

* The Provincial Assembly barred Sewall from Massachusetts, but he had already been
barred from his own home. His house and property had been confiscated and sold in
1776.

In December 1778 a conversation with Martin Howard, a Loyalist recently arrived from Rhode Island, convinced Sewall of the rightness of his judgments and expectations.

[Howard] tells me that a number of gentlemen of influence and property, who have been lying on their oars to see which way the game would finally go, as I suppose, have lately come in * . . . that they, together with Mr. Galloway, are unanimously of opinion, that from the unexpected tyranny of the Congress and their sub-devils, the almost universal poverty and distress of the people, and the general aversion to French connections, the quondam union of the thirteen states is upon the point of dissolution, and that nothing is wanting but a single effort to crush the rebellion, root and branch. . . . From all these appearances I augur well. [8]

Although Sewall occasionally wished for a war directed by ''an unfeeling, politic King of Prussia or Empress of Russia,'' rather than George III in whose ''composition is too much of the Milk of human Nature,'' still he projected a sanguine faith in the struggle's favorable outcome. [9] For even if Britain would not stir, even if the Americans would not throw over their Congress, still victory would come to the patient, and ''the point of dissolution'' would make a new imperial unity necessary. ''The situation of American loyalists, I confess, is enough to have provoked Job's wife, if not Job himself,'' Sewall wrote as the year ended; ''but still we must be men, philosophers, and Christians.'' And he greeted 1779 with thoughts of seeing his exiled friends again in Cambridge.

Sewall's hopefulness was reinforced in 1779 by the good news that January of expected victory in Georgia and the Carolinas. In the wake of their submission, Sewall was confident that the surrender of all the Southern colonies would follow. Then, he said with obvious relish, ''All the artillery of Heaven & Great Britain may be turned against the four New England provinces—and may it rain fire & brimstone, an horrible Tempest, upon all the Cities of Sodom & Gomorrah.'' Yet in

* One of the gentlemen Sewall names as ''lying on his oars'' was William Smith of New York, whose daughter Harriet was to marry Sewall's son Jonathan Jr. in Canada.

the contemplation of such glorious victory, he again became generous, and even protective toward his native New England. "I confess," he told Tom Robie,

> entre nous, I have a predilection for my *natale Solum*—and notwithstanding all that I with a thousand other innocents, have suffered from the ambition and Envy of the *few,* backed by the Delusion and Ignorance of the many headed Monster, the State Leviathan, or, if you please, the Mob, the worst I wish them is speedy repentence, and a general pardon, with as few exceptions as is consistent with sound policy.[10]

Even the entry of France into the war could not—on the surface at least—provoke Sewall's anxiety. He was "rather inclined to rejoice & laugh, than to grieve and cry at this Event." [11] He confessed to Isaac Smith that summer that he had actually wished for this outbreak of hostilities with France, for Catholic pledges of neutrality could be trusted no more than the promises of the devil himself, and an open war was preferable to a betrayal of promise. Faced with this threat from France, England might at last "unite & exert its innate Strength." [12] Some gloomy Croakers might cry out that summer of 1779, but he, as always, was "disposed to look for the bright side."

Sewall busied himself in 1780 with comet-watching and the national lottery. In June he set off on another country outing with traveling companions Sam Sewall and Samuel Curwen.* And in November Sewall was cheered by the news of Benedict Arnold's return to his proper loyalties. Without the usual straining of facts, Sewall was able to give an optimistic prediction for the future of the war, an optimism shared in late 1780 by most of his fellow Loyalists. "The Rebel Arnold's return to his Allegiance" and the southern victories seemed to promise a British victory.[13]

By December 1781, however, no one held such hope for a British victory. Ward Chipman, usually as unwarrantedly optimistic as his friend Sewall, broke a long silence of depression: "The mortification of seeing our Enemies and such Enemies triumphant in such a cause is

* There is a long account of this journey, on which Sewall and his companions were robbed, in *JSC*.

too much for my Spirits. . . . the general view is that the American
war will be given over & this place evacuated. . . . many are appre-
hensive that Savannah & Charlestown will fall before Spring." [14] In
March 1782, political upheaval followed the military defeats. That
month the North ministry fell. Sewall viewed this political event prag-
matically. Although he personally respected North's "consummate
wisdom and Patriotism," he believed the resignation appropriate:
"With all their consummate abilities & disinterested integrity, they
have been *Unfortunate* and of all possible objections that the most vir-
ulent opposition can make to the Continuance of a Minister or a General in office, this is the most weighty." But the outcome of this
change in government Sewall would not and could not predict. "I
have no Opinion to hazard—I am involved in Egyptian darkness—I see
nothing ahead—I conjecture nothing—its such a sudden jirking Whirle
as has confounded my Ideas." [15] His hopes, however, remained that
his American countrymen would themselves grant a British victory.
He expected daily that Americans would renounce their leaders, who
had delivered them into the hands of the Bourbons. "How, by what
singular infatuation," he asked Chip, "could my Countrymen, tear
themselves from the fond Embraces of an English protestant parent—
and throw themselves into the Arms of the ancient, natural, implacable
Enemy to Englishmen and the protestant Religion? Of a power which
every english Child knows, has so long aimed at universal Monarchy,
and as a leading step to that, at first subjugating English America?" [16]
His only concern was that the Americans would waken to their senses
too late, and find themselves locked in the grasp of the "most Chris-
tian King—the Grand Bulwark of that dreaded ecclesiastical Mon-
ster," the Catholic Church.

The stupid senselessness of the war had always been the cornerstone
of Sewall's arguments against it, but the intensity of his frustration at
his countrymen reached its fullest during the following months of
1782. In April he judged his state of mind to be so agitated that he
"could give loose to political Madness." An intelligent analyst of politics and power, he argued, could not fail to see the folly of American

independence. As long as the three powers of France, Spain, and England exist America must belong to one or be at war with all. At the same time as he might argue this point, Sewall also made two observations from the European point of view. First, Europe could not afford to allow an independent power to establish itself in America, for "An Independent power there would not only be Masters of all N. and S. America, but of the West Indies Islands, and of Course, in process of time, of Europe itself." Yet this war had shown that no single European country could control the American population. From these conclusions, Sewall produced—only partially in jest—a master plan, a Machiavellian solution to the American dilemma:

> My plan is simply this. Give France all her ancient possessions to the Northland, Spain all hers to the Southward, England to retain the Middle Colonies, and the three powers mutually to guarrantee to each other their several possessions *against rebels to either of the Crowns.* This would effectually secure their Allegiance in times of Peace, and in Case of a War between the three European powers, or any two of them, the Colonists would not think of rebellion while they had powerful inimical Colonies in their Neighborhood. Interest governs States as well as Individuals, universally—and upon this plan, it would eternally be the Interest of France, Spain and G. Britain, to discourage revolts in the Colonies.[17]

In short, Sewall was willing, even anxious to turn back the clock by the decades, and to risk the safety of frontier-area Americans in order to return Massachusetts to Britain.

Sewall's scheme probably reached no ears but Chipman's. This political "hobby horse," as he called it, was set aside that summer as the peace talks began. By winter he knew of the recognition of independence, and by year's end he learned from New York correspondents that British strongholds were being evacuated and Loyalists from New York were pouring into Canada in the dead of that winter.[18]

To the injury of the apparent American victory was added this insult: the British government was rumored to be reevaluating its policy of support for the now permanently exiled Loyalists in England. It was clear that these men were viewed as permanent burdens upon the

Treasury, and many Loyalists feared they would be abandoned by the Government they had risked their careers and fortunes to honor. With some justification Ward Chipman wrote in December of 1782: "We now find that loyalism has been a crime and an attachment to government the source of disgrace & neglect." [19]

Sewall took little satisfaction from his own firm belief that independence spelled ruin for rebels and refugees alike. As always he was furious with his countrymen. Instead of rising up against the demagogues of Congress, they had permitted themselves to be ridden to certain ruin like a herd of jackasses. "This opinion," he told Chip, "is founded on my own Experience, on both sides the Atlantic, and on the History of all Ages and Nations from the time of Moses to the present day. Look back, Chip," he urged:

> to the beginning of American Troubles, and trace them down to Independence, and say whether you dont see clearly the Mark of the Beast, Jack Ass, on the forehead of every American below a Committee-man—poor Beasts, I pity them from my Soul—how have their more cunning leaders coaxed them on, like dray horses with Bells by the empty sounds of Liberty and Property, redress of Grievances, the Majesty of the People—INDEPENDENCE! Good God, where is now their Liberty, property, Majesty and Independence?—what is the fruit of all their folly but an exchange of imaginery for real and substantial Grievances? [20]

For himself, Sewall could muster little of the usual show of optimism and hope. "I have got to an end of all my wishes & prayers—hopes and fears—resentments of all kinds—in short, as the late belligerent powers, now are, I am all peace within, every passion is hush'd to a perfect stupid Calm." [21]

The exercise of reason, in which he believed he had always placed his confidence, no longer seemed applicable to politics. And his own judgments had been proved by recent events to have been foolishly premised. "I am now clearly convinced," he added to Chip, "that I have all along been an Ass, a fool, and a blockhead—I have thought, Nincompoop that I was, that Justice, Mercy, Honesty, Gratitude, and other Attributes with which we Shackle our Passions and Appetites, were uniformly the same thro all Nature—but Ld Bolinbrok [*sic*] tells me they are not the same in the Deity; and Experience has now taught me they are not the same with the Gods of this world. . . . So be it. We can't alter the Nature of things.'' And if his own notions of right and wrong were so afoul of political reality, then he could only bid "Adieu again, & forever, to politics.'' [22]

His adieu followed seven years of wild speculation on military and political events, credulousness, inaccurate prediction, and a myopia regarding the fate of the American masses shared with each of his Loyalist correspondents. His foolishness and theirs can only be explained by their own emotional needs and their longing to have things set right again. Sewall, like many of his companions, reduced the Revolution to a war directed against his own happiness and well-being. Although he might make angry judgments and self-righteous ones, not one moment of objective self-reappraisal occupied him. He saw nothing and searched for nothing in his own political behavior in Massachusetts to warrant exile, or even opprobrium.

CHAPTER TWELVE

The Causes and Cure of Personal Madness
1785-1787

THE 1780s BROUGHT an end to Jonathan Sewall's personal war against melancholy and depression. Events, Sewall conceded to Chip, now seemed entirely out of his influence or control; if once he had optimistically believed himself master of circumstances, he now admitted that they were master of him.[1] But this surrender of will brought him little peace, even when Sewall coupled it with a physical retreat from those realities he could not affect. He had established such a retreat for himself when he changed lodgings in the winter of 1783, claiming as his sanctum sanctorum a large room above a kitchen detached from the main house. Here he surrounded himself with favorite furniture and favorite books; his only companions were a pair of goldfinches and an "italianized" cat. He allowed no human being to enter this "Cynical tub." [2]

Yet even in this sanctuary Sewall was disturbed by thoughts of America. The permanence of exile had not, as he had perhaps hoped, resolved his ambivalence toward that country; it had only sharpened it. His continuing conflict of emotion made him bitter. He could, and did, renounce his ties with America through stubborn gestures: he changed his name from its immigrant spelling, "Sewall," to what he insisted was its rightful English spelling, "Sewell." And he could console himself by arguments that loyalty, with its secure Vice Admiralty commission, was more profitable than rebellion would have been. But neither these gestures of renunciation nor assertions of confidence led him to the neutrality of feeling toward his native country that would have freed him from his past for the sake of his future.

There were some certainties in that future which could not be avoided. He knew he could not remain much longer in England. Life here had proven too expensive, even in the provinces. From a combination of necessary costs such as his sons' schooling, and costs which Sewall complained arose from a "total want of resolution in the Government of my Family," [3] he had already fallen into debt. His budget was so tight in 1782 that he had reduced his Vice Admiralty deputy's salary from £150 to an embarrassing sum of £50 a year. [4] Now in 1783 Sewall was inclined to see even that sum as an extravagance. These thoughts led him logically, though reluctantly, to contemplate his own residence in Halifax. He had no more enthusiasm for that cold pioneer region now than he had at the time of his appointment to the Court in 1768, but he could live there among friends, draw the full salary from his court, and provide more intelligently for his sons' futures.

This last consideration weighed most heavily in Sewall's decision. In recent years a note of morbidity had crept steadily into his discussions of his two boys, Jonathan and Stephen; he had formed a conviction in 1780 that he was soon to die, leaving his children without income or career. For his own sake, he told Chip, death made little difference. But it would leave his sons to repeat their father's own childhood history. "If I never see you again," he wrote in 1780, "you may possibly see my dear Boys—they are fine boys, Chip—and may be fatherless.—thats the only Question that ever unmans me—let Wars of Rebellion continue, let my little all go, let me be banished from my Native Country, which heaven knows I dearly love, give me my life till my dear, dear boys are upon their own Legs and take it heaven, when you please." [5]

Sewall's prophecies of an early death seemed more a comment on the uncertainty of the future than a medical diagnosis, despite some signs of declining health. For his part, Chip tried earnestly to reassure his friend. ''I am distress'd at your extreme anxiety about your dear Boys,'' he responded.

> Merit and industry never yet wanted Friends or failed of success in life; and it is impossible you can be without the firmest confidence, that those dear objects of your care are equally so to me; Rest assured that they will, they shall answer your fondest expectation, they shall live prosper and be great in life. I anticipate the satisfaction I shall feel in seeing the Sons of him who has been more than a father to me, tread in his Steps and revive the full remembrance of all his goodness to me, and while I have the means of enjoyment in life they shall never be without the fullest participation, nothing on my part shall ever be too great a sacrifice to promote their interest, happiness or welfare. . . . tell them this and more, convince them that they have one Friend, whose anxiety and wishes are and whose endeavors will be as great to promote their success in life as yours. Tell them tis Chip.[6]

But Sewall continued to envision only the bleakest futures for his sons. ''You know I have a poor scurvey Constitution at best,'' he reminded Chipman in April 1782. ''This damp climate has brought on a scorbutic habit, which possibly may, eer long, put an End to a Life, which but for my two poor boys, I can confess to you, I should have no great regret at parting with—but I am anxious for my dear Boys, who, if I die, will be helpless, friendless, pennyless, fatherless Orphans.''[7]

There was little Chip could do but urge Sewall to put aside brooding and make constructive plans for his children's futures. This Sewall finally began to do in 1783 as he contemplated the move to Canada.

Sewall had provided his sons Jonathan and Stephen excellent secondary educations during the years in Bristol. But he preferred not to continue their English schooling, despite their academic successes. He was certain that a university education, without the social and economic standing necessary to make it meaningful, would be pretentious and damaging to the boys' self-esteem. To be trained a gentleman English style, when one had no inheritance of rank or income to live as taught, he saw as foolish and unkind. Instead, Sewall now concluded that his sons should be "bred to the law"—in a colonial setting.

Although they differed in character and talents, Sewall was convinced both sons would be successful in their father's profession. "Their powers are of a different cast," he explained in a long, musing letter to Chip.

> Jack's are impetuous and penetrating—Stephen's are calm and solid— Jack's impetuosity is such as hurrys him thro Errors and Mistakes, because he cannot stop to look a second time, at what he does not comprehend at first Glance—while on the other hand such is the Majors [Stephen Sewall] cool patience, that untill he is certain his first Step is right, nothing can induce him to attempt the Second. The one Submits his Judgment to rules—the other trusts to the Quickness of his Apprehension. [8]

Jonathan, Sewall concluded, could base his legal success on courtroom oratorical skills; Stephen could build a solid practice upon a reputation for thoroughness and efficiency.

Following this thinking, Sewall determined to apprentice his older son, Jonathan, to Chip when all were settled in Canada. But circumstances threatened to delay even his best laid plans. His financial situation had grown steadily worse while he, like other near-desperate Loyalists, waited for the Government to hear his claims for compensation of lost property, wealth, and professional income. By August of 1784, Sewall confessed with great agitation to Chip that he could not quit Bristol honorably "unless Dame Fortune favors me in this years Lottery . . . or the Commissioners make me some Recompence for Losses—or someone will trust me with a Loan of £600 to be paid at three yearly payments." [9]

No lucky lottery ticket and no loan eased Sewall's difficulties. He was helpless to do anything but wait. This waiting increased his general anxiety, and it added to a growing tension already apparent between Sewall and his wife. In 1784 Sewall had suggested leaving Esther in Bristol while he and his sons went out to Canada. It was a planned separation which revealed more than the exigencies of debt.

In fact, Sewall blamed Esther for his financial difficulties (although he sometimes attributed these to the Government or the Devil). If he died a pauper, he grew fond of saying, he had no pity for a widow who would only be suffering the consequences of her spendthrift ways. But Esther's real or imagined extravagance was not the true source of his irritation; Esther's fault was not the openness of her purse but the openness of her expression of homesickness. Her displays of feeling stirred Sewall's own painful longings for Massachusetts. Esther Sewall spoke freely of her yearnings for Boston and of her desires to be reunited with family and old friends. She lacked the wit or the skill to hide her feelings—or her despair at the Sewalls' future. Her unhappiness with Bristol was sheer contentment when compared to her gloom at the prospect of Canada.

Sewall felt his wife's unhappiness as an accusation, although Esther was neither a vindictive nor a censorious woman. She passively obeyed her husband all her life. But this was not enough if she could not hide her emotions from him. By 1787 Sewall could sarcastically wish his wife out of his sight forever, either returned to Massachusetts, "or at Nova Zembla,* or in the Georguine Sidus, or tyed to the Tail of the Comet of 1668." [10]

In the early winter of 1784 Sewall was at last called down to London to testify before the Royal Commission on the Losses and Services of American Loyalists. Here he presented a claim for almost £6000 in property, furnishings, and personal articles, all confiscated or destroyed by the American rebels.[11] He found other Loyalists willing to give him what aid they could; Andrew Oliver, Lieutenant Governor of Massachusetts before the Revolution, testified to Sewall's wealth and his loyalty. In turn, Sewall spoke in behalf of those who sought his help.[12] But when this exchange of favors was completed, there was little purpose his presence in London could serve. He re-

---

* The reference to Nova Zembla is taken from Sterne's *Tristram Shandy,* Sewall's favorite novel, and a book all the rage in England during his exile. Sewall's letters are sprinkled with these references throughout the 1780s.

turned to Bristol uncertain, as were all his companions in exile, of when the Commissioners would complete their investigations and deliberations.

The impression Sewall left with his old friends in London disturbed them. His appearance as well as his temperament had greatly changed. "Mr. Sewall was in Town about three or four weeks ago," Thomas A. Coffin reported in December of 1784. "I saw him several times— he is much altered, he not only looks older but his face is full of carbuncles." [13]

One year later Coffin might not have recognized Sewall at all. For events in 1785 brought to a head the turmoil brewing inside him. The Commissioners appeared determined to drag their heels, and their delay left Sewall a prisoner to his Bristol creditors. The waiting was only monotony and boredom for most of the family, but for Jack, each day wasted postponed his start upon a career. Reluctantly, Sewall decided to send his oldest son out to Canada alone. In March 1785 Jonathan Sewall Jr. sailed in the *John and Ann*. This enforced separation from his son angered Sewall, and it removed one of his only links to the world outside himself.

Only the prospect of reunion with his son kept Sewall's spirits from flagging. All his expectations focused that spring on the claims settlement: a generous settlement, and thus by Sewall's standards a just one, would free him to quit Bristol and to begin his new life with some degree of the luxury and security he had watched diminish over the last few years. But the settlement, when it came that June, was a disappointment and a humiliation. "I rec'd, such was the amazing generosity of Government, the enormous Sum of £480 as a Compensation for a Loss which at a Modest Computation my Claim set at £6000." [14] Sewall's anger clouded his understanding of his settlement; the £480 was, in fact, only the first installment of a £1600 compensation. Still, this sum could do little more than pay his most pressing debts: £50 went for the expense of Jack's voyage; £50 paid the long overdue salary of his Vice Admiralty clerk; and £150 went to various creditors. Of the £480, £280 remained for family expenses.

Sewall's pockets should not have been this empty, for in April of 1785 his half-yearly salary for the Vice Admiralty Court had come due. As a matter of course he had petitioned the Treasury for his salary warrant, but now, as late as June, no action had been taken on his request. The delay appeared at first just another financial inconvenience, the result of the Government's usual bureaucratic inefficiency. But the cost of such an inconvenience was high. Sewall was now forced to move his family into more economical lodgings while they awaited the money, and their emigration to Canada. The change in residence and the disappointment of the claims settlement Sewall treated with his familiar black humor. ''I had rather been in the Belly of a Whale or Shark,'' he said, ''or parcelled out among the Cod, Haddocks, Mackerel and Shrimps, than to be where I am now.'' [15]

But the delay proved to be more than a delay. In August Sewall learned that the Treasury department was deliberating the abolition of his Court at Halifax. And, as a postscript to this news, he was told that no salary warrant would be drawn for his back pay until the matter was decided.

That month Sewall entrusted to his friend Samuel Curwen the delivery of a petition to Philip Stephens of the Admiralty, pleading for the continuation of his court. Curwen, who owed his own pension to Sewall's influence and personal exertion in his behalf,[16] made every effort to deliver the document to its addressee. But Stephens was out of town—officially—and the clerk insisted the case had already been determined. Curwen could not even learn the government's decision unless Sewall sent a letter of authorization to the Admiralty. All Curwen could do was offer his further services to Sewall if needed, and ''most heartily wish the continuance of your commission to be commensurate with your life.'' [17]

Although Mr. Ramus, the Admiralty clerk, insisted the case had been determined, the truth was that the Admiralty had not yet considered Sewall's fate at all. In fact, they knew nothing of the Treasury department's deliberations on the Vice Admiralty court matter. The Treasury memo to Stephens on the subject still lay, as it had lain for

months, on the desk of one of that department's many underlings. The
Treasury would make no decision without the Admiralty's judgment;
the Admiralty was in official ignorance of the matter: Sewall's memorial pleaded a nonexistent case.

Perhaps more than anything else, the futility of this situation affected Sewall. By the winter of 1785 the rapid succession of disappointments and frustrations, added to "the many plagues and vexa-
tions with which I have been persecuted for many years" took their
full toll of him. In November of 1785 he closeted himself in his bed-
room, and he did not come out until eighteen months later.[18]

Throughout these months Sewall's doctor prescribed for his physical
symptoms—for headaches, stomach pains, dizziness—but Sewall recognized his sickness was psychological. By his own frank admission,
he was an invalid not of the body, but of the mind. "My malady was
altogether mental," he later explained in an extraordinary account of
his eighteen-month retreat. The contagion to which he had at last succumbed was spread by a persecuting world of government, wife, and
creditors. In the safety and privacy of his room, Sewall confronted his
demons with the only means of resistance he had remaining to him: he
burned, he said, with a resentment which he "kept in one continual
fervent glow." His anger at his circumstances and those who made
them wholly preoccupied him. It abated only in his sleep, when for
nine to ten hours a day his fury gave way to a peaceful, dreamless
oblivion, and he slept "as sweetly and quietly as a sucking infant or a
labouring peasant." It was, he said, those very daily outpourings of
anger which allowed him this salutary quiet sleep.

Sewall passed these months with little food, no exercise, and without fresh air. His doctor gave a prognosis of death unless his patient
cared for these most basic physical needs. Yet Sewall made no effort
to comply. The doctor, he wrote, "did not understand my constitution
as well as I did myself." It was emotional nourishment that would determine his body's fate, not ordinary food; and it was his resentment
that protected and nurtured his physical frame. "Had [my malady]
taken a melancholy turn, no doubt my flimsy corps would soon have

fallen a victim; but it took a more favorable turn: I was mad as the Devil the whole time.''

Yet from this hiding place Sewall made one final effort to rescue himself from his myriad persecutors. In June 1786 news came that the letter between the Treasury and Admiralty departments was at last *en traine*. Before the month was up, Sewall had mastered his anger sufficiently to compose a respectful but self-vindicatory memorial to the Lords of the Treasury. He urged them to continue his court, for the Canadian district was now heavily populated with exiled Loyalists ''in Consequence whereof, the Trade & Commerce of the District is increased & probably will be still further increasing.'' But the major portion of his memorial was devoted to a history of personal expectations, promises made, and broken, and injustices done. Your memorialist, he wrote,

> considered his Appointment as permanent and from that Confidence, has lost irrecoverably the Oppo which he once had, of obtaining a Subsistance by his professional practice at Halifax—a Measure which he could not embrace with propriety while he was honor'd with the Comn of Judge of V. Admty for that Department and which, from a Variety of Circumstances, it is now impossible for him to adopt.[19]

By the long and unexpected detention of his salary, Sewall concluded, he was ''reduced to the most humiliating and distressing Situation.'' Whatever their pleasure respecting his future, he begged his due for the past.

The summer passed without reply, the silence adding fuel to the fires of his anger. In September 1786 Sewall sent a long despairing letter to his son Jack. By that time two full years had passed without payment of salary. ''It has not been in my power to see you,'' he wrote bitterly, ''which was the first wish of my Soul—nor, which was the next, to send you out those tokens of Love and Affection, which I wish'd to send . . . the evil one, or Fate, or ye Treasury counteracted all my fine schemes.'' [20]

Yet he was determined that neither the Devil nor the Treasury would thwart his only remaining wish—reunion with his son. Despite all disappointments and delays, Sewall pledged to Jack that "if I live to the next Spring," the whole family would embark for St. John. This resolution finally drew Sewall out of his retreat. In April 1787, still uncertain of his court's fate, he left Bristol for London, and there booked passage for his family to Canada.

While in London, Sewall broke a continuing solitude to receive a visit from his old friend, John Adams, now Minister Plenipotentiary to the Court of St. James. It had been twelve years since the two men had spoken, yet there was not even a momentary awkwardness in reunion. "When Mr. Adams came in, he took my hand in both his, and with a hearty squeeze, accosted me in these words—*how do you do my dear old friend!*—our conversation was just as might be expected at the meeting of two old sincere friends after a long separation." [21] The two men talked for three hours. Adams pleaded with Sewall to join him for dinner, so that their time together might be extended. But Sewall, true to his peculiar need for a separation from the world outside his doors, refused to leave his lodgings. He had refused his Loyalist friends, he told Adams, and must refuse his American friend as well. All that could be said must be shared here, in Sewall's London roominghouse.

This warm reunion did not mean that either man's judgment of his friend's role in the Revolution had changed. Adams believed until his death that Sewall had sacrificed principle for office; Sewall believed that Adams's patriotic zeal was "the ofspring [*sic*] perhaps, in part, tho imperceptible to himself, of disappointed ambition." But the issues that had divided them were long dead, and there no longer seemed a need to take each other's measure as a political opponent. That conflict which had forced them to define their relationship only in political terms had been resolved: they saw each other again as complete personalities. Sewall was drawn once more to his friend's generosity, openness, his "heart formed for friendship, and susceptible to its finest feelings." Above all men in the world, Sewall would choose John Adams for his *fidus Achates* in the anticipated asylum of Canada. [22]

Although the reunion was a welcomed event, the meeting must have been difficult for Sewall. The contrast between his own disappointments and Adams's satisfactions was too obvious to be put out of mind. Perhaps a gentle envy sharpened, or distorted, Sewall's sensitivity to his friend's mood and circumstances. "If I am not mistaken," Sewall concluded after the visit, "now [Adams] has reached the summit of his ambition, he finds himself quite out of his element; and looks back with regret to those happy days, when in a snug house with a pretty farm about him at Braintree he sat quiet in the full possession of domestic happiness." Sewall judged Adams unqualified by nature or education to shine in the courts of Europe as an ambassador must. He was quick to grant Adams's ability to execute the purely intellectual and political duties of his office; but the John Adams he knew could neither "dance, drink, game, flatter, promise, dress, swear with the gentlemen, [or] talk small talk & flirt with the Ladys." In short, Sewall concluded, "he has none of the essential *arts* or *ornaments* which constitute a courtier." [23]

Adams carried away an even more troubled image of Sewall. The exile from Massachusetts and the disappointments of career his friend had suffered had left Sewall a morose and melancholy man, without purpose in life save the rearing of his children. He lived for his sons, Adams remembered later on. And years later, when Sewall died, Adams diagnosed his illness as a broken heart. [24]

CHAPTER THIRTEEN

Permanent Retreat

1787-1796

THE SEWALLS' JOURNEY to Canada took seven weeks. Perhaps the diversion of the sea voyage worked favorably upon Sewall, or perhaps the thoughts of returning home to America dispelled his long-standing gloom. Whatever the cause, Sewall experienced a drastic change in mood on board ship. The months filled with "foolish hobgoblin fears" gave way to a sense of well-being and enthusiasm. His appetite revived, his health improved, his daily headaches disappeared.

He continued in this mood throughout his first summer in New Brunswick. What he saw in that province buoyed his spirits, for it was not the barren wilderness he had expected. The city of St. John particularly pleased him. It was a neat, attractive town, with broad streets and comfortable homes. It was not, of course, a replica of Boston, but it bore a decided New England stamp. From his window, Sewall could watch the commerical activities of a harbor that differed only in magnitude of business from Boston's port. City politics and city government were reminiscent of Boston, even to the existence of a noisy, troublesome political faction drawn from the lower ranks.[1] And in St. John, as in Boston, Sewall's friends were social and political leaders, not men swallowed up in the oblivion of English society.

When he set down his thoughts on himself and his situation that September, Sewall spoke with confidence of maintaining his mental health. He knew his limitations, and would not make heavy demands upon himself. He could not and would not try to reverse the misanthropic patterns of his years in exile. He would be content to live in peaceful retirement and isolation. But, if his present mood could be sustained, he would venture out occasionally into "the great World" of St. John, to enjoy adventures that would break the awful monotony of his isolation.[2]

Only one thing threatened Sewall's equilibrium: the still-pending decision on his Vice Admiralty court. But on this point, as on others, he was now optimistic. Sometime before July he had learned that the matter had been placed in the hands of Sir Guy Carleton, now Lord Dorchester. The Treasury had turned to Dorchester because his experience as Governor of Lower Canada seemed to make him the best judge of the Court's usefulness. Sewall believed that this development operated to his advantage, for he had valuable contacts within Dorchester's Canadian circle. In July Sewall drafted an informal memorial to his young friend Edward Winslow, whose service during the war had made him the confidant of Dorchester. In this letter Sewall briefed Winslow on the best arguments for the court's continuance:

> If a Court of Appeals was ever necessary and convenient in order to give the Subject a right to two Tryals [sic], without the trouble and expense of carrying an Appeal to England, certainly it should seem, that Necessity and Convenience is greatly increased by the Change of Circumstances in the District; and if a New Commission is necessary in order to include New Brunswic [sic], it may be deserving of Consideration whether St. Johns, as being the most central part of the District, is not the most proper and convenient place for the establishment of the Court; * as by this Arrangement the two extremities of the District would be equally accomodated, and Halifax subjected to no other inconveniences than St. Johns must experience while the Court remains established at Halifax; and at the same time Quebec would be greatly eased of a heavy burthen by having the Travel and expence so much lessened in Cases of Appeal.[3]

---

* Sewall's argument for a central location for his court fitted nicely, of course, with his personal preference for life in St. John.

Objectively, however, Sewall's case was insupportable. The local Vice Admiralty court was adequate for the modest maritime activity of Lower Canada. And the inescapable fact remained that Sewall's court had rarely, if ever, entertained a case.

Whatever the merits of Sewall's cause, Winslow would undoubtedly have lobbied for his friend. Unfortunately, Sewall's move came too late. Dorchester had delivered his opinion, probably before Sewall arrived in Canada. Only days after Sewall posted his letter to Winslow, notification of the Court's abolition was on its way from London to St. John.[4]

The news did not reach Sewall until November. On the 27th of that month he learned of his court's closing.[5] He greeted the Government's decision with relative calm; he had prepared himself for the loss of the office. But he was not prepared for the compensation which the Treasury department offered him. He had hoped for a full pension; he had expected a half-pension. Yet the Government granted him only £ 200 a year as recompense for the loss of his court.

The Treasury had dealt shabbily with him, Sewall concluded. And further evidence to support his judgment came when he read that the Government intended to pay him only three-fourths of his salary for the past year. Although the court was still functioning in November, the Treasury department thought it necessary to pay Sewall only until its decision to abolish the court in July.

Sewall's old anger returned. On December 12 he drafted a letter of protest to his London agent, Lewis Wolfe: "The report of Lord Dorchester, and the determination of their Lordships thereon for abolishing my Office, is no more than I had prepared myself to expect—but the curtailing me of one Quarter of the last Years Salary, and the reducing me below half pay is more than my fears ever suggested." The full salary, he argued to Wolfe, was due him because his commission granted a salary on a yearly, not a quarterly basis. It was not divisible, as the Treasury officials had made it in their settlement, even though for convenience' sake it had been paid in two installments. More importantly, Sewall insisted, the court itself had continued to function for four months after the decision for its abolition. By law, and for obvious practical considerations, the Treasury must concede that a court's authority continues until notification of its dissolution is received. If this were not the case, on what footing would legal actions stand which were determined in the intervening months between decision and notification? The Treasury's interpretation, signified by the salary settlement, raised the possibility of damage suits against the judges in all such interim cases, as well as the necessity of retrial in each instance. Unless the Treasury were willing to tolerate such an inconsistency of logic and law, Sewall's term of office must be reckoned until the date notification was received.

But the heart of the petition was not its legal or logical arguments. It was Sewall's complaint that "I have sacrificed to my Duty, my property in America, for which I laboured hard many years—and all other future prospects which once opened for myself and my Children." [6]

That sacrifice was real enough. But Sewall's claim to compensation for a loss of office he had never truly administered, in a province he had come to only because of exile, never struck him as hollow. His was the eighteenth-century officeholder's perspective. Although the office proved valueless to the Government, and though it had been won through political favoritism, still it belonged to Sewall and had been taken away. Its loss was a personal insult as much as a financial disaster.

Over the winter and spring Sewall waited for a response to his memorial. He expected no relief from Government, and viewed his present and future through a "dismal gloom." He wrote to Thomas Robie, who was himself genuinely bankrupt and in desperate financial straits, that he was "in point of property, Deviltry, and matrimony, about in Job's situation." In short, Sewall believed the entire world, in the form of Mr. Pitt, Mrs. Sewall, Fate, and the Devil, was again conspiring against him. [7]

Despite this array of enemies, Sewall's situation "in point of property" did improve steadily over the next months. A warrant for the £441 in salary arrears eased his financial situation over the winter of

1787 and the spring of 1788.[8] And in July of that year, his agent at
Stedman and Company reported that the Treasury had accepted many
of the arguments in Sewall's memorial. The department conceded
Sewall's right to a full year's salary, and agreed to issue a warrant for
the remaining £144. They also agreed to raise Sewall's pension. The
concession on this point was, of course, a great deal more modest than
Sewall had demanded, for the Treasury would not grant a full pension.
It promised instead to consider what additional sum was necessary to
raise Sewall's settlement to an equal footing with other refugees' compensation for loss of office. Using the standards for compensation established that June by Parliament Lewis Wolfe estimated that Sewall
would receive an additional £80.[9]

Thus, by 1789, concessions and compensations made Sewall an af-
fluent man once again. His Admiralty pension had, as his agents
predicted, been raised to £280 per annum.* A second pension
"granted you under the address of the House of Commons for your
Loss of Profession" † added £150 each year to his income.[10] And,
after four years of wrangling over the legitimacy of his claims for lost
property and wealth, the Government released all of the remaining
£1160 from his claims settlement.[11]

But if Sewall's settlement was ample, he never believed it was just.
He shared with many Loyalists a confusion about the ways in which
decisions were made on claims, for the process was shrouded in mystery. Few understood the basis on which their claims to compensation

* Sewall's admiralty pension was determined under the rules of the Loyalist compensation rather than as an independent Treasury matter. Thus on a claim of £600 per annum
Sewall received a settlement of one-half, subject to certain deductions set by the Claims
Commission on all figures over £400. When these deductions are taken into consideration, the £280 figure rather than £300 is made understandable.

† Sewall had claimed £300 for the loss of profession in Massachusetts. The £150 settlement he received was in keeping with the Commission's rule of one-half compensation on this category of claims up to £400. Sewall's claim is low considering his extensive legal practice, which, even though reduced in the 1770s by anti-Crown sentiments,
must have remained a profitable one. The modest claim is probably explained by the fact
that at the time it was filed, Sewall still enjoyed his £600 yearly stipend as Vice-Admiralty judge.

were judged, and fewer understood how well or poorly they had fared in relation to others with comparable claims. Their ignorance on both scores probably led them to see the government's decisions as arbitrary. Clearly Sewall did. He always feared he had been discriminated against, but whether because his loyalty was doubted, his connections in government were inadequate, or the Devil and Mr. Pitt conspired against him he did not know.

Even had Sewall clearly understood the bases on which his claims for professional and property compensation were judged, it is doubtful that he could have reconciled himself to his settlement. The situation was inevitably frustrating for a Loyalist like Sewall because the Government set both the stakes of the game and the rules by which it was played. The government's criteria were the measurable, concrete aspects of the Loyalist's life—his property holdings, his salary, his professional income. And the guidelines for compensation were determined largely by impersonal budgetary and political considerations. Sewall was bound to feel cheated, because his subjective demands could not be met. He looked for a reward for his loyalty and amends for his lost past and sacrificed potential. He needed both to satisfy his sense of justice; he also needed them to vindicate his personal opinion of himself. Perhaps this vindicatory aspect of compensation was central to Sewall and to others like him; and the government's failure to raise the Loyalists to honor was like a public denial of the wisdom of loyalty.

For the rest of his life Sewall brooded over his bad fortune. It was not the actual compensation that continued to agitate him, for he conceded his financial security and soon ceased all his complaints about the monetary settlement. He knew that his real fears of poverty, and especially the lack of patrimony for his sons, had been alleviated. Although less wealthy that he had been in Massachusetts, Sewall was able to satisfy most of his wishes and needs: he put aside enough money to finance both sons' lean first years in the practice of law; * he

* Both Stephen and Jack became lawyers, and both were to become leading members of their profession. Jonathan Jr. was Solicitor and Attorney General of Quebec by 1796,

built a home in St. John, elegant for its time and place; [12] and he was free to indulge in such whims as the purchase of a sizeable lottery ticket each year. [13] He could, when he died, leave for his wife and children "those tokens of Love and Affection" which, in 1786, he could not give his son.

Yet Sewall's life continued to face the past and not the present or future. Edward Winslow cautiously but correctly observed to Jack Sewall that "your worthy Father (conscious of superior abilities—of unimpeached honor—Loyalty and Integrity) is mad at a rascally World because they have not done Justice to his merit." But Sewall's anger slipped more frequently into the passive melancholy he had once abhorred. To observers like Winslow it was exactly that habit of "indulging in a train of melancholy reflections" that lost Sewall to society. [14] Which was cause and which effect, Sewall himself might be less certain than his friends; but the melancholy and the habit of isolation surely fed each other, and together made their own complete world for him.

Sewall's physical decline kept pace with his emotional one. He ate little, and took only one meal a day. He relied, perhaps too heavily, upon port wine in hot water, which, Esther Sewall explained, braced her husband's nerves. [15] He suffered a seemingly endless series of minor ailments: colics, colds, headaches, piles, rheumatism, and a relentless constipation. [16] Each illness gave concrete cause for the deepening withdrawal from human society. Even communication with his sons grew less frequent, though he loved them deeply and felt a constant concern for them. In August 1790, Stephen Sewall, still home with his father, wrote to his brother in Quebec that "My father has had a bad disorder in his bowels . . . [and] does not yet feel bold enough to attempt a letter." [17] Such apologies grew frequent over the next years.

---

two appointments on which Sewall lived to congratulate his son. He was later promoted to judge of the Vice Admiralty court, and in 1808 he became the Chief Justice of Quebec. Jack's career in particular fulfilled his father's every hope, and his later achievements on the bench represented that blooming of legal talents and personal career which the Revolution had denied his father.

Illness was often an excuse for inactivity as much as its cause. "You seem anxious to know the reason of his not writing as often as if you thought he was not well," Stephen wrote Jack a few days later: "but be assured that his health is as good now and better than when you left us and I need not tell you he loves you as affectionately as a father can a Son, but he has not always materials for a letter (which he likes to make good)—[and] *does not like to write* unless he has something to write upon." [18] Because Sewall rarely left his own room, he had little "to write upon."

By November 1790, Sewall's restriction to his bedchamber was a matter of medical necessity as well as personal choice. On November 13 Esther Sewall wrote to her brother-in-law, Governor John Hancock, that her husband's constitution had been shattered by his confinement, and he was in need of constant care.[19] This need for constant attention permitted Sewall ample revenge upon his wife for the imagined evils she had caused him in their exile. Esther—lively, gregarious, and still pathetically homesick—became his companion prisoner in their home. By 1790 even the little snatches of social life she had enjoyed in St. John were impossible to maintain. And the attention to her husband, which she considered her unquestionable duty, barred all possibility of a visit to Boston and her family.

The company of her sons was also denied Esther. In May of 1789 Jonathan Jr., had left St. John for Quebec, a city less infested with lawyers and more likely to provide him with the financial rewards of his profession. Sewall was highly possessive of his sons, whose lives and futures were his sole interest outside himself; yet he recognized the wisdom of Jack's decision to move farther west.[20] So also did Esther Sewall, who felt the separation as keenly as her husband. Sewall promised the family would join Jack the following spring, but Esther realized her husband could not fulfill this pledge.

By April 1791 Jonathan Jr. had realized this as well. The knowledge prompted him to enlist Chip's help in arranging his brother Stephen's emigration. In a letter to Chipman, which respectfully skirted Sewall's psychological handicaps, Jack explained why Stephen must no longer wait for his father to act. "My father is on in years," he wrote, "he is of a sedentary disposition and Habit, And a debilitated Frame has rendered him disposed to consider the slightest Exertions as events of difficulty and importance." [21] Jack accepted his father's limitations but he would not allow Sewall's infirmities of body or mind to wreck his younger brother's future. Both sons had waited two years for their father to act. Stephen had dutifully postponed his own career as a lawyer in order to remain with his father. But now Jack urged Chip: "Stephen must come out."

In 1791 Stephen Sewall left St. John. Only Esther remained behind. Sewall realized his wife's predicament, but he was helpless to relieve her. Their relationship had deteriorated during the years of penny-pinching and waiting in England, and Sewall felt, now as then, that he had failed her expectation. They were little more to each other now than patient and nurse, or at best, demanding invalid and dutiful wife. Esther strove constantly to please Sewall, and to do her duty to him, but her efforts only exacerbated the situation. Her homesickness, which she could not hide, remained a persistent reminder to Sewall of his own longings and of his mistreatment by Government and Fate. Her unhappiness was, as it had been since their exile began, a personal rebuke. Thus, when Sewall saw the necessity of Stephen's departure, he voiced a desire to see his wife gone as well. He complained to Chip that her presence kept him from the peace and solitude he sought. Let Esther go to Quebec, he said, and he would find his own happiness in some far-off asylum like Wales.[22] Chipman saw the bravado of the outburst and dismissed it. It was clear that Sewall wished his wife gone because he knew she wished to be gone.

In the spring of 1792 Sewall's health grew worse. Although he recovered from this bout of illness, he was left so weak that in May he still could not write his name without effort. By October even the walk from bed to fireplace was difficult for Sewall to execute. It was clear that he was slowly dying.[23] But more painful to him than this physical decline was his incapacity to communicate with his sons. "At your father's request," Chip wrote to Jack in October of 1792:

> I enclose a bill for Stephen which he desires you will realize and forward
> to him by the first opportunity and he desires me to tell you both how

truly and feelingly he regrets that he finds himself unable to write himself.—he says with Tears in his eyes, "tell them I have taken up my pen
twenty, yea an hundred times to write them, when so many thousand
ideas have crowded upon my mind, such sensations have agitated me and
so violently that I found myself overpowered and unequal to the task—
but they must continue their attention in writing to me—I have no happiness now remaining but a continuation of the intelligence of their welfare
and success." [24]

From that winter forward, the family was prepared for Sewall's
death. He continued to live, a weak and skeleton-like figure, until the
fall of 1796. On September 17 of that year Sewall's physician, Dr.
Paddock, found his patient unable to rise from the bed. The doctor,
Esther Sewall, and Chip kept a daily vigil until the evening of September 27, when, at quarter to seven, Jonathan Sewall died a peaceful
death, "without a struggle or a groan." [25]

CHAPTER FOURTEEN

Conclusion: A Man at Odds with His Times

JONATHAN SEWALL CAME of age in an era of relative social and political stability in Massachusetts, an era when basic shared assumptions reigned without need of articulated philosophy. There was no organized opposition to imperial authority as such, and the political battles that raged in the Massachusetts of the 1740s and 1750s concerned matters of place and patronage rather than constitutional issues. Crown and provincial interests were not yet defined as mutually exclusive.

In such a decade without full-blown ideologies, Sewall, like most young men, looked to his own career. His goals were for the most part practical, and he worked to secure a position for himself in the society as he found it. His uncertain status as a fringe member of Massachusetts' social elite gave to Sewall's ambition its cast rather than its direction: he was more susceptible to the security of bureaucratic position than to the potentials of entrepreneurial law, and he desired respect more than fame.

Sewall did enjoy from the start the two definite advantages of family name and versatile intelligence. Both served him well. The former created opportunities; the latter insured his ability to exploit them. A third advantage lay in Sewall's own affinity for protege relationships in a society—and a profession—highly paternalistic in structure.

It was in one of his patrons, Chambers Russell, that Sewall found a model for his own expectations for himself. But both early mentors, Russell and Edmund Trowbridge, were crucial in determining the particular direction Sewall's life was to take. Chambers Russell's generous grant of the Charlestown law practice kept Sewall away from the urban, commercially oriented, and ultimately radical atmosphere of Boston law. And Edmund Trowbridge's patronage, which opened the way to a Government career for Sewall, linked Sewall's interest early with the Crown.

Jonathan Sewall's success in the 1760s was enviable. For a decade his career advanced rapidly, exclusively under the aegis of the Crown. Within three years, from 1767 to 1769, he was appointed to every important post within his professional competence. He became Solicitor General, Advocate General, Attorney General, and Judge of Admiralty. In the course of this success, his political orientation was shaped. Success confirmed to Sewall the basic justness of the social and political status quo. His personal experiences firmly fixed his image of the British government as benign and generous. And this conviction activated that highly developed sense of loyalty to benevolent authority which had been a personal hallmark throughout his youth and early manhood. Thus, when the political conflicts of the late 1760s began to brew, it was difficult for Sewall to accept criticism of the Government as substantive. At the same time it made defense of that government a matter not only of practical interest but of personal honor. Both during the years of conflict, and throughout his life, Sewall could make sense of the political protest that led to revolution only by dismissing the content of the radicals' political arguments, and declaring them a ruse to conceal the actual motives of personal ambition and private jealousy. Quite simply, he continued to see the bases of the political battles in the 1760s and 1770s as identical with those of the 1750s: a challenge of "outs" to "ins," in a battle that remained "who shall *serve* at home."

Yet if the battle remained the same, it was clear to Sewall that the tactics employed were new, and, to his mind, dangerous. In their fight for power, these men he called "outs" attacked not merely the officeholders but also the offices they held. Throughout the 1760s a notion was carefully nurtured by them that Crown and provincial interests were no longer mutual but conflicting. Although Sewall insisted that this was a groundless and irresponsible ploy, he nevertheless saw it take root in the public mind and create a frustrating and ultimately defeating dilemma for all conservative native sons like himself. For during the years of his greatest success, holding an office in which a talented colonial lawyer might understandably take pride, Sewall found himself faced with a crisis of political allegiance that he did not believe real, but could not avoid. Nevertheless, much of his energy went into a futile, almost quixotic effort to avoid it. As Attorney General he sat directly in the crossfire between imperial authority and provincial opposition. Yet, he sought to establish a neutrality by imposing his own terms upon the combatants. He demanded from all a special immunity based on his professional integrity: from the community he demanded recognition that judicious execution of his duties justify the duties themselves; from his superiors he demanded independence from any partisan behavior which, when order and harmony were restored, might be seen to have tarnished his reputation. In short, Sewall expected professional integrity to serve as a talisman against the growing polarization between the Crown and the colony he served.

The world did not, of course, agree to make this separate peace with Jonathan Sewall. His insistence on behaving as if things had remained the same even as they were changing around him moved him as surely into a partisan position as any conscious declaration might. His mere continuation in appointive office, his acceptance of the Admiralty commission—both sides saw these as clear choices in a conflict that allowed of no neutrality.

Throughout his lifetime Sewall clung to his belief that, in an artificial conflict, he had taken the high ground of reason and duty. It was in this light that he interpreted his active role as a newspaper essayist in the prerevolutionary decade. Both Government and Opposition viewed him as the apologist for Crown policy and personnel that he was. But Sewall saw himself only as an opponent of slander and irresponsible agitation. Such a self-image is not uncommon among those who defend the status quo.

Sewall's political essays do constitute one of the best of the Loyalists' defenses of that status quo. In "J," in "Philanthrop," and in "Philalethes" he carefully enshrined British constitutional government in its equipose between tyranny and anarchy. He could envision no constructive alternative to that constitution, and had no faith that it could be improved upon by the innovations of mass participation in government or by the changes in leadership he believed the radicals sought. Although he conceded the possibility of imperfections and injustices within the imperial system he urged that they be tolerated. For Sewall, the process of correcting any one political or social ill was itself potentially more dangerous to the social body than the affliction might prove to be. He particularly urged toleration of those real or imagined imperfections whose cure would loose the bonds of empire. He did not believe, as Sam Adams might, that America could reproduce the blessings of the British constitution outside the context of its imperial structure. Of this he was certain: the only fruits of successful rebellion and political independence would be social disintegration.

Sewall's concern with warning against radical experimentation with independence shows that he occasionally conceded the deeper implications of what he called petty struggles for political office. Yet he did little to stem any movement toward independence. Like most prominent Loyalists, Sewall never doubted that, if it became necessary, England herself would move to preserve the colonial status quo. This conviction comforted the American Tory, and helped to further dull his political senses. Ultimately it proved his undoing. In the face of a rising opposition, conservative leaders like Sewall did little save remind the colonists of their blessings, exhort them to remember their obligations, and warn them against arousing Britain's wrath. It was the unshakable belief in Britain's power and support that helps explain why men like Sewall never felt a need to fully confront the political situation, to urge constructive compromise with the opposition, or to effectively combat it. Perhaps Sewall and his fellow conservatives simply yielded, as historian William Nelson put it, "to the common temptation of those who are satisfied with things as they are to expect things to remain as they are." [1]

Things did not remain as they were. In April 1775 a depressed and bitter Sewall fled Boston for England, one of the earliest of the Tory refugees. Although he left believing that he would return to a chastised province, he never saw Massachusetts again.

His years of exile were years of a steady and complete personal disintegration. In England he experienced the disorientation of the uprooted. His life lacked meaningful activity, the sense of purpose a man's work provides, and even the comfort familiar daily routine offers to every human being. He was acutely aware of his career having been interrupted in its ascent: he was 47 and in his prime, a man accustomed to an active and vital role in his profession and in political decision-making. Now he found himself in a limbo of waiting and inactivity. As with all his fellow New Englanders, Sewall's waiting was disturbed by desperate and unabating homesickness. The longing for familiar ways and familiar things grew more intense as the years passed. No act of renunciation, no ventings of hatred against the "plotters, instigators, & cherishers of this most unnatural, causeless distructive [sic] rebellion," [2] and no unfavorable comparisons of provincial life with the glamor of British society could alleviate the pain of separation from New England.

Deeper even than the craving for newton apples and New England cranberries, and at the core of Sewall's heightened Americanism, was the fear of what permanent residence in Britain might mean. British society would accept Loyalists like Sewall only on its own terms; it would absorb them, almost without notice, into its anonymous middling ranks, tucking them away in provincial cities like Bristol and Ipswich. Sewall quickly realized how high the price of this adjustment would be: even the accomplishments of his lifetime would be reduced in scale, for the "miniature Yankee puppet-show" of America was dwarfed by the British society he had admired from a distance.

For a while Sewall took refuge from disquieting thoughts of assimilation by gathering with fellow New Englanders in New England clubs and in the American residential ghettos on Brompton Row or in Bristol. But he realized that his fate hung upon the outcome of the war. His stake in victory became far more than the restoration of property, office, or profession; like all Loyalists, he wanted a victorious England from which he could flee.

To the drain of inactivity and homesickness were added the practical worries of living in England. At first, Sewall was luckier than most. Throughout the war years he enjoyed the relatively steady income of his Canadian Vice Admiralty post. This spared him for some time the humiliation familiar to other exiles who had to rely on government charity. But for Sewall, as for most Loyalists, every year in the prolonged war brought a new tightening of the British government's pursestrings, and with it a decline in his standard of living. His letters record the frequent moves to smaller quarters, the dismissal of servants, the trimming away of amenities, and the rising personal debt.

These anxieties, humiliations, and practical problems were, of course, the common lot of the American exiles. But against them Sewall proved without resiliency or inner resources. For he brought to the confrontation with exile that extreme sense of his own innocence of wrongdoing and continuing integrity that had sustained him—and diverted him from reality—in the past. His certainty that he was not deserving of punishment and was an innocent in a "rascally world" caused him to cast himself more than most in the role of victim—victim of unnecessary rebellions, of evil men, of foolish men, of ungrateful dependents, and irresponsible and unthinking superiors. Satisfied that there was no reason why he should find himself denied his proper position and respect, Sewall refused to accept any lesser place in the world. As early as 1783 he had begun to withdraw, revealing to his friends and family that acute and paralyzing sense of helplessness in the face of so many enemies. Perhaps more than anything else, the abolition of his Vice Admiralty Court—a blow that destroyed his faith in the British government as a benevolent patron—caused him to end his relations with that rascally world and retreat into himself.

When Sewall died in 1796 the independent nation he did not believe could—or should—survive its revolutionary birth was thirteen years old. About that nation Sewall had said and written little. But from his last major political writing, in 1785, the measure of his political growth or stagnation might be taken. In the summer of 1785, while Sewall awaited news of his claim settlement, he had composed a "Plan of Union" for the loyal Canadian provinces.* The plan revealed the lesson of the Revolution as Sewall saw it: that the proper colonial government should act as an antidote to republicanism and as a safe-guard against rebellion. He envisioned for Canada an indigenous oli-garchy, supported and maintained in power by the British government in exchange for that oligarchy's guarantee of provincial allegiance to the Crown. This provincial ruling class would, in essence, be given all the broad powers necessary to crush republicanism. Its agency would be an intercolonial privy council, presided over by a Lord-Lieutenant. This council would supervise all colonial political activity, exercise the right to disallow any colonial legislation; and if necessary, it could suspend any weak colonial governor. Such a powerful centralized gov-ernment, free to respond immediately to crisis situations, would be able to detect and correct political deviance before it became danger-ous. Thus Sewall espoused independence for the rulers rather than the ruled and showed himself willing to accept repression if consensus could not be had.

* The Sewall plan was originally thought to be one of the many plans of union com-posed by Joseph Galloway (Julian Boyd, *Anglo-American Union: Joseph Galloway's Plans to Preserve the British Empire, 1774–1788* [Philadelphia, 1941]). This error was first pointed out by Robert Livingston Schuyler in a review article of Boyd's book in the *Political Science Quarterly*, LVII, No. 2. Schuyler showed that the plan employed dis-tinctly New England terminology, such as "Legislative Court" for Assembly, a phrase the Pennsylvania Loyalist would not have used. Further, the plan, unlike Galloway's many others, was designed for the organization of the remaining Canadian provinces and not for the empire before the Revolution. Schuyler's speculation was followed up in 1951 by William Nelson. Nelson confirms Jonathan Sewall as the author of the plan. Nelson's analysis of the plan is excellent, and this discussion relies upon it (William Nelson, "The Last Hope of the American Loyalists," *Canadian Historical Review*, XXXII, No. 1 [March, 1951], 22–42).

Every detail of Sewall's plan revealed how fresh the memory of Massachusetts politics remained in his mind. He grudgingly conceded that legislative assemblies must be allowed, but he sought to hedge any democratic spirit within those assemblies by setting high property qualifications for its members and by abolishing any residence requirements for its candidates. His colonial judiciary—unlike the bench and subsidiary legal offices of the Bay Colony—would be Crown appointed, independent, and well paid.

Sewall's plan was not visionary but reactionary; it showed no mature understanding of the problems of empire and imperial organization. Unlike the farsighted William Smith, Sewall could not see that continued colonial loyalty required that the general populace, as well as its leaders, be drawn into the mainstream of imperial politics. Only in this way could the isolation which bred independent development be ended. Where Smith proposed a "liberal government, admitting all, whether French or English, to office, Honor, and popular Suffrage and Trust without any contracted privilege," [3] Sewall proposed an oligarchy to act as a policing agent over fellow colonials.

Cecelia Kenyon has written of the anti-Federalists that they were "men of little faith." The epitaph is more fittingly laid upon Loyalists like Jonathan Sewall. Sewall's pessimism about reform, his cynicism about men's motivations, and his total lack of confidence in the masses of men were common traits among the officeholding Loyalists. This was more than a self-serving view of life, though it was indeed that. It was an approach to human society that suppressed growth and crippled innovation. It is personally tragic that Jonathan Sewall was exiled from a New England he loved and believed to his death he had served faithfully and well. Yet there was no room for him in the country Massachusetts and her sister colonies hoped to become.

$\mathcal{N}otes$

CHAPTER ONE

1. The Sewall family genealogy from which this account is drawn was compiled in 1885. See Mr. and Mrs. E. E. Salisbury, eds., *Family Histories and Genealogies of the Families of Mac Curdy, Mitchell, Lord, etc.* (New Haven, 1892).

2. Samuel Sewall to Benjamin Sewall, November 22, 1731, JS Mss.

3. This inventory and other business records regarding the sale of the merchant's goods can be found in JS Mss.

4. See C. K. Shipton, *New England Life in the Eighteenth Century: Representative Biographies from "Sibley's Harvard Graduates"* (Cambridge, 1963), p. 565. See also the preface to *Novanglus,* p. iii. In 1746 and 1747 Sewall's schooling was also financed by Harvard through fellowship monies such as the Thomas Hollis Fund. See "Minutes of the President and Fellows of Harvard College, Cambridge, May 7, 1746" in *Publications of the Colonial Society of Massachusetts,* XVI, *Collections* (Boston, 1925), pp. 759–60; CP-HU, I, Book 6.

5. For a discussion of class ranking, its importance and its manipulation by the wealthy, see Robert Zemsky, "The Massachusetts Assembly, 1730–1755" (Ph.D. dissertation, Yale University, 1967). For a history of Harvard College, see Samuel E. Morison, *Three Centuries at Harvard, 1636–1936* (Cambridge, 1936).

6. FR-HU, I, 70.

7. For a description of Harvard life, see Page Smith, *John Adams,* Vol. I, 1735–1785 (Garden City, New York, 1962), pp. 15–21; see also, Gilbert Chinard, *Honest John Adams* (Boston, 1961), pp. 12–16.

8. FR-HU, I, 256–57.

9. This account is taken from the records of Harvard College. See, FR-HU, I, 285–92. See also Shipton, *New England Life,* p. 565.

10. FR-HU, I, 318–19, 339, 341; CP-HU, II, 10–11.

11. "Report of the School Committee on the Browne and other Donations, September 14, 1835," CP-HU, II, 326.

12. See Chinard, *Honest John Adams,* p. 19.

13. Smith, *John Adams,* I, 25, 28, 33.

14. Jonathan Sewall to [John Higginson], May 10, 1757, R-S Mss. For the family connection, see "Biographical Notice of Officers of Probate for Essex County," *Essex Institute Historical Collections,* III (1861), 6.

15. *Harvard University Quinquiennial Catalogue of the Officers and Graduates, 1636–1920,* p. 148.

16. Eulogy on Chambers Russell, draft in JS Mss.

CHAPTER TWO

1. Jonathan Sewall to Thomas Robie, September 25, 1773, R-S Mss.

2. For the best discussion of Massachusetts' legal development, see Richard B. Morris, "Legalism versus Revolutionary Doctrine in New England," *NEQ,* IV (1931), 195–215, reprinted in David Flaherty, ed., *Essays in the History of Early American Law* (Chapel Hill, 1969), pp. 418–32.

3. "Suffolk Bar," *MHSP,* XIX, 1st series (1881–1882), 142; see also Murrin, "Anglicizing"; Washburn, *Sketches.*

4. Charles Warren, *History of the Harvard Law School and of Early Legal Conditions in America,* Vol. I (Cambridge, 1908), pp. 7–8.

5. *MHSP,* 1st series, V (1860–1862), 108–26.

6. For a discussion of the amateur nature of the lawyer in the seventeenth century, see William Davis, *Bench and Bar of the Commonwealth of Massachusetts,* Vol. I (Boston, 1895). See also, William Davis, *History of the Judiciary of Massachusetts* (Boston, 1900).

7. Washburn, *Sketches,* 52–53.

8. These same factors seem to have been at work in other colonies. See Milton M. Klein, "The Rise of the New York Bar: The Legal Career of William

Livingston,'' in Flaherty, ed. *Essays in the History of Early American Law,* pp. 392–417.

9. Quoted in Chinard, *Honest John Adams,* p. 37.

10. For a vivid description of these circuit riding tours, see Joseph Williamson, ''The Professional Tours of John Adams in Maine,'' *Collections of the Maine Historical Society,* 2d series, I, 301–8; Washburn, *Sketches,* pp. 162–63.

11. Jonathan Sewall to William Cushing, August 30, 1758, Miscellaneous Collection, Massachusetts Historical Society.

12. See RSCM.

13. See RSCM.

14. *Novanglus,* p. 1v.

15. John Adams to Jonathan Sewall, February 1759, Ad Mss, published in *WJA,* I, 51–55.

16. Jonathan Sewall to John Adams, February 13, 1760, Ad Mss, published in *WJA,* I, 50–51.

17. Jonathan Sewall to John Adams, September 29, 1759, Ad Mss.

18. See, for example, ''Lindamera'' to Simon Bradstreet, March 8, 1757; Jonathan Sewall to Thomas Robie, March 17, 1757; Thomas Robie to Jonathan Sewall, March 18, 1757; Jonathan Sewall to Thomas Robie, March 22, 1757, R-S Mss.

19. Jonathan Sewall to Thomas Robie, September 25, 1773, R-S Mss.

20. Thomas Perkins et al. v. Obediah Merrell, York Superior Court (York), June 1770, RSCM.

21. Hugh Wilson v. Samuel Winchell, Cumberland and Lincoln Superior Court (Falmouth), June 1764, RSCM.

22. Edward Jewett v. Joseph Baker Jr., Middlesex Superior Court (Charlestown), April 1770, RSCM; William Gallop v. John Giddings, Essex Superior Court (Ipswich), June 1774, RSCM.

23. Jonathan Sewall to John Adams, October 1765, RTP Mss. For the case itself, see Colonel Northrop v. John Oliver and Michael Nagail, Bristol Superior Court (Taunton), October 1765, RSCM.

24. James Fowle v. Joshua Wyman, Middlesex Superior Court (Charlestown), April, 1772, Middlesex Superior Court (Cambridge) October 1773;

Nathan Taylor et al. v. Obadiah Brown, Worcester Superior Court (Worcester), September 1769, RSCM.

25. Jonathan Brewer v. Joseph Waite, Worcester Superior Court (Worcester), September 1765, RSCM.

26. *Novanglus*, p. iv.

27. These three family names appear repeatedly in Sewall's later practice. See for example, Silas Walker v. John Gould, Worcester Superior Court (Worcester), September 1765, in an action involving £104 in money damages; J. A. Tyng v. Elizah Fletcher, Middlesex Superior Court (Cambridge), October 1766, in an action for trespass; James Tyng v. Abel Lawrence, Middlesex Superior Court (Cambridge), October 1766; John Gould et al. v. Joseph Phips, Middlesex Superior Court (Charlestown), April 1765 (Cambridge), October 1765 (Charlestown), April 1776 (Cambridge), October 1766 (Charlestown), April 1767 (Cambridge), October 1767 (Charlestown), April 1768 (Cambridge), October 1768 (Charlestown), April 1769; Jonathan Hunt v. John Holland, Middlesex Superior Court (Charlestown), April 1771, in an action for trespass; John Hunt v. John Murray, Middlesex Superior Court (Cambridge), October 1772 (Charlestown), April 1773, in an action for trespass, RSCM.

28. Charles Warren's evaluation, quoted in DAB, XVIII, 653–54.

29. Quoted in *Novanglus*, p. iv; in John Adams to Jedidiah Morse, November 20, 1815, *WJA*, X, 179.

CHAPTER THREE

1. For an account of the funeral and of Mayhew's eulogy, see Freiberg, "Prelude," pp. 3–4; see also, Hutchinson, *History*, III, 63.

2. Sarah Cushing Paine, comp. and Charles Henry Pope, ed., *Paine Ancestry: The Family of Robert Treat Paine, Signer of the Declaration of Independence, including Maternal Lines* (Boston, 1912), p. 104; Hutchinson, *History*, III, 63–64; William Tudor, *Life of James Otis* (Boston, 1823), p. 54.

3. For a sympathetic interpretation of Hutchinson's behavior, see Bernard Bailyn's new biography, *The Ordeal of Thomas Hutchinson* (Cambridge, 1974), pp. 47–50.

4. *JOURNALS*, Vol. 1760–1761, p. 265.

5. *Novanglus,* pp. iv–v; John Adams to Jedidiah Morse, November 20, 1815, *WJA,* X, 178–179.

6. Quoted in Tudor, *Life of James Otis,* p. 118, 119–20.

7. The account of this exchange can be found in Tudor, *Life of James Otis,* ch. 9; see also, Freiberg, "Prelude," p. 42.

8. *Boston Evening Post,* February 14, March 14, 28, April 4, 25, May 23, June 13, 1763; *Boston Gazette and Country Journal,* March 29, April 4, 1763.

9. "J," *Boston Evening Post,* March 14, 1763.

10. Richard Frothingham, *Life and Times of Joseph Warren* (Boston, 1865), pp. 49–50; Freiberg, "Prelude," pp. 90–91n; Zobel, *Massacre,* p. 27.

11. *Boston Gazette and Country Journal,* March 29, 1763; *Boston Evening Post,* April 4, 1763.

12. *Boston Gazette and Country Journal,* April 18, 1763.

13. *Boston Gazette and Country Journal,* August 29, 1763.

14. Jonathan Sewall to Thomas Robie, June 16, 1759, R-S Mss.

15. *JOURNALS,* Vol. 1760–1761, p. 150.

16. See Edmund S. Morgan, "Thomas Hutchinson and the Stamp Act," *NEQ,* XXI (1948), 459–92; Freiberg, "Prelude," pp. 66–80, Bailyn, *Ordeal,* pp. 62–69.

17. Hutchinson, *History,* III, 107–8.

18. *Ibid.,* p. 108.

19. Hutchinson, *History,* III, 88–01, 109–15; Freiberg, "Prelude," pp. 158–59; Edmund S. Morgan and Helen Morgan, *The Stamp Act Crisis: Prologue to Revolution* (New York, 1963), chs. 8 and 9.

20. "A" and "Paskelos," "AA," "Y," and various other anti–government authors appear in the *Boston Gazette and Country Journal;* Sewall's articles as "Philanthrop" are published in the *Boston Evening Post,* December 1, 15, 22, 29, 1766; January 5, 12, 26, February 9, March 2, July 27, August 3, 10, 1767.

21. "Philanthrop," *Boston Evening Post,* January 12, 1767.

22. Edmund S. Morgan, "Thomas Hutchinson and the Stamp Act," *NEQ,* XXI (1948), 459–92; Freiberg, "Prelude," pp. 66–80.

23. Francis Bernard to Charles Paxton, January 21, 1767, FB Mss.

24. *Records of the Council of Massachusetts-Bay,* Vol. 16 (Boston, 1761), p. 212.

25. Francis Bernard to Phillip Stephens, April 10, 1767; Francis Bernard to Charles Paxton, January 21, 1767, FB Mss.

26. "Jeremiah Gridley," *DAB,* VII, 611.

27. *Records of the Council of Massachusetts-Bay,* Vol. 16, pp. 262–63.

CHAPTER FOUR

1. For the best discussion of the institutional strains between the customs and the civil agents in America, see Thomas Barrow, *Trade and Empire: The British Customs Service in Colonial America, 1660–1775* (Cambridge, 1967). Barrow outlines fully the development of the customs service in America. See also the study of the customs service in Oliver M. Dickerson, The *Navigation Acts and the American Revolution* (Philadelphia, 1951).

2. John Temple to James Cockle, September 28, 1764, PRO/AO–821; for the documents in this affair, see PRO/AO–821; see also, B-T Mss, 1762–1768; Barrow. *Trade and Empire,* pp. 193–94; Hutchinson, *History,* III, 117; Zobel, *Massacre,* pp. 20–22; "Bowdoin-Temple Correspondence," *MHSC,* 6th series, IX (1897).

3. See the account of Robert Hale, in Barrow, *Trade and Empire,* pp. 194–95.

4. Barrow, *Trade and Empire,* p. 222; Zobel, *Massacre,* p. 65.

5. John Temple to [Robert Hallowell], November 25, 1767, PRO/AO–821; Francis Bernard to John Pownall, February 18, 1768, FB Mss; Francis Bernard to Lord Barrington, February 20, 1768, FB Mss.

6. "Opinion on 7 George 3rd Ch 46," February 1, 1768, JS Mss.

7. *MINUTES,* p. 96.

8. The *Lydia* case is discussed in Barrow, *Trade and Empire,* pp. 228–29; William T. Baxter, *The House of Hancock: Business in Boston, 1724–1775* (New York, 1965), pp. 256–68; Hiller Zobel, "Jonathan Sewall: A Lawyer in Conflict," *Cambridge Historical Society,* XL (1964–1966), 125; Oliver M. Dickerson, "John Hancock: Notorious Smuggler or Near Victim of British

Revenue Racketeers," *Mississippi Valley Historical Review,* XXXII (1946), 517–33.

9. Samuel Venner to Jonathan Sewall, April 15, 1768, JS Mss.

10. Sewall's opinion on the *Lydia* libel is printed in O.M. Dickerson, "Opinion of Attorney General Sewall of Massachusetts in the Case of the Lydia," *WMQ,* 3rd series, IV, 500–504.

11. Zobel, *Massacre,* p. 72.

12. Commissioners of Customs to Lords of Treasury, May 12, 1768, PRO/T/1–465.

13. *Ibid.*

14. Francis Bernard to Commissioners of Customs, January 6, 1769, FB Mss.

15. The *Liberty* affair is more than a twice-told tale. Nevertheless, the two most important discussions of the case come from Zobel, *Massacre,* ch. VI and *LPJA,* II, 173–210 and from Dickerson, "John Hancock." Dickerson's is a Whig interpretation, vindicating Hancock as the victim of Government greed and political repression. Zobel and Wroth are concerned less with the moral implications of the affair and more with the light it sheds on the problems of law enforcement within the imperial structure. I have chosen to develop the Zobel interpretation because my own focus is on intergovernment, or structural strain between Sewall and the Commissioners and how the *Liberty* affair affected this, rather than on the Whig-Tory struggle itself. (On the Liberty affair, see also, G. G. Wolkins, "Hancock's Sloop Liberty," *MHSP,* LV [1921–1922], 239–84, and Baxter, *House of Hancock,* pp. 256–68.)

16. For a discussion of the use of the Stamp Act as an "emotional issue which [the radicals] could exploit to arouse public opinion," that is, in a propaganda war, see Joseph Thomas Leslie, "Partisan Politics in Massachusetts During Governor Bernard's Administration, 1760–1770" (Ph.D. dissertation, University of Wisconsin, 1960), ch. 8.

17. See Barrow, *Trade and Empire,* p. 235.

18. Dickerson believes this is a major issue in the Hancock case (in "John Hancock").

19. Francis Bernard to the Earl of Hillsborough, June 11, 1768, FB Mss. See also Hutchinson, *History,* III, 138; Zobel, *Massacre,* pp. 74–77.

20. Francis Bernard to the Earl of Hillsborough, June 11, 1768, FB Mss; Francis Bernard to the Earl of Hillsborough, July 9, 1768, extract in PRO/T/1–468.

21. Robert Hallowell's Testimony to the Board of Treasury, July 21, 1768, PRO/T/1–468.

22. Zobel, *Massacre,* p. 73.

23. *MINUTES,* August 8, 1768.

24. Jonathan Sewall to Samuel Venner, February 9, 1769; Francis Bernard to Commissioners of Customs, January 6, 1769, PRO/T/1–771.

25. See Barrow, *Trade and Empire,* ch. 11. See also Henry Hulton, *Some Accounts of the Proceedings of the People of New England from the Establishment of a Board of Customs in America to the Breaking out of the Rebellion in 1775, divided into Seventeen Chapters, with an index, ending with an Account of the Sufferings of the Commissioners of Customs, 1767–1776,* p. 40.

26. See Francis Bernard to Commissioners of Customs, January 6, 1769, PRO/T/1–771.

27. Jonathan Sewall to Samuel Venner, February 9, 1769, PRO/T/1–771; David Lisle to Commissioners of Customs, November 18, 1768, PRO/T/1–771.

28. Francis Bernard to Commissioners of Customs, January 6, 1769; Jonathan Sewall to Samuel Venner, February 9, 1769, PRO/T/1–771. For a different version, see Samuel Venner's Memorial to the Lords of Treasury, B-T Mss.

29. *MINUTES,* August 8, 1768.

30. Francis Bernard to Commissioners of Customs, January 6, 1769, PRO/T/1–771; Thomas Hutchinson to Commissioners of Customs, September 17, 1768, TH Mss.

31. *MINUTES,* August 8, 1768.

32. Jonathan Sewall to Commissioners of Customs, August 5, 1768, PRO/T/1–771.

33. Samuel Venner to Jonathan Sewall, August 8, 1768, PRO/T/1–771.

34. Richard Reeves to Jonathan Sewall, August 25, 1768, JS Mss.

35. Sewall's italics. Jonathan Sewall to Samuel Venner, August 10, 1768, PRO/T/1–771.

36. Robert Auchmuty to Four Commissioners (Hulton, Robinson, Burch, and Paxton), September 16, 1768, B-T Mss.

37. Thomas Hutchinson to Commissioners of Customs, September 17, 1768, TH Mss.

38. Thomas Hutchinson to Commissioners of Customs, September 17, 1768, TH Mss.

39. Four Commissioners to the Governor, Lieutenant Governor, and Robert Auchmuty, September 13, 1768, PRO/T/1–771.

40. Thomas Hutchinson to Commissioners of Customs, October 29, 1768, TH Mss. John Temple did not see this letter until December 1769.

41. *MINUTES*, November 3, 1768.

42. David Lisle to Commissioners of Customs, November 18, 1768, PRO/T/1–771.

43. *MINUTES*, November 18, 1768.

44. Samuel Venner to Commissioners of Customs, November 21, 1768, PRO/T/1–771.

45. *MINUTES*, November 29, 1768.

46. Burch, Robinson, Hulton to Jonathan Sewall, December 20, 1768, PRO/T/1–771.

47. Francis Bernard to Commissioners of Customs, January 6, 1769, PRO/T/1–771.

48. *MINUTES*, January 19, 1769.

49. *MINUTES*, January 26, 1769.

50. Hulton, "Accounts of the Proceedings," p. 181.

51. See the Venner memorial in the B-T Mss.

52. John Temple to Thomas Whately, November 4, 1768, printed in *MHSC*, 6th series, IX, 111–12.

53. Bernard was appointed Commissioner of Customs for Ireland. See John Temple to William Samuel Johnson, December 4, 1771, printed in *MHSC*, 6th series, IX, 280–81.

54. John Temple to William Samuel Johnson, December 4, 1771, printed in *MHSC*, 6th series, IX, 280–81.

CHAPTER FIVE

1. For an account of the fleet's arrival, see Dickerson, *BUMR*, p. 1; see also, Zobel, *Massacre*, ch. 9.

2. Dickerson, *BUMR,* p. 20.

3. See "Journal of the Times," November 3, 1768, in Dickerson, *BUMR,* p. 18.

4. For a discussion of the "Journal" and its effectiveness, see Dickerson's introduction to his compilation.

5. "Journal of the Times," April 22, 1769, Dickerson, *BUMR,* p. 92.

6. "Journal of the Times," January 7, 1768, Dickerson, *BUMR,* pp. 46–47.

7. "Journal of the Times," January 30, 1769, Dickerson, *BUMR,* p. 57.

8. Dickerson, "John Hancock," p. 522.

9. For a fine discussion of the uses of hate in Revolutionary war propaganda, see Philip Davidson, *Propaganda and the American Revolution, 1763–1783* (Chapel Hill, 1941), ch. 8, pp. 139–52. Zobel discusses the advantages of creating local hate figures in Zobel, *Massacre,* p. 111.

10. "Journal of the Times," June 30, 1769, Dickerson, *BUMR,* p. 113.

11. Zobel musters evidence for this view in Zobel, *Massacre,* ch. 12, pp. 132–144.

12. "Journal of the Times," January 9, 1769, Dickerson, *BUMR,* p. 47.

13. Zobel, *Massacre,* p. 292.

14. "Journal of the Times," March 27, 1768, Dickerson, *BUMR,* p. 84.

15. John Hancock to Jonathan Sewall, November 2, 1772, JS Mss.

CHAPTER SIX

1. Francis Bernard to Philip Stephens, Secretary of the Admiralty, March 15, 1769, FB Mss.

2. "Journal of the Times," June 29, 1769, Dickerson, *BUMR,* pp. 112–13.

3. "Diary of John Rowe," *MHSP,* 2d series, X (1895–1896), 72.

4. See Freiberg, "Prelude," p. 225.

5. See for example, Francis Bernard to Charles Paxton, January 21, 1767; Francis Bernard to Lord Barrington, October 20, 1768; Francis Bernard to the Earl of Hillsborough, December 12, 1768, FB Mss. On the need for independent salaries, see O.M. Dickerson, *American Colonial Government, 1696–1765* (New York, 1912; reprinted New York, 1962), pp. 181–224.

6. Thomas Hutchinson to ———, January 8, 1770, TH Mss.; Bailyn, *Ordeal*, pp. 169–95.

7. Thomas Hutchinson to ———, January 8, 1770, TH Mss.

8. See Carl Ubbelohde, *The Vice-Admiralty Courts and the American Revolution* (Chapel Hill, 1960), ch. 6, pp. 128–47.

9. Jonathan Sewall to Secretary of the Board of Admiralty, 1769 (draft), JS Mss.

10. Tudor, *Life of James Otis*, pp. 365–66; Zobel, *Massacre*, pp. 146–50; John Robinson to Thomas Hutchinson, November 1, 1769, TH Mss.

11. Thomas Hutchinson to ———, January 8, 1770, TH Mss. Mary Beth Norton has published one of the Hutchinson letters on this proposed exchange of offices in the *MHSP*. She discusses the entire episode in a somewhat more abbreviated form than it is discussed here. See Mary Beth Norton, ''A Recently Discovered Thomas Hutchinson Letter,'' *MHSP*, LXXXII (1970), 105–9.

12. For a complete discussion of the Seider murder and the Boston Massacre, see Zobel, *Massacre*. For a more Whiggish interpretation, see Frederic Kidder, *History of the Boston Massacre, March 5, 1770* (Albany, 1870). See also, Harry Hansen, *The Boston Massacre: An Episode of Dissent and Violence* (New York, 1970).

13. *WJA*, X, 201; quoted in Zobel, ''Jonathan Sewall,'' p. 126.

CHAPTER SEVEN

1. For the ''Vindex'' articles, see *Boston Gazette and Country Journal*, December 10, 17, 24, 31, 1770; January 7, 14, 21, 28, 1771.

2. This is Zobel's evaluation as well. Zobel, *Massacre*, p. 299.

3. Sewall's ''Philanthrop'' pieces appear in the *Boston Evening Post*, December 24, 1770; January 14, 28, February 4, 18, 1771.

4. *Boston Gazette and Country Journal*, December 10, 1770.

5. ''Vindex,'' December 24, 1770, *Boston Gazette and Country Journal*.

6. Thomas Hutchinson to [Francis Bernard], January 30, 1771, TH Mss.

7. Thomas Hutchinson to ———, January 8, 1770, TH Mss.

8. Thomas Hutchinson to [Francis Bernard], January 30, 1771, TH Mss.

9. Francis Bernard to Thomas Hutchinson, April 6, 1771, FB Mss.

10. Thomas Hutchinson to Jonathan Sewall, September 16, 1771, printed in Mary Beth Norton, "A Recently Discovered Thomas Hutchinson Letter," *MHSP* (1970), LXXXII, 105–9.

11. Thomas Hutchinson to ———, March 16, 1772, TH Mss.

12. Thomas Hutchinson to John Robinson, October 23, 1772; Thomas Hutchinson to Francis Bernard, October—, 1772, TH Mss.

CHAPTER EIGHT

1. Samuel G. Drake, *History of Middlesex County,* Vol. I (Boston, 1880), p. 338.

2. Jonathan Sewall to Secretary of the Admiralty, 1769, JS Mss.

3. Jonathan Sewall to Ward Chipman, August 3, 1775, WC Mss.

4. *Ibid.*

5. *JOURNALS,* May–June 1773, p. 27.

6. See Hutchinson, *History,* III, 287–95; James Kendall Hosmer, *The Life of Thomas Hutchinson, Royal Governor of the Province of Massachusetts-Bay* (Boston, New York, 1896), pp. 363–442.

7. *JOURNALS,* May–June 1773, pp. 27–44.

8. For these proceedings, see *JOURNALS,* May–June 1773, pp. 58–61; *Boston Evening Post,* Supplement, June 28, 1773.

9. The "Philalethes" series is printed in the *Massachusetts Gazette,* June 17, 24, July 1, 15, 22, August 5, 12, 1773; see Bailyn, *Ordeal,* pp. 246–51.

10. "Philalethes," *Massachusetts Gazette,* July 1, 1773.

11. Hutchinson, *History,* III, 295.

12. For a full description and discussion of the famous Boston Tea Party, and the events which led up to it, see B. W. Labaree, *The Boston Tea Party* (New York, 1864). See also, Ralph V. Harlow, *Sam Adams: Promoter of the American Revolution* (New York, 1923), pp. 211–19.

13. See, for example, Andrew Oliver to———, February 13, 1769, printed in the pamphlet, *Copy of Letters Sent to Great Britain by His Excellency Thomas Hutchinson, the Hon. Andrew Oliver, and several other persons born and*

educated among us, Which original Letters have been returned to America, and laid before the Honorable House of Representatives of this Province, 1773, p. 13.

14. Bernard's correspondence is filled with accounts of his veto decisions. See, for example, Francis Bernard to Earl of Hillsborough, May 30, 1768, May 8, 1769; Francis Bernard to Viscount Barrington, May 30, 1769, FB Mss.

15. See Richard D. Brown, *Revolutionary Politics in Massachusetts: the Boston Committee of Correspondence and the Towns, 1772–1774* (Cambridge, 1970); Agnes Hunt, *The Provincial Committees of Safety of the American Revolution* (New York, 1968).

16. For the best discussion of the radicals' ideology, see Bernard Bailyn, *The Ideological Origins of the American Revolution* (Cambridge, 1967); see also, Bernard Bailyn, "The Origins of American Politics," *Perspectives in American History,* I (1967), 9–120.

17. John Adams to Abigail Adams, July 9, 1774, printed in Adams Family Archives, *Adams Family Correspondence,* ed. by L. H. Butterfield, Vol. I, 1761–1776 (Cambridge, 1963), 136–37; for a dramatization of this farewell, see Smith, *John Adams,* I, 159.

CHAPTER NINE

1. John Andrews to William Barrell, September 2, 1774, "Letters of John Andrews," *MHSP,* VIII (1864–1865), 351.

2. Sewall's young friend John Colman has left an eyewitness account of the day's events. It is found in the JS Mss. For other, less complete accounts, see Drake, *History of Middlesex County,* p. 341; Richard F. Frothingham Jr., *The History of Charlestown, Massachusetts* (Charlestown and Boston, 1845–1849), p. 302; Frank Moore, *Diary of the American Revolution* (New York, London, 1860), I, 37–42.

3. Loyalist Association, 1774 (draft), JS Mss.

4. "Letters of John Andrews," *MHSP,* VIII (1864–1865), 408.

5. *Ibid.*

6. Andrew Eliot to Thomas Brand Hollis, April 25, 1775, "Letters of Andrew Eliot," *MHSP,* XVI (1878), 281.

7. Jonathan Sewall to Thomas Robie, July 15, 1775, R-S Mss.

8. *Ibid.*

9. "Massachusettensis" appeared in the *Boston Gazette and Country Journal* on December 12, 19, 26, 1774; January 2, 9, 16, 23, 30, February 6, 13, 20, 27, March 6, 13, 20, 27, April 3, 1775. They are reprinted in *Novanglus*. In *Novanglus*, "Massachusettensis" is credited to Jonathan Sewall.

10. John Adams, in *Novanglus*, p. vi.

11. The WC Mss contain two documents that serve as sources for the "Massachusettensis" legal arguments. See "Notes on Taxation of the Colonies" and "Notes on the Post Office as Revenue Tax," WC Mss.

12. Moore, *Diary of the American Revolution*, I, 92–93.

13. 3rd Provincial Congress of Massachusetts, June 16, 1775, printed in *JOURNALS*, Vol. 1774–1775, 344–47.

14. *A Cure for the Spleen, or Amusement for a Winter's Evening; being the substance of a Conversation on the Times, over a Friendly Tankard and Pipe* (1775), reprinted in *The Magazine of History*, XX, no. 79, 119–55.

15. Jonathan Sewall to General Frederick Haldimand, May 30, 1775, JS Mss.

16. See William Nelson's discussion of this Tory interpretation of the Revolution in *The American Tory* (Boston, 1968), ch. 9, 170–90. See also, Joseph Galloway's *Historical and Political Reflections on the Rise and Progress of the American Rebellion* (London, 1780).

17. James Warren to Mercy Warren, May 18, 1775, "Warren-Adams Letters: Being Chiefly a Correspondence among John Adams, Sam Adams and James Warren," *MHSC*, LXXII–LXXIII (1917), 50.

18. Jonathan Sewall to Thomas Robie, June 7, 1775, R-S Mss.

19. Jonathan Sewall to Thomas Robie, August 12, 1775, R-S Mss.

20. *Ibid.*

CHAPTER TEN

1. Jonathan Sewall to Ward Chipman, August 3, 1775, WC Mss.

2. See Norton, *British-Americans*, for a fuller discussion of the social patterns of the New England exiles.

3. Jonathan Sewall to Ward Chipman, November 29, 1775–January 14, 1776, WC Mss.

4. Jonathan Sewall to Ward Chipman, September 22, 1775, WC Mss.

5. Jonathan Sewall to Ward Chipman, November 29, 1775–January 14, 1776, WC Mss.

6. Jonathan Sewall to Edward Winslow, January 10–20, 1776, EW Mss.

7. Jonathan Sewall to Thomas Robie, March 12, 1777, R-S Mss.

8. Jonathan Sewall to Edward Winslow, January 10–20, 1776, EW Mss; Jonathan Sewall to John Foxcroft, March 14, 1776, JS Mss. For requests for American items, see, for example, Jonathan Sewall to Thomas Robie, August 17, 1776, February 21–22, 1778, R-S Mss; Jonathan Sewall to Ward Chipman, April 17, 1780, WC Mss; Esther Sewall to Edmund Quincy, January 10, 1783, JS Mss.

9. *JSC,* pp. 45, 48; Norton, *British-Americans,* p. 100.

10. See Lewis Einstein, *Divided Loyalties: Americans in England During the War of Independence* (London, 1933), p. 202.

11. For criticisms and reports on the military conduct of the war by the Loyalists remaining in New York, see *Historical Anecdotes Civil and Military, in a Series of Letters written from America, in the Years 1777 and 1778, to Different Persons in England; containing Observations on the General Management of the War, and on the Conduct of our Principal Commanders, in the Revolted Colonies, during that Period* (London, 1779).

12. Jonathan Sewall to Edward Winslow, January 10–20, 1776, EW Mss.

13. Jonathan Sewall to Ward Chipman, November 25, 1775–January 14, 1776, WC Mss.

14. Jonathan Sewall to Edward Winslow, January 10–20, 1776, EW Mss.

15. Jonathan Sewall to John Lowell, April 24, 1777, printed in *MHSP,* xiv (1875–1876), 182–84.

16. See the discussion of Loyalist confidence in British victory in Einstein, *Divided Loyalties,* pp. 215–17.

17. For a discussion of the British military and its inadequacies, see Eric Robson, *The American Revolution, in its Political and Military Aspect, 1763–1783* (London, 1955), esp. ch. 5.

18. For a description of Burgoyne's campaign, see John Richard Alden, *The American Revolution, 1775–1783* (New York, 1962), pp. 115–48.

19. James Putnam to Jonathan Sewall, July 22, 1777, JS Mss.

20. Ward Chipman to Jonathan Sewall, September 11, 13, 20, 1777, JS Mss.

21. Ward Chipman to Jonathan Sewall, November 7, 1777, JS Mss.

22. *JSC,* p. 160.

23. Jonathan Sewall to Mrs. John [Mehetabel Robie] Higginson, March 4–April 1, 1778, R-S Mss; printed in *MHSP,* 2d series, X (1895–1896), 418–20.

24. Samuel Curwen to Jonathan Sewall, December 31, 1776, *JSC,* pp. 92–94; Jonathan Sewall to Thomas Robie, March 12, 1777, R-S Mss, printed in *MHSP,* 2d series, X (1895–1896), 417–18; Esther Sewall to Sisters, February 18, 1778, JS Mss.

CHAPTER ELEVEN

1. *JSC,* p. 154.

2. For a description of the Bristol refugee community, see Wilbur H. Siebert, "The Colony of Massachusetts Loyalists at Bristol," *MHSP,* XLV (1911–1912), 409–14.

3. Jonathan Sewall to Edward Winslow, September 20, 1778–January 4, 1779, EW Mss; see also, Jonathan Sewall to Isaac Smith, May 9, 1778, SmC Mss; Jonathan Sewall to Thomas Robie, January 29, 1779, R-S Mss.

4. Samuel Curwen to Jonathan Sewall, February 4, 1782, *JSC,* p. 332; Thomas A. Coffin to Mrs. Coffin, December 3, 1784, TC Mss.

5. Jonathan Sewall to Edward Winslow, September 20, 1778–January 4, 1779, EW Mss. For shared sentiments on the Carlisle peace offer, see Samuel Curwen to Jonathan Sewall, March 23, 1778, *JSC,* pp. 181–85.

6. Jonathan Sewall to Isaac Smith, May 9, 1778, SmC Mss.

7. Jonathan Sewall to Thomas Robie, January 29, 1779, R-S Mss.

8. Jonathan Sewall to Samuel Curwen, December 18, 1778, *JSC,* pp. 206–7.

9. Jonathan Sewall to Edward Winslow, September 20, 1778–January 4, 1779, EW Mss.

10. Jonathan Sewall to Thomas Robie, January 29, 1779, R-S Mss.

11. Jonathan Sewall to Isaac Smith, June 22, 1779, SmC Mss.

12. *Ibid.*

13. Jonathan Sewall to Elisha Hutchinson, November 25, 1780, H-W Mss.

14. Ward Chipman to Jonathan Sewall, December 9, 1781, JS Mss.

15. Jonathan Sewall to Ward Chipman, March 23–April 4, 1782, WC Mss.

16. *Ibid.*

17. Jonathan Sewall to Ward Chipman, April 22, 1782, WC Mss.

18. See Ward Chipman to Jonathan Sewall, October 6, 1782, December 18, 1782, JS Mss.

19. Ward Chipman to Jonathan Sewall, December 18, 1782, JS Mss. For the best discussion of the reevaluation policy and its results, see Norton, *British-Americans;* see also, Einstein, *Divided Loyalties,* pp. 226–43.

20. Jonathan Sewall to Ward Chipman, 1782, JS Mss.

21. Jonathan Sewall to Ward Chipman, February 1, 1783, WC Mss.

22. *Ibid.*

CHAPTER TWELVE

1. Jonathan Sewall to Ward Chipman, February 1, 1783, WC Mss.

2. Jonathan Sewall to Thomas Robie, March 11, 1782, December 6, 1782–August 27, 1783, R-S Mss.

3. Jonathan Sewall to Thomas Robie, March 11, 1782, R-S Mss.

4. *Ibid.*

5. Jonathan Sewall to Ward Chipman, March 15, 1780, JS Mss.

6. Ward Chipman to Jonathan Sewall, December 9, 1781, JS Mss.

7. Jonathan Sewall to Ward Chipman, April 22, 1782, JS Mss.

8. Jonathan Sewall to Ward Chipman, February 1, 1783, WC Mss.

9. Jonathan Sewall to Ward Chipman, August 31, 1784, WC Mss.

10. Jonathan Sewall to Thomas Robie, December 25, 1787, R-S Mss.

11. For Sewall's memorials and correspondence regarding his claim, see PRO/AO/12–48. See also, E. Alfred Jones, *The Loyalists of Massachusetts*

(London, 1930), p. 259; Hugh Edward Egerton, ed., *The Royal Commission on the Losses and Services of American Loyalists 1783–1785* (Oxford, 1915), p. 233.

12. Sewall's testimony for Jonathan Simpson of Boston and for Sir William Pepperrell can be found in Egerton, *Royal Commission,* pp. 235–36, 152–53.

13. Thomas A. Coffin to Mrs. Coffin, December 3, 1784, TC Mss.

14. Jonathan Sewall to Jonathan Sewall Jr., September 29, 1786, JS Mss.

15. Jonathan Sewall to Jonathan Sewall Jr., June 5, 1786, JS Mss.

16. For Sewall's help in gaining a pension for Curwen, see Samuel Curwen to Jonathan Sewall, October 3, 1776, SC Mss.

17. Samuel Curwen to Jonathan Sewall, August 16, 1785, December 14, 1785, SC Mss.

18. For Sewall's own extraordinary account of these eighteen months see Jonathan Sewall to Judge Joseph Lee, September 21, 1787, LF Mss.

19. Jonathan Sewall to the Lords of the Treasury (Draft), June 28, 1786, JS Mss.

20. Jonathan Sewall to Jonathan Sewall Jr., September 29, 1786, JS Mss.

21. Jonathan Sewall to Judge Joseph Lee, September 21, 1787, LF Mss.

22. *Ibid.* See also John Adams's account in the introduction to *Novanglus,* pp. vi–vii; see Smith's dramatization in *John Adams,* II, 645–46.

23. Jonathan Sewall to Judge Joseph Lee, September 21, 1787, LF Mss.

24. *Novanglus,* p. vii.

CHAPTER THIRTEEN

1. See Jonathan Sewall Jr. to Jonathan Sewall, December 5, 1785, JS Mss.

2. Jonathan Sewall to Judge Joseph Lee, September 21, 1787, LF Mss.

3. Jonathan Sewall to Edward Winslow, July 25, 1787, EW Mss.

4. See Lewis Wolfe to Jonathan Sewall, July 31, 1787; George Rogers to Jonathan Sewall, August 2, 1787, JS Mss.

5. Lewis Wolfe to Jonathan Sewall, July 31, 1787, JS Mss.

6. Jonathan Sewall to Lewis Wolfe, December 12, 1787, JS Mss.

7. Jonathan Sewall to Thomas Robie, December 26, 1787, R-S Mss.

8. Charles Stedman to Jonathan Sewall, January 20, 1788, Lewis Wolfe to Jonathan Sewall, August 31, 1789, JS Mss.

9. Stedman and Wolfe to Jonathan Sewall, July 11, 1788, JS Mss. For a discussion of the Commission's standards and procedures, see Norton, *British-Americans;* see also, Egerton, *Royal Commission;* Jones, *The Loyalists of Massachusetts;* Wallace Brown, *The Kings Friends, the Composition and Motives of the American Loyalist Claimants* (Providence, 1965); George Wrong, *Canada and the American Revolution* (New York, 1935), pp. 464–70; North Callahan, *Flight from the Republic* (New York, 1967), pp. 120–41; Einstein, *Divided Loyalties,* pp. 226–43.

10. Lewis Wolfe to Jonathan Sewall, February 15, 1789, JS Mss.

11. Charles Munro to Jonathan Sewall, July 11, 1788, Lewis Wolfe to Jonathan Sewall, July 6, 1790, December, 1790, JS Mss. For an account of the claims made against Sewall's settlement, see Jonathan Sewall to Charles Munro, December 8, 1789, PRO/AO/13–137.

12. *The Evening Times-Globe,* St. John, New Brunswick, April 4, 1960.

13. Lewis Wolfe to Jonathan Sewall, February 15, 1789, August 31, 1789, December 31, 1790, JS Mss.

14. Edward Winslow to Jonathan Sewall Jr., November 1, 1790, JS Mss.

15. Esther Sewall to Jonathan Sewall Jr., August 22, 1789, November 4, 1789, JS Mss.

16. The correspondence among family from 1789 until Sewall's death is filled with reports on Sewall's health. See Esther Sewall to Jonathan Sewall Jr., August 22, 1789, September 6, 1789, October 1, 1789, November 4, 1789, March 22, 1790, April 11, 1790, August, 1790, June 18, 1793, November 17, 1794; Jonathan Sewall to Jonathan Sewall Jr., March 21, 1790; Stephen Sewall to Jonathan Sewall Jr., June 7, 1790, June 22, 1790, August 11, 1790, March 14, 1791; Ward Chipman to Jonathan Sewall Jr., April 9, 1792, May 29, 1792, October 4, 1792, February 23, 1793, JS Mss; Jonathan Sewall Jr. to Ward Chipman, April 16, 1791, WC Mss.

17. Stephen Sewall to Jonathan Sewall Jr., August 11, 1790, JS Mss.

18. Stephen Sewall to Jonathan Sewall Jr., August 24, 1790, JS Mss.

19. Esther Sewall to John Hancock, November 13, 1790, Boston Public Library.

20. Jonathan Sewall to Thomas Robie, May 6, 1789; Jonathan Sewall to Thomas Robie, July 26, 1789, R-S Mss.

21. Jonathan Sewall Jr. to Ward Chipman, April 16, 1791, WC Mss.

22. Ward Chipman to Jonathan Sewall Jr., May 20, 1791, JS Mss.

23. Ward Chipman to Jonathan Sewall Jr., April 9, 1792; Ward Chipman to Jonathan Sewall Jr., February 23, 1793, JS Mss.

24. Ward Chipman to Jonathan Sewall Jr., October 4, 1792, JS Mss.

25. Edward Winslow to Jonathan Sewall Jr., September 27, 1796; Esther Sewall to Stephen and Jonathan Sewall Jr., October 9, 1796, JS Mss.

CHAPTER FOURTEEN

1. William Nelson, *The American Tory* (Boston, 1968), p. 18.

2. Jonathan Sewall to Thomas Robie, March 12, 1777, R-S Mss.

3. "Observations by Mr. Smith, late Chief Justice of the Remaining Colonies," January 17, 1785, William Smith Papers, New York Public Library, partially printed in *New York History,* XXIII (1942), 323–40.

Bibliography

The largest collection of Sewall documents is found in the Public Archives of Canada at Ottawa. The papers of Jonathan Sewall, containing letters of father and son, begin with documents as early as the 1731 letter on the death of Sewall's merchant father. The bulk of the senior Sewall's letters, however, cover the years of exile, 1775–1796. They are carefully catalogued and divided into volumes. Letters among family members are also contained in this collection, as are letters to Sewall from his English agents and from Ward Chipman. The Papers of Ward Chipman, Sewall's son by sentiment if not by birth, are also collected in the Public Archives and contain Sewall's letters to Chipman as well as Sewall's family members' correspondence addressed to Chip. Between the two collections a vivid portrait of the Sewall family can, I believe, be drawn. Sewall's somewhat distorted views on events during his exile years, especially in Canada, are given perspective by the correspondence between Chipman and Jonathan Sewall Jr. A third major collection among the Public Archive's Loyalist papers is the Papers of Edward Winslow. This collection offers insight into Canadian politics as well as specific information and documents concerning Sewall.

The Massachusetts Historical Society houses the Sewall-Robie Collection, a correspondence between Sewall and his cousin Thomas Robie which spans almost forty years. It is the best source of information on Sewall's personal life before the Revolution. As Robie was never politically active, Sewall's letters to him tend to be more personal and related to family matters. These letters contain the best examples of Sewall's wit and social satire.

The Massachusetts Historical Society also holds the papers of several of Sewall's colleagues and friends. Letters to and from Sewall are found in the Coffin Papers, the William Heath Collection, the Higginson Collection, the Hutchinson-Watson Collection, the Smith-Carter Papers, and the Lee Family Papers—in which the extraordinary letter of September 21, 1787, from Sewall to Judge Joseph Lee, detailing Sewall's eighteen-month retreat from society is found. Also at the Massachusetts Historical Society are the Adams Papers, containing letters between John Adams and Jonathan Sewall, and legal records of Adams's practice. These legal records provided information on Sewall's major cases, the Hancock trials, and the two suits by blacks for their freedom. These cases are printed with thorough explanatory notes in Hiller Zobel and L. Kinvin Wroth, eds., *The Legal Papers of John Adams,* 3 Vols. (Cambridge, 1965). Part of the Adams Papers are published, and are available on microfilm.

Other collections yielding Sewall correspondence or materials related to his life are the Samuel Curwen Papers, Essex Institute, part of which are published as the *Journal and Letters of the late Samuel Curwen* (New York, 1845); The Papers of William Smith, New York Public Library; Papers of Beverly Robinson, in the Sir Henry Clinton Papers at Wm. L. Clements Library, University of Michigan; Oxenbridge Thacher Papers, and John Hancock Papers, Boston Public Library; and the correspondence of the Hutchinson Family in the British Museum's Egerton Manuscripts.

Sewall's Harvard career is pieced together from the Harvard University Archives. His political career is investigated in the transcripts of the Papers of Sir Francis Bernard, at Harvard University's Houghton Library; in the Henry Hulton Letterbooks, also at Houghton; in the Thomas Hutchinson Papers, Vols. XXV–XXVII of the Massachusetts Archives, State House, Boston. Sewall's political writings of the 1760s and 1770s, as well as those of his opponents, are found in the Massachusetts newspapers: *Boston Evening Post, Boston Gazette and Country Journal, Massachusetts Gazette,* and *The Boston Censor.* These newspapers are available on microcard, or in almost complete collections at Harvard University, Houghton Library. Harbottle Dorr's *Annotated Massachusetts Newspapers, 1765–1776* (4 vols., Massachusetts Historical Society) provided the identification of political essayists and a running contemporary commentary on the political events of pre-Revolutionary Massachusetts.

Sewall's own legal records did not survive his exile. Some were sequestered along with other personal papers in Massachusetts; others were destroyed in passage from Bristol to Halifax and St. John. His legal library, which contained over 150 volumes—including Coke's *Reports,* Strange's *Reports,* Blackstone's *Commentaries,* Bolingbroke's *Philosophical Works,* and Montesquieu's *Reflections*—was lost in the years of exile, en route from England to Canada. The only sources for Sewall's legal practice are the *Legal Papers of John Adams,* and the incomplete records for the pre-Revolutionary Massachusetts Courts preserved in the Suffolk County Courthouse, Boston. Only superior court records have survived: thus no materials on Sewall's Middlesex County inferior court practice are available. The Admiralty Court records for Sewall's period are not extant. However, materials on Sewall's legal opinions as Attorney and Advocate General can be found scattered among his papers at the Public Archives, and in the Public Record Office collections of Great Britain. The Public Record Office, Treasury Papers, I, bundle 463, and Treasury Papers, 64, bundle 188, contain correspondence on Sewall's *Lydia* and *Liberty* decisions.

The Treasury Office Papers also contain the official records of the Venner affair, in Treasury 1, bundles 465, 468, and 771. Transcripts of bundles 463–482 are located in the Library of Congress, but bundle 771—which contains the bulk of the material on the Venner affair—is not available in this country. The minutes of the Customs Board investigation of the affair are found in the Public Record Office, Commissioners of Customs in America, Records and Minutes, 1762–1770, Vol. V, Minutes Extracted from the Board's Records, Book 1, 1767–1769. It is available in microfilm from the University of Michigan. Materials relating to the Bernard-Temple feud, and to the Venner affair from Temple's point of view, are found respectively in Public Record Office, Declared Accounts, Customs, bundle 821, and the Temple-Bowdoin Manuscripts at the Massachusetts Historical Society.

For Sewall's Loyalist claims and pension payments, the first source is the New York Public Library's transcript of the *Calendar of the Original Memorials, Vouchers and Other Papers deposited with the Commission of Enquiry into the Losses and Services of the American Loyalists held under Acts of Parliament of 23, 25, 26, 28, and 29 of George III preserved amongst the Audit Office Records in the Public Record Office of England, 1783–1790* (1903). His claims and details of the claims made upon his estate are found in the Public Record Office, Audit Office 13, bundles 136–137. The account of his pension payments is available in Treasury 50, Miscellanea 31–33, Loyalist Quarterly Pension Lists, 1788–1796. Mary Beth Norton's extensive study of the Loyalist claims and claimants, *The British Americans: The Loyalist Exiles in England, 1774–1789* (Boston, 1972) puts Sewall's compensation and his attitude toward it in perspective.

Among other secondary sources I would mention John Murrin's "Anglicizing an American Colony: The Transformation of Provincial Massachusetts" (Ph.D. dissertation, Yale University, 1966), helpful in organizing the discussion of the legal profession in Sewall's era. Malcolm Freiberg's "Prelude to Purgatory: Thomas Hutchinson in Provincial Massachusetts Politics, 1748–1776" (Ph.D. dissertation, Brown University, 1950) is a fine supplement to Thomas Hutchinson's own *History of the Colony and Province of Massachusetts-Bay,* still one of the best American histories. Bernard Bailyn's excellent new biography, *The Ordeal of Thomas Hutchinson* (Cambridge, 1974), was useful for all discussions of Sewall's political career during the early 1770s. The best general study of the Tories remains William Nelson's *The American Tory,* although it needs the refinement of more detailed and intensive research on the various Tory subgroups. Bailyn's work on radical ideology, *Pamphlets of the American Revolution, 1750–1776* (Cambridge, 1965), is essential to any discussion of revolutionary Massachusetts, while Thomas Barrow's *Trade and Empire: The British Customs Service in Colonial America, 1660–1775* (Cambridge, 1967) is essential to the understanding of the customs apparatus and its relationship to radical and government factions. Hiller Zobel's *Boston Massacre* (New York, 1970) has been relied upon for the discussions of the military occupation of Boston and for the author's understanding of the institutional problems of imperial government in the province of Massachusetts.

PRIMARY SOURCES

I. Manuscripts and Documents

Ann Arbor	W. L. Clements Library, University of Michigan. Papers of Beverley Robinson, Sir Henry Clinton Papers.
Boston	Boston Public Library. John Hancock Papers.
——	Boston Public Library. Oxenbridge Thacher Papers.
——	Massachusetts Archives. Vols. IX, CXXX.
——	Massachusetts Archives. Papers of Thomas Hutchinson.
——	Massachuhsetts Historical Society. Papers of John Adams.
——	Massachusetts Historical Society. Bowdoin-Temple Manuscripts.

—— Massachusetts Historical Society. Coffin Papers.

—— Massachusetts Historical Society. Harbottle Dorr's Annotated Massachusetts Newspapers, 1765–1776. 4 Vols.

—— Massachusetts Historical Society. William Heath Collection.

—— Massachusetts Historical Society. Higginson Family Collection.

—— Massachusetts Historical Society. Hutchinson-Watson Collection.

—— Massachusetts Historical Society. Lee Family Papers.

—— Massachusetts Historical Society. Robie-Sewall Collection.

—— Massachusetts Historical Society. Smith-Carter Papers.

—— Suffolk County Courthouse. Records of the Superior Court of Massachusetts.

Cambridge   Harvard University. Papers of Sir Francis Bernard.

—— Harvard University. Henry Hulton Letterbooks.

—— Harvard University Archives. College Papers and Faculty Records.

London   British Museum. Correspondence of the Hutchinson Family, Egerton Manuscripts, 2659.

—— Public Record Office. Audit Office, 13. 136–37.

—— Public Record Office. Audit Office. Declared Accounts, Customs. 821.

—— Public Record Office. Customs Commissioners in America. Records and Minutes, 1762–1770, V. Minutes Extracted from the Board's Records. Book I, 1767–1769.

—— Public Record Office. Treasury 1. In-Letters. 771.

—— Public Record Office. Treasury 28. 1.

—— Public Record Office. Treasury 50. Miscellanea 31–33. Loyalists Quarterly Pension Lists, 1788–1790.

—— Public Record Office. Treasury 64. 188.

New York   Columbia University. Special Collections. *Journals of the House of Representatives of Massachusetts.*

—— New York Public Library. Manuscript Room. *American Loyalists, Calendar of the Original Memorials, Vouchers and other Papers deposited with the Commission of Enquiry into the Losses and Services of the American Loyalists held Under Acts of Parliament of 23, 25, 26, 28, and 29 of George III preserved amongst the Audit Office Records in the Public Record Office of England, 1783–1790* (1903).

—— New York Public Library. Manuscript Room. Balch Papers, 1775–1782, Loyalist Box.

Ottawa   Public Archives of Canada. Papers of Ward Chipman, Lawrence Collection.

—— Public Archives of Canada. Papers of Jonathan Sewall.

—— Public Archives of Canada. Papers of Edward Winslow.

Salem   Essex Institute. Papers of Samuel Curwen.

Washington   Library of Congress. Public Record Office. Admiralty 2. 1056–58 (Photostat).

—— Library of Congress. Public Record Office. Colonial Office 5. 92 (Transcript).

―――― Library of Congress. Public Record Office. House of Lords Manuscripts. Item 226. Papers Concerning the Superior Court of Vice Admiralty at Halifax, Nova Scotia (Photostat).

―――― Library of Congress. Public Record Office. Treasury 1. In-Letters. 463, 465, 466, 468, 471, 474, 482, 623 (Transcripts).

II. Pamphlets

New York Columbia University. Special Collections. Bernard, Francis. *Select Letters on the Trade and Government of America; and the principles of Law and Polity applied to the American Colonies.* 1774.

―――― Columbia University. Special Collections. *Case and Claim of the American Loyalists impartially Stated and Considered.* London, 1783.

―――― Columbia University. Special Collections. *Copy of Letters Sent to Great Britain by His Excellency Thomas Hutchinson, the Hon. Andrew Oliver, and several other persons born and educated among us, Which original Letters have been returned to America, and laid before the Honorable House of Representatives of this Province.* 1773.

―――― Columbia University. Special Collections. Galloway, Joseph. *Historical and Political Reflections on the Rise and Progress of the American Rebellion.* London, 1780.

―――― Columbia University. Special Collections. Hulton, Henry. *Some Accounts of the Proceedings of the People of New England from the Establishment of a Board of Customs in America to the breaking out of the Rebellion in 1775, divided into Seventeen Chapters, with an index, ending with account of Sufferings of the Commissioners of Customs, 1767–1776.* Andre de Coppet Collection of American Historical Manuscripts in Princeton University Library.

―――― Columbia University. Special Collections. *Letters to the Ministry from Governor Bernard, General Gage and Commodore Hood. And also Memorials to the Lords of Treasury from the Commissioners of the Customs.* Edes & Gill, 1769.

―――― Columbia University. Special Collections. *The Speeches of His Excellency Governor Hutchinson, to the General Assembly of the Massachusetts-bay. At a Session begun and held on the sixth of January 1773. With the Answers of His Majesty's Council and the House of Representatives, respectively.* 1773.

SECONDARY SOURCES

Adair, Douglass, and Schutz, John A., eds. *Peter Oliver's Origins and Progress of the American Rebellion.* San Marino, California: Huntington Library, 1963.

Adams, Charles Francis. *The Works of John Adams.* 10 Vols. Boston: Books for Libraries Press, 1851–1866.

Adams, John. *Novanglus and Massachusettensis; or Political Essays, published in the Years 1774 and 1775, on the Principal Points of Controversy, between Great Britain and her Colonies*. New York: Russell and Russell, 1968.

Alden, John Richard. *The American Revolution, 1775–1783*. New York: Harper and Row, 1962.

Alger, Arthur M. "Barristers at Law in Massachusetts." *New England Historical and Genealogical Register*, XXXI (1877), 206–8.

Ames, Nathaniel. *An Astronomical Diary, 1726–1775*. Boston: by the author, 1725–1774.

Andrews, Charles M. *The Colonial Period in American History*. 4 Vols. New Haven: Yale University Press, 1934–1937.

——. *Guide to the Materials for American History, to 1783, in the Public Record Office of Great Britain*. 2 Vols. Washington: Kraus, 1912–1914.

Austin, James T. *Life of Elbridge Gerry*. Boston: Wells and Lilly, 1828–1829.

Bailyn, Bernard. *The Ideological Origins of the American Revolution*. Cambridge: Harvard University Press, 1967.

——. *The Ordeal of Thomas Hutchinson*. Cambridge: Belknap Press of Harvard University, 1974.

——. "The Origins of American Politics." *Perspectives in American History*, I (1967), 9–120.

Baker, William K. *The Loyalists*. London: G. Routledge and Son, 1921.

Barrow, Thomas C. *Trade and Empire: The British Customs Service In Colonial America, 1660–1775*. Cambridge: Harvard University Press, 1967.

Baxter, William Threipland. *The House of Hancock: Business in Boston, 1724–1775*. New York: Russell and Russell, 1965.

Beardsley, E. E. *Life and Correspondence of the Right Reverend Samuel Seabury*. Boston: Houghton, Mifflin, 1881.

Belcher, Henry. *The First American Civil War*. 2 Vols. London: MacMillan, 1911.

Bentley, William. *The Diary of William Bentley*. Salem: The Essex Institute, 1907.

Benton, William A. *Whig-Loyalism: An Aspect of Political Ideology in the American Revolutionary Era*. Rutherford, New Jersey: Fairleigh Dickinson University Press, 1969.

Billias, George A., ed. *Law and Authority in Colonial America*. Barre, Massachusetts: Barre Publishers, 1965.

"Biographical Notice of Officers of Probate for Essex County." *Essex Institute Historical Collections*, III (1861), 6.

Bond, B. W. Jr. "The Colonial Agent as a Popular Representative." *Political Science Quarterly*, XXXV (1920), 372–92.

"Bowdoin-Temple Papers." *Massachusetts Historical Society*, 6th Series, IX (1897).

Boyd, Julian P. *Anglo-American Union: Joseph Galloway's Plans to Preserve the British Empire, 1774–1788*. Philadelphia: University of Pennsylvania Press, 1941.

Boyle, John. "Journal of Occurrences in Boston, 1759–1778." *New England Historical and Genealogical Register*, LXXXIV (1930), 262.

Bradford, Alden, ed. *Speeches of the Governors of Massachusetts, from 1765–1775*. Boston: Russell and Russell, 1818.

Bradley, A. G. *Colonial Americans in Exile: Founders of British Canada*. New York: E. P. Dutton, 1932.

Brebner, J. B. *The Neutral Yankees of Nova Scotia*. New York: Columbia University Press, 1937.

Brennan, Ellen E. "James Otis: Recreant and Patriot." *New England Quarterly*, XII (1939), 722–26.

——. *Plural Office Holding in Massachusetts 1760–1780*. Chapel Hill: University of North Carolina Press, 1945.

Brown, Gerald Saxon. *The American Secretary: The Colonial Policy of Lord George Germain, 1775–1778*. Ann Arbor: University of Michigan Press, 1963.

Brown, Richard D. *Revolutionary Politics in Massachusetts: The Boston Committee of Correspondence and the Towns, 1772–1774*. Cambridge: Harvard University Press, 1970.

Brown, Wallace. *The Good Americans*. New York: Morrow, 1969.

——. *The King's Friends: The Composition and Motives of the American Loyalist Claimants*. Providence: Brown University Press, 1965.

Butterfield, L. H., ed. *Diary and Autobiography of John Adams*. Cambridge: Belknap Press of Harvard University, 1961.

Callahan, North. *Flight from the Republic*. New York: Bobbs-Merrill, 1967.

——. *Royal Raiders: The Tories of the American Revolution*. Indianapolis; Bobbs-Merrill, 1963.

Canniff, William. *History of the Settlement of Upper Canada with special reference to the Bay Quinte*. Toronto: Dudley and Burns, 1869.

Carter, C. E., ed. *The Correspondence of General Gage with the Secretaries of State, 1763–1775*. 2 Vols. New Haven: Archer Books, 1931–1933.

Chalmers, George, ed. *Opinions of Eminent Lawyers on Various Points of English Jurisprudence Chiefly Concerning the Colonies*. 2 Vols. London: Reed and Hunter, 1814.

Channing, Edward, and Coolidge, A. C., eds. *The Barrington-Bernard Correspondence and Illustrative Matter, 1760–1770*. Cambridge: Da Capo Press, 1912.

Chinard, Gilbert. *Honest John Adams*. Boston: Little, Brown, 1961.

Chroust, Anton H. *The Rise of the Legal Profession in America*. 2 Vols. Norman, Oklahoma: University of Oklahoma Press, 1965.

Clark, D. M. "American Board of Customs, 1767–1783." *American Historical Review*, XLV (1940), 777–85.

Cunningham, Anne Rowe. *Letters and Diary of John Rowe, Boston Merchant, 1759–1762, 1764–1779*. Boston: W. B. Clarke Company, 1903.

Dahl, Robert A. *Who Governs? Democracy and Power in an American City*. New Haven and London: Yale University Press, 1966.

Davidson, Philip. *Propaganda and the American Revolution, 1763–1783*. Chapel Hill: University of North Carolina Press, 1941.

Davis, William T. *Bench and Bar of Massachusetts*. 2 Vols. Boston: The Boston History Company, 1895.

——. *History of the Judiciary of Massachusetts*. Boston: The Boston Book Company, 1900.

Davol, Ralph. *Two Men of Taunton, in the Course of Human Events, 1731–1829.* Taunton: Davol Publishing Company, 1912.

"Diaries of George Inman: Extracts." *Pennsylvania Magazine of History,* VII (1883), 237–48.

"Diary of John Rowe." *Massachusetts Historical Society Proceedings,* 2d Series, X (1895–1896).

Dickerson, Oliver M., ed. *Boston Under Military Rule, 1768–1769, as Recorded in a Journal of the Times.* Boston: Chapman and Grimes, 1936.

———. "John Hancock: Notorious Smuggler or Near Victim of British Revenue Racketeers?" *Mississippi Valley Historical Review,* XXXII (1946), 517–33.

———. *The Navigation Acts and the American Revolution.* Philadelphia: University of Pennsylvania Press, 1951.

Dorson, Richard M. *American Rebels.* New York: Pantheon, 1953.

Doughty, Arthur George. *Documents relating to the Constitutional History of Canada, 1759–1791.* Ottawa: C. H. Parmelee, 1918.

Dow, George F., ed. *Diary and Letters of Benjamin Pickman.* Newport, Rhode Island: Wayside Press, 1929.

Drake, Samuel G. *History of Boston.* Boston: L. Stevens, 1854.

Drake, Samuel G. *History of Middlesex County.* Boston, 1880, I, 338.

East, Robert. "The Business Entrepreneur in a Changing Economy, 1763–1795." *Journal of Economic History,* Supplement VI (1946), 489–505.

Eddis, William. *Letters from America, Historical and Descriptive, Comprising Occurrences from 1769–1777.* London: printed for the author, 1792.

Einstein, Lewis. *Divided Loyalties: Americans in England During the War of Independence.* London: Cobden-Sanderson, 1933.

Eliot, John. *Biographical Dictionary, Containing a Brief Account of the First Settlers, and other Eminent Characters . . . in New England.* Salem: Cushing and Appleton, 1809.

Fergusson, C. B. *Diary of Simeon Perkins, 1790–1796.* Toronto: Publications of the Champlain Society, 1961.

Flaherty, David H., ed. *Essays in the History of Early American Law.* Chapel Hill: University of North Carolina Press, 1969.

Flick, Alexander C. *Loyalism in New York during the American Revolution.* New York: Columbia University Press, 1901.

Forbes, Harriette. *New England Diaries, 1602–1800.* Topsfield, Massachusetts: private printing, 1923.

Freiberg, Malcolm. "Prelude to Purgatory: Thomas Hutchinson in Provincial Massachusetts Politics, 1748–1776." Ph.D. dissertation, Brown University, 1950.

———. "Thomas Hutchinson: The First Fifty Years (1711–1761)." *William and Mary Quarterly,* 3d series, XV (1958), 35–55.

French, Allen. *General Gage's Informers.* Ann Arbor: University of Michigan Press, 1932.

Frothingham, Richard F. Jr. *The History of Charlestown, Massachusetts.* Charlestown and Boston: Little and Brown, 1845–1849.

———. *Life and Times of Joseph Warren*. Boston: Little, Brown and Company, 1865.

Gilroy, Marion. *Loyalists and Land Settlement in Nova Scotia*. Halifax: Public Archives of Nova Scotia, 1937.

Gipson, Lawrence H. *Jared Ingersoll: A Study of American Loyalism*. New Haven: Yale University Press, 1920.

Gordon, William. *The History of the Rise, Progress, and Establishment of the Independence of the United States of America: Including an Account of the Late War; and of the Thirteen Colonies, from their origin in that Period*. 4 Vols. London: printed for the author, 1788.

Granger, Bruce I. *Political Satire in the American Revolution, 1763–1783*. Ithaca, New York: Cornell University Press, 1960.

Grey, Lennox. "John Adams and John Trumball in the 'Boston Cycle.' " *New England Quarterly* IV (1931) 509–14.

Greene, Evarts B. *The Revolutionary Generation*. New York: Macmillan, 1943.

Gruber, Ira D. "The American Revolution as a Conspiracy: The British View." *William and Mary Quarterly*, 3d series, XXVI (1969), 360–72.

Haight, Canniff. *Before the Coming of the Loyalists*. Toronto: Haight and Company, 1897.

Hansen, Harry. *The Boston Massacre: An Episode of Dissent and Violence*. New York: Hastings House, 1970.

Harlow, Ralph. *Sam Adams: Promoter of the American Revolution*. New York: Holt and Company, 1923.

Harris, E. *History and Historiettes, United Empire Loyalists*. Toronto: W. Briggs, 1897.

Harvard University. *Harvard University Quinquennial Catalogue of the Officers and Graduates, 1636–1930*. Cambridge: Harvard University Press, 1930.

Higginson, T. W. *Life and Times of Stephen Higginson*. Cambridge: Houghton, Mifflin and Company, 1907.

Historical Anecdotes, Civil and Military; in a series of letters written from America, in the Years 1777 and 1778, to different Persons in England; containing Observations on the general management of the war, and on the conduct of our principal commanders, in the revolted colonies, during that period. London, 1779.

Hosmer, James Kendall. *The Life of Governor Thomas Hutchinson, Royal Governor of the Province of Massachusetts-Bay*. Boston, New York: Houghton, Mifflin and Company, 1896.

Hunt, Agnes. *The Provincial Committees of Safety of the American Revolution*. New York: Haskell House, 1968.

Jones, Edward Alfred. *The Loyalists of Massachusetts, their Memorials, Petitions, and Claims*. London: St. Catherine Press, 1930.

Kidder, Frederic. *History of the Boston Massacre, March 5, 1770*. Albany: J. Munsell, 1870.

Klein, Milton. "Prelude to Revolution in New York: Jury Trials and Judicial Tenure." *William and Mary Quarterly*, 3d series, XVII (1958), 439–62.

Knapp, Samuel L. *Biographical Sketches of Eminent Lawyers, Statesmen and Men of Letters*. Boston: Richardson and Lord, 1821.

Knollenberg, Bernard. *Origins of the American Revolution, 1759–1766*. New York: Collier Books, 1961.

Labaree, L. W. *Conservatism in Early American History*. Ithaca, New York: Cornell University Press, 1959.

———. *Royal Government in America*. New Haven: Yale University Press, 1930.

———. "The Nature of American Loyalism." *American Antiquarian Society, Proceedings*, LIV (1944), 15–58.

Lawrence, Joseph W. *Footprints, or Incidents in Early History of New Brunswick, 1783–1883*. St. John: J. and A. McMillan, 1883.

———. *The Judges of New Brunswick and Their Times*. St. John: printed for the author, 1907.

"Letters of Andrew Eliot." *Massachusetts Historical Society Proceedings*, XVI (1878).

"Letters of John Andrews." *Massachusetts Historical Society*, VIII (1864–1865).

"Letters of Jonathan Boucher." *Maryland Historical Magazine*, VIII, 44.

"Letters of Nathaniel Walker Appleton." *Publications of the Colonial Society of Massachusetts*, VIII (1902–1904), *Transactions*, 295–97.

"Letters of Richard Lechmere." *Massachusetts Historical Society Proceedings*, 2d series, XVI (1902).

Lincoln, William, ed. *History of Worcester, Massachusetts, from Its Earliest Settlement to September, 1836*. Worcester: Hersey Company, 1837.

Loring, James S. *The Hundred Boston Orators*. Boston: J. P. Jewett, 1852.

Maier, Pauline. "John Wilkes and American Disillusionment with Britain." *William and Mary Quarterly*, 3d series, XX (1963), 373–95.

Main, J. T. *Rebel versus Tory: The Crisis of the Revolution, 1773–1776*. Chicago: Rand McNally, 1963.

Martin, Chester. "The Loyalists in New Brunswick." *Ontario Historical Society, Papers and Records*, XXX (1934), 160–70.

Mathews, Hazel. *The Mark of Honour*. Toronto: University of Toronto Press, 1965.

Matthews, William. *American Diaries, an annotated bibliography of American Diaries, written prior to the year 1861*. Boston, 1959.

Mayo, C. B., ed. "Additions to Hutchinson's History." *American Antiquarian Society Proceedings*, LIX (1950), 11–74.

Mayo, Lawrence S., ed. *Hutchinson's The History of the Colony and Province of Massachusetts-Bay*. 3 Vols. Cambridge: Harvard University Press, 1936.

"Minutes of the President and Fellows of Harvard College, Cambridge, May 7, 1746." *Publications of the Colonial Society of Massachusetts*, XVI, *Collections* (1925), 759–60.

Moody, James. *Lieutenant James Moody's Narrative of his Exertions and Sufferings*. New York: Richardson and Urquhart, 1968.

Moore, Frank. *Diary of the American Revolution*, Vol. I. New York and London: C. Scribner, S. Low and Company, 1860.

Morgan, Edmund S. "Thomas Hutchinson and the Stamp Act." *New England Quarterly,* XXI (1948), 459–92.

Morison, Samuel E. "The Commerce of Boston on the Eve of the Revolution." *American Antiquarian Society Proceedings,* XXXII (1922), 24–51.

——. *Three Centuries at Harvard, 1636–1936.* Cambridge: Harvard University Press, 1936.

Morris, Richard B. "Legalism versus Revolutionary Doctrine in New England." *New England Quarterly,* IV (1931), 195–205.

——. *Studies in the History of American Law.* New York: Columbia University Press, 1930.

Morse, Jedidiah. *Annals of the American Revolution.* Port Washington, New York: Kennikat Press, 1968.

Murrin, John M. "Anglicizing an American Colony: The Transformation of Provincial Massachusetts." Ph.D. dissertation, Yale University, 1966.

Myers, T. B. *The Tories or Loyalists in America.* Albany: J. Munsell Press, 1882.

Nelson, William. *The American Tory.* Boston: Beacon Press, 1968.

——. "The Last Hopes of the American Loyalists." *Canadian Historical Review,* XXXII (1951), 22–42.

Norton, Mary Beth. *The British-Americans: The Loyalist Exiles in England, 1774–1789.* Boston: Little, Brown, 1972.

——. "A Recently Discovered Thomas Hutchinson Letter." *Massachusetts Historical Society Proceedings,* LXXXII (1970), 105–9.

O'Brien, Conor Cruise, ed. *Edmund Burke's Reflections on the Revolution in France.* Baltimore: Penguin Books, 1968.

Oliver, F. E. *The Diaries of Benjamin Lynde and of Benjamin Lynde Jr. with an appendix.* Boston: Riverside Press, 1880.

Paine, Sarah Cushing, comp., and Pope, Charles Henry, ed. *Paine Ancestry: The Family of Robert Treat Paine, Signer of the Declaration of Independence, Including Maternal Lines.* Boston: D. Clapp, 1912.

Parker, David. *Guide to the Materials for United States History in Canadian Archives.* Washington: Carnegie Institute, 1913.

Parkes, H. B. "New England in the 1730's." *New England Quarterly,* III (1930), 397–419.

"Payne Family Notes." *Massachusetts Historical Society Proceedings,* XIII (1873–1875), 416–17.

Quincy, Edmund. *Life of Josiah Quincy of Massachusetts.* Boston: Ticknor and Fields, 1868.

Quincy, Josiah. *The History of Harvard University.* 2 Vols. 2d edition. Boston: Crosby, Nichols, Lee and Company, 1860.

——. *Memoir of the Life of Josiah Quincy, Junior of Massachusetts, 1744–1775.* Boston: Press of J. Wilson, 1874.

Raymond, W. O. *The River St. John, its physical features legends and history from 1604 to 1784.* Sackville, New Brunswick: Tribune Press, 1943.

——, ed. *The Winslow Papers*. St. John, New Brunswick: The Sun Printing Company, 1901.

Reed, W. B., ed. *Life and Correspondence of Joseph Reed*. 2 Vols. Philadelphia: Lindsay and Blakiston, 1847.

"Report of the School Committee on the Browne and other Donations, September 14, 1835." *Harvard College Papers,* 2d series, VII (1835–1836), 326.

Rife, C. W. *Edward Winslow, Jr. Loyalist Pioneer*. Report of the Canadian Historical Association, 1928.

Ritcheson, Charles. *British Politics and the American Revolution*. Norman, Oklahoma: University of Olahoma Press, 1954.

Robson, Eric. *The American Revolution, in its Political and Military Aspect, 1763–1783*. London: Batchworth Press, 1955.

Robson, Robert. *The Attorney in Eighteenth Century England*. Cambridge, England: Cambridge University Press, 1959.

Ryerson, A. E. *Loyalists of America and their Times: from 1620 to 1816*. Toronto: W. Briggs, 1880.

Sabine, Lorenzo. *The American Loyalists: or, Biographical Sketches of Adherents to the British Crown in the War of the Revolution*. Boston: Little, Brown, 1847.

——. *A Historical Essay on the Loyalists of the American Revolution*. Springfield, Massachusetts: Walden Press, 1957.

Sachse, W. L. *The Colonial Americans in Britain*. Madison, Wisconsin: University of Wisconsin Press, 1956.

Salisbury, Mr. and Mrs. Edward E. *Family Histories and Genealogies . . . of the Families of Mac Curdy, Mitchell, Lord, Etc*. New Haven: private printing, 1892.

Sargent, W. *The Loyalist Poetry of the Revolution*. Philadelphia: Collins Press, 1857.

Schutz, John A. *William Shirley, King's Governor of Massachusetts*. Chapel Hill: University of North Carolina Press, 1961.

Schuyler, Robert L. "Galloway's Plans for Anglo-American Union." *Political Society Quarterly,* LVII (1942), 281–85.

"Sewall Letters." *Massachusetts Historical Society Proceedings,* 2d series, X (1896).

Sewall, Jonathan. *A Cure for the Spleen, or Amusement for a Winter's Evening, being the Substance of a Conversation on the Times, over a Friendly Tankard and Pipe*. New York: James Rivington, 1775.

Shipton, Clifford K. *New England Life in the Eighteenth Century: Representative Biographies from 'Sibley's Harvard Graduates.'* Cambridge: Belknap Press of Harvard University, 1963.

Siebert, Wilbur. H. "The Colony of Massachusetts Loyalists at Bristol England." *Massachusetts Historical Society Proceedings,* XLV (1912), 409–14.

Smith, Page. *John Adams*. 2 Vols. New York: Doubleday, 1962.

Smith, P. H. *Loyalists and Redcoats*. Chapel Hill: University of North Carolina Press, 1964.

Smith, William. *The Diary and Selected Papers of Chief Justice William Smith, 1784–1793*. 2 Vols. Toronto: Champlain Society, 1963.

Sosin, Jack. *Agents and Merchants: British Colonial Policy and the Origins of the American Revolution, 1763–1775.* Lincoln, Nebraska: University of Nebraska Press, 1965.

Stark, James H. *The Loyalists of Massachusetts.* Boston: printed for the author, 1907.

Stevens, B. F. *Facsimiles of Manuscripts in European Archives Relating to America, 1773–1783.* 25 Vols. London: Malby and Sons, 1889–1898.

Sutherland, L. S. *The Correspondence of Edmund Burke, Vol. II, July 1768–June 1774.* Cambridge and Chicago: Cambridge University Press, University of Chicago Press, 1960.

Thomas, Leslie J. "Partisan Politics in Massachusetts during Governor Bernard's Administration, 1760–1770." Ph.D. dissertation, University of Wisconsin, 1960.

Tiffany, N. M. *Letters of James Murray, Loyalist.* Boston: private printing, 1901.

Townsend, Annette. *The Auchmuty Family of Scotland and America.* New York: The Grafton Press, 1932.

Trumball, J. *McFingal: A Modern Epic Poem, Or, the Town Meeting.* Philadelphia, 1776.

Tudor, William. *Life of James Otis.* Boston: Wells and Lilly, 1825.

Ubbelohde, Carl. *The Vice-Admiralty Courts and the American Revolution.* Chapel Hill: University of North Carolina Press, 1960.

Van Tyne, C. H. *Loyalists in the American Revolution.* Gloucester, Massachusetts: The Macmillan Company, 1959.

Walett, Frances G. "The Massachusetts Council 1766–1774: The Transformation of a Conservative Institution." *William and Mary Quarterly,* 3d series, XV (1958), 508–20.

Wallace, W. Stewart. *The United Empire Loyalists.* Vol. XIII of *Chronicles of Canada.* Edited by George M. Wrong and H. H. Langton. Toronto: Brook and Company, 1914.

"Ward Chipman's Diary." *Essex Institute Historical Collections,* LXXXVII (1951), 211–41.

Ward, George A., ed. *The Journal and Letters of the Late Samuel Curwen.* New York: Leavitt, Trow, and Company, 1845.

"Warren-Adams Letters: Being Chiefly a Correspondence among John Adams, Sam Adams, and James Warren." *Massachusetts Historical Society Collections,* LXXII–LXXIII (1917).

Warren, Charles. *History of the Harvard Law School and of Early Legal Conditions in America.* Vol. I. Cambridge: Lewis Publishing Company, 1908.

Washburn, Emory. *Sketches of the Judicial History of Massachusetts from 1630 to the Revolution in 1775.* Boston: Little, Brown, 1840.

Whitmore, William H. *The Massachusetts Civil List for the Colonial and Provincial Periods, 1630–1774.* Albany: J. Munsell, 1870.

Williamson, Joseph. "The Professional Tours of John Adams in Maine." *Collections of the Maine Historical Society,* 2d series, I, 301–8.

Wolkins, G. G. "Hancock's Sloop Liberty." *Massachusetts Historical Society Proceedings,* LVI (1920), 239–84.

Woodbury, Ellen. *Dorothy Quincy, Wife of John Hancock with Events of Her Time.* Washington: The Neale Publishing Company, 431 Eleventh Street, 1901.

Wright, E. C. *The Loyalists of New Brunswick.* Fredericton, New Brunswick, Canada: printed by the author, 1955.

Wrong, George M. *Canada and the American Revolution.* New York: Macmillan Company, 1935.

———. "The Background of the Loyalist Movement, 1763–1783." *Ontario Historical Society, Papers and Records,* XXX (1934), 171–80.

Wyman, Thomas Bellows. *The Genealogies and Estates of Charlestown, in the County of Middlesex and Commonwealth of Massachusetts, 1629–1818.* Vol. 2. Boston: D. Clapp, 1879.

Zemsky, Robert M. "Power, Influence, and Status: Leadership Patterns in the Massachusetts Assembly, 1740–1755." *William and Mary Quarterly,* 3d series, XXVI (1969), 502–20.

———. "The Massachusetts Assembly, 1730–1755," Ph.D. dissertation, Yale University, 1967.

Zobel, Hiller B. "Jonathan Sewall: A Lawyer in Conflict." *Proceedings of the Cambridge Historical Society,* XL (1964–1966), 123–36.

———. *The Boston Massacre.* New York: Norton, 1970.

———. and Wroth, L. Kinvin. *Legal Papers of John Adams.* 3 Vols. Cambridge: Belknap Press of Harvard University, 1965.

Index